THE RECORDS
OF MEDIEVAL EUROPE

CAROLLY ERICKSON was born in 1943. She obtained her B.A. in French and in History simultaneously from the University of Washington, Seattle. She received her M.A. from Columbia University in 1964 and her Ph.D. in 1969. Mrs. Erickson has taught at Barnard College, Brooklyn College, San Fernando Valley State College, and presently teaches at Mills College. She is the author of several scholarly articles in medieval history and of a forthcoming book entitled *Protest and Western History*. At the present time she is working to complete two books, one on *Francis Exalted: Bartholomew of Pisa's De Conformitate in Franciscan Thought,* and the other on women's role in history and culture.

THE RECORDS
OF MEDIEVAL
EUROPE

EDITED WITH AN INTRODUCTION BY

CAROLLY ERICKSON

ANCHOR BOOKS
DOUBLEDAY & COMPANY, INC.
GARDEN CITY, NEW YORK
1971

The Anchor Books edition is the first publication of
The Records of Medieval Europe

Anchor Books edition: 1971

Library of Congress Catalog Card Number 72–131112

Grateful acknowledgment is made
to the Master and Fellows of Corpus Christi College, Cambridge,
for their permission to use the cover reproduction.

TO NORMAN F. CANTOR

PREFACE

I put together this collection of source readings for an undergraduate course in medieval civilization at Mills College in the summer and fall of 1968. Since then, several groups of students have tested it and suggested changes in the original version. In choosing the passages, I have tried to maintain a balance between those illustrative of political and institutional change and those which reveal dimensions of both the popular and the scholarly mind. Many familiar documents will be sought here in vain— the omissions are only too obvious to me as I conclude the tasks of editing. Still, though I have avoided including any source simply because it has become traditional, I have tried at the same time not to succumb to the opposite temptation of obscurantism. Even though most of these selections have not, to my knowledge, appeared in medieval anthologies before, each has been chosen because it illustrates unusually clearly an important component of medieval life.

The introductory essay, "A Framework for Interpretation," is intended to fill the gap between the student's general knowledge, acquired through lectures and textbook study, and these documents. My purpose in the essay has not been to impose a particular set of conclusions, but merely to provide a general orientation; long explicatory and narrative passages have been omitted from it, as these should more appropriately come from the instructor and the text.

I would like to thank John Noonan and Thomas Bisson for advice and help with specific documents. Latinists Judith Jastram and Roland Mayer have tried valiantly to save me from blunders in the forty-odd new translations that appear here; those errors that remain are, of course, entirely my responsibility.

Susan Massotty, Sheila Underwood, Jim Albertson, Sally Ballinger and Peter Ballinger have helped greatly with many burdensome details in the preparation of the manuscript; Lisa Johnson and Ronnie Shushan of Anchor Books has smoothed away many technical difficulties with deceptive ease. Finally, I want particularly to thank Warren Hollister for his generous and unfailing encouragement throughout.

Oakland, California

C.E.

CONTENTS

PART TWO:
THE CENTRAL MIDDLE AGES

THE CHANNELS OF PUBLIC LIFE

GOVERNMENT, COMMERCE AND COMMUNICATIONS

THE REPOSITORIES OF THOUGHT

THE MONASTERY

THE SECULAR CLERGY

LITERATURE

PART THREE:
THE HIGH MIDDLE AGES

THE CHANNELS OF PUBLIC LIFE

GOVERNMENT, COMMERCE AND COMMUNICATIONS

THE SOCIAL ORDER

THE REPOSITORIES OF THOUGHT

THE MONASTIC AND MENDICANT ORDERS

THE SECULAR CLERGY

A FRAMEWORK FOR INTERPRETATION

The area we call Western Europe underwent great change in its governmental and social organization between the early fourth century and the death of Charlemagne in the early ninth. It has often been said that the most conspicuous manifestation of this change was a shift in the geographical focus of the West—a shift from the Rome-centered hegemony of a Mediterranean empire to the centrifugal anarchy of the northern Germanic states.

Some of the best evidence for this gravitation toward the north comes from Roman historians like Dio Cassius (DOCUMENT 1) and Zosimus (DOCUMENT 2), who chronicle the preoccupation of Roman rulers with the Germanic threat. Marcus Aurelius, one of the most capable of these rulers, was forced during the greater part of his reign to remain not at Rome but at the most vital and important part of the Empire's territory— the military frontier. There he was preoccupied with diplomatic maneuvering among the tribal groups in a way that suggests he had abandoned all attempts to arrive at a definitive settlement of the intermittent belligerency between Romans and barbarians, and was only hoping to forestall it.

Zosimus' *History* confirms the continuation of this unsettled situation into the fourth century, although by then at least some of the maneuvering was being carried on by barbarians raised to positions of military responsibility within the Empire. Zosimus' black picture of indolence at high levels of government and corruption at lower ones suggests that internal fragmentation of its political power was as damaging to the Empire as pressure inward upon its frontiers. His account of Alaric's siege of Rome gives evidence not so much of Alaric's invincibility as of confusion and division among the Roman authorities.

Perhaps nothing else reveals a state's weaknesses quite so clearly as its legislation; the Code of Roman law drawn up under the Emperor Theodosius II in the first half of the fifth century (DOCUMENT 4) tells historians much about the disintegration of late-Roman central government. In it the once-exalted Roman Senate is reduced to the indignity of repetitiously chanting its decrees in a sort of legislative litany. The Code also reveals that those born into the curial class, which since the early fourth century had been responsible for running municipal government and producing the local tax assessment, preferred to give up their status rather than remain at their posts and be bankrupted. Finally, it makes it clear that by the fifth century (and, in fact, long before it) systems of personal and legal interdependence were strongly in force which tended to be disruptive of traditional loyalties to state and local government.

To be sure, remnants of the Roman economic system—a system which, at the height of its sophistication, had achieved some degree of mutual dependence among the various provinces in the Western half of the Empire—remained in evidence long after the Germanic states developed. But it became apparent under the successors of the first important Merovingian king, Clovis (481–511), that local, or at most regional trade was rapidly becoming the only workable solution to the severe economic crises that plagued the last centuries of imperial rule.

Fredegar's *Chronicle* (DOCUMENT 5) describes the everyday workings of the government presided over by these successors of Clovis. Operating largely in ignorance of the framework of legal and administrative institutions that had characterized the Empire, the Merovingian rulers of Gaul normally manipulated their subjects by violence and the constant threat of violence. Treachery became the ordinary substitute for bureaucracy, and membership in the royal household brought no guarantee of immunity from arbitrary attack.

The capitularies of Charlemagne (DOCUMENT 7) are a sharp

2

contrast to Fredegar's *Chronicle*. They seem at first to indicate that, by the late eighth century, a Germanic ruler had succeeded in achieving orderly government and had recaptured a clear notion of the state. The capitulary on military service prescribes stringent punishments for offenders, and central and local administration seem to be operating in enviable balance. In the capitulary of Aachen, Charlemagne's legislative strength is used to support the system of ecclesiastical law promulgated in earlier church councils, which would seem to signify the practical fulfillment of his theory of theocratic monarchy. Yet beneath the surface, there are signs that these laws do not indicate an eighth-century revival of the Roman imperial government at all: they lack a framework of explicit enforcement procedures. Their content is an astonishing mixture of the weighty and the trivial, and, far from resembling a systematic "code," they often appear to be summaries of the emperor's statements which have taken on the quality of binding legislation.

The transition from Roman to Germanic government that these documents reveal, then, is not cyclical—from empire to short-lived chaos to empire again—but linear. It is a transition from the imperial system of complex, positive decentralization through a phase of nearly absolute anarchy to another empire, but one which has revived only the rhetoric and symbolic ritual of its earlier model. The Carolingian system represented, in fact, a short-lived effort to combat the characteristically medieval tendency to wed civil jurisdiction to dynastic power at all levels of government, a tendency already strongly in evidence in most Western areas in the eighth and ninth centuries.

The increasing personalization evident in government was paralleled in the social order by the growth of dependent relationships outside the framework of civic life. Public duties ceased to weigh on men's consciences; *The Theodosian Code* (DOCUMENT 9) includes many decrees against fleeing the "compulsory public service" required of all tradesmen. Service in the army had become an unthinkable burden to many, a burden to be avoided by even the most drastic means—assumption of

3

the clerical life. The government's increasing inability to meet its military payroll forced soldiers (a growing number of whom were former slaves) to the extreme of pillaging the property of citizens.

The Code reveals a social setting beset with extremes, in which the patterns of human interaction normal before the chaos of the third century have been irretrievably lost. What is more, there is no longer any definable set of social ideas prevalent throughout the Empire. Instead, several parallel groups of customs have come to be recognized as equally legitimate, particularly after the Germanic peoples, living under Roman influence, were moved to set down their previously unwritten laws. *The Burgundian Code* (DOCUMENT 10) was one of these codes, written in the late fifth and early sixth centuries. Among other issues, these laws dealt extensively with the problem of settling disputes between peoples who did not share the same law; they provided for settlement of disputes between Christian and Jew, between Roman and Roman (when a German had ill-advisedly "involved himself"), and, finally, prescribed the German procedure of oath swearing as a proof of innocence in a criminal suit. Beyond these procedural guidelines, the Code enunciates certain vital assumptions, common to the barbarians, about the way a community regulates itself: that authentication of an assertion must be through the quantitative oral support of respected local witnesses; that the enforcement of social norms must be a local responsibility and must rely on a broad base of honest men within the community; that offenses are best measured and the offender redeemed by money payments, even in cases of bodily harm; and that each man has a different degree of social importance (also measurable in money), determined by his positive value to the entire group. All these ideas were foreign to Roman law. It proved to be impossible to reconcile the two kinds of law, so that by the close of the medieval period, Europe was divided between them. Those areas where the Roman population and influence remained strong (Italy and southern France) continued to live under Roman law, and those where Roman influence had never penetrated (northern France, and most areas of Germanic speech) or had been obliterated (England) lived under Germanic customary law.

As the governmental focus of the West shifted northward, so too did the centers of culture, resulting in a measurable loss of the urbanity and sophistication that had characterized Roman literature and thought. The intellectual atmosphere of the late Empire and early Middle Ages was characterized by three processes: first, the rise of a heterogeneous body of Christian thought; second, the attempt to maintain and pass on a tradition of Roman education, emphasizing literature, philosophy and a devotion to participation in civic affairs; and third, the gradual establishment among the Germanic peoples of a new group of intellectuals who eventually created a synthesis of Christian and Roman thought, and added their own cultural predispositions to it. The third process, in many ways the most difficult to trace, was only beginning to be evident at Charlemagne's court; its full development came in the next three centuries.

The ascetic tendencies in Hebraic tradition, evident in *The Manual of Discipline* (DOCUMENT 11) (written probably between the early second century B.C. and the end of the first A.D.), with its economic communism and its concept of dualism, not only in deity, but in the very spirit of man, strongly influenced Jesus of Nazareth and his early followers. The Christian gospel, at first not readily distinguishable from other Eastern, salvationist religions popular in Rome, in fact went far beyond them in its radical social message. Jesus preached voluntary withdrawal from the sinful world of material possession into the ranks of a persecuted elite whose reward would come in the life after death (DOCUMENT 12). His followers, recruited, in the beginning, from among the lowest strata of Roman society, puzzled and finally infuriated the Roman authorities by their refusal to resist persecution and their lust for martyrdom.

The strain of ascetic withdrawal in Christianity survived the institutionalization of the religion in the two broad forms of monastic life that became dominant in the West. One, the Bene-

5

dictine, came to prevail on the Continent, while the other, Greek in origin, and exemplified in the *Rule* of St. Columban (DOCUMENT 14), was best preserved among the Celtic peoples, especially in Ireland.

Many of the implicit assumptions of the early Christian monks were echoed in the works of a mysterious thinker known to the medieval West as "Dionysius the Areopagite." Although he was most probably a Syriac monk who lived in the fifth century, medieval men associated him with the Athenian disciple of Paul mentioned in Acts 17, 34, and venerated his works accordingly. The Pseudo-Dionysius' *Mystical Theology* (DOCUMENT 13) established the incomprehensible remoteness of a deity who is beyond love, logic and time. His *Celestial Hierarchies* describes a host of heavenly beings that flank God, carry some of his attributes, and serve to link God to man in a chain of created life. The author borrowed the concept of a hierarchy of being from the Neo-Platonist philosophers; his imaginative blending of their doctrines with Christian theology seemed to prove that pagan and Christian thought were not irreconcilable.

The Christian community in the late Empire, having had power thrust upon it first by Constantine's complex legislation (granting Christianity equal legal status with other religions of the Empire) and then by Theodosius' decrees of the 390s (which made it the only legal religion), was forced for the first time to define its ideology as an institution, rather than as a collectivity of individual believers. Even before the fourth century, Christian apologists like Clement of Alexandria (d. 215) had tried to speak on behalf of "the church." His method in the *Exhortation to the Greeks* (DOCUMENT 15) was to argue with educated Romans on their own terms, pointing to the (in his view) futile inconsistencies in Greek philosophical thought and trying to identify Christian monotheism with Plato's "knowledge of the existence of the true God."

The greatest of the Church Fathers, Augustine (354–430), Bishop of Hippo in North Africa, was less conscious that he was establishing theological doctrine that would become the norm of a far-flung institution. Although he wrote on virtually every problem confronting the church during his lifetime, he was particularly important in articulating what became the prevailing doctrine of sexual abstinence (DOCUMENT 16), and in creating a powerful interpretation of contemporary history—with the Gothic pillaging of Rome in 410 as its pivot—in which human affairs represent only the superficial, and finally unimportant, evidence of God's will moving through time and change (DOCUMENT 17). In *The City of God,* the idea of the ancient *polis* was exalted to a transcendent, religious concept that at once ennobled the pagan idea and reconciled it with Christian belief.

Vincent of Lérins' treatise *Against Heresy* (DOCUMENT 18) deals with an equally vital interpretative problem—how to determine orthodoxy. His solution was to prefer that belief which seemed to represent a majority view, or which had the support of custom behind it, or which (these two criteria being absent) had been recommended by an "ancient General Council." In brief, this was the tendency of orthodox Christian theologians to depend on tradition, a tendency that was to remain prevalent until the fourteenth century. The need for some such arbiter of theological truth is evident from Vincent's own description of contemporary heresies. These were by no means the only "new doctrines" eventually to receive the condemnation of the church.

In the more mundane area of day-to-day ecclesiastical administration, *The Life of Bishop Bonitus* (DOCUMENT 19) chronicles the rise of an upper-class youth to court preferment and then into the episcopacy. In the early Christian centuries, such a career was not uncommon, particularly in areas where Roman tradition remained strong; the exemplary lives of men like Bonitus were ennobled by the growth of a new Christian didactic genre—hagiography. St. Columban's letter to the pope (DOCUMENT 20) also dealt with a problem that was ostensibly trivial —how to calculate the precise date of Easter. Yet the controversy over this calculation succeeded in dividing the Roman and

7

Celtic churches until they were finally united at the Synod of Whitby in 664.

Strong currents of secular Roman culture continued to flow within what was, by the fourth century, becoming the mainstream of Christian thought. This was conspicuously true in the city of Rome itself, where paganism and a cultivation of the old civic virtues were associated with freedom from an increasingly despotic imperial government now centered at Constantinople. Rutilius Namatianus and other writers continued to blend poetry with patriotism and civic religion in panegyrics like *The Homecoming* (DOCUMENT 22) until well into the medieval period.

One form of philosophical thought that received the devotion of large numbers of educated Romans (including, at one point in his life, Augustine) was Neo-Platonism. The leading proponent of Neo-Platonism, Plotinus (205–270), built his thought on certain of Plato's assumptions about the nature of reality. In his *Enneads* (DOCUMENT 21) Plotinus advanced ideas which, in their almost mystical loftiness, more nearly approached the style of religion than that of philosophy. Plotinus envisioned a permanent and purposed universe in which the tenuous links between ideas and physical objects were not merely unquestioned but obvious. What was more significant for medieval thought, the importance of absolute concepts in his writings—the highest love, perfect beauty, the Good—made them at many points compatible with Christian doctrine.

The vast ranks of men of the early Middle Ages who were neither professional intellectuals nor functional irrationalists have left few records of their ideas. It is possible, however, here and there to discern currents of thought which bear their stamp. One such current is reflected in the large body of Jewish and Christian apocalyptic literature appearing in the early centuries of the Christian era. Works of this kind, usually associated in the West with periods of persecution, provided a hope of escape for a population caught between the fragmentation of Roman authority and the unknown terrors of barbarian rule. The *Reve-*

8

lation (DOCUMENT 23) is a Christian apocalypse. Its prophecies of the war, famine and death that were to precede the "last days" (when those marked as God's faithful would be spared) envision the humbling of the powerful of the earth and the disruption of an intolerable economic system. The fact that the *Revelation* became a part of the canonical New Testament ensured the continued respectability of millennarian prophecy throughout the Middle Ages; waves of popular conviction that the end of the world was at hand found encouragement and justification in the recorded vision of John on Patmos. As for the church on earth, the popular imagination was fired by *The Legend of Simon Magus* (DOCUMENT 24), the demonic magician, and his humbling at the hands of the "first pope," Peter. This legend served to create a miraculous and almost superhuman aura about the papal office, particularly among the vast majority of believers who would never see a pope.

Finally, the transmutation, in the Saxon *Heliand* (DOCUMENT 25), of the story of Jesus' life and passion into the story of a Germanic chieftain's betrayal by a member of his war band shows another influence of the popular mind. If the Germanic peoples in continental Europe and England had, by the ninth century, been Christianized, it was equally apparent that their Christian beliefs had been radically Germanized.

PART TWO: THE CENTRAL MIDDLE AGES

Although the grandsons of Charlemagne were still fighting for control of an empire that embraced a large part of Western Europe in the 840s (DOCUMENT 27), it was an empire that could no longer call itself Rome's heir. Charlemagne's court scholars had revived the rhetoric of imperial rule but could not ensure the continuance of a dynasty worthy of it. Emperors are in any case survived not by sons but by bureaucracies, and Charlemagne had never found the means or the men to organize an efficient administrative system.

The large volume of well-regulated commerce and pilgrim

traffic ascribed to the tenth-century Lombard kingdom in the *Regulations of the Royal Court at Pavia* (DOCUMENT 26) seems to bely Nithard's image in his *History of the Sons of Louis the Pious* of primitive and opportunistic shifts of power at the highest level of Carolingian government. Yet the fact that a small group of minor customs officials could carry out their jobs in an orderly way while princes had to fight for their very lands reveals that the links between central and local government had been lost. Neither of the centripetal forces that would bind Western kingdoms together by 1150 was yet in evidence—a system of royal feudalism and a tradition of sanctity surrounding the kingly office. In the Holy Roman Empire, the idea of sacred monarchy had appeared by the time of *The Deeds of Conrad II* (DOCUMENT 28), in the first part of the eleventh century; the importance of the royal election, consecration, acclamation by the Roman people and papal blessing are evident from the document. But the German realms failed (at least until the late twelfth century) to develop feudal relationships and a feudal law. Consequently, when the imperial supremacy was attacked by strong challenges from the papal curia after 1073, it had no second line of defense. Despite the loyal counterattack of Henry IV's ecclesiastical vassals in their *Renunciation of Gregory VII* (DOCUMENT 29), the emperor was forced to bow to papal authority at Canossa in 1077. Because the temporal antagonist in the first great clash of church-state ideologies was a relatively weak emperor, the spiritual ideology was temporarily victorious.

The resurgence of town life in Western Europe on a large scale came primarily after 1150, although small centers of commercial life could spring up under the circumstances outlined in the description of ninth-century Bruges (DOCUMENT 30). But by far the greater number of Europeans lived under the restrictions of a predominantly self-sufficient rural economy. The combined action of customary inheritance through the eldest son and an overweening piety on the part of landowners of modest possessions brought about a large concentration of property under ecclesiastical jurisdiction (DOCUMENT 31). This fact, plus the greater abundance of records relating to church-owned lands, makes it almost inevitable that examples of manorial jurisdiction as well as manorial economy be taken from ecclesiastical documents. Abbot Sehier's census for Chaumousey describes the system of peasant taxes in labor and in kind which are at the heart of the manorial system.

Disputes also arose among those who owned the manorial estates, the landed nobility. Until well into the ninth century, in the absence of a convenient and trustworthy system of royal justice, the blood feud continued to vie with less barbaric procedures as a popular means of settling differences of opinion within the knightly class (DOCUMENT 32). Nevertheless, a body of feudal custom gradually came into existence to regulate relationships among free men, much of it based on an ideal of knighthood that developed slowly in the tenth and eleventh centuries.

Feudalism was the term later applied to ties of dependence among medieval knights; just as knighthood provided the ideology, so feudalism provided the external framework within which they lived. At its height, feudal law decisively influenced the ownership and transfer of land and the organization of armies, and even circumscribed the jurisdiction of kings (DOCUMENT 33). But because feudal loyalties rested primarily on mutual good faith, feudalism was an extremely unstable means of promoting order in society. It was not until the late eleventh century that kings began to proclaim themselves to be chief, or liege, lords in their kingdoms, and to use feudal law, now backed by royal armies, to coerce their unruly vassals.

The years between about 814 and 1100 were a period of great fruitfulness in the life of the mind, most of it centered in the Benedictine monasteries of the West. During these three centuries the Benedictines enjoyed an intellectual hegemony that they were never to regain. In the full correspondence of Servatus Lupus of Ferrières (DOCUMENT 34), theologian and devoted student of classical letters, and even in the vexed career of Anselm of Canterbury (DOCUMENT 35), forced to pursue a genuine monastic vocation amid the pressures of political clashes and administrative frustrations, it is clear that the Rule of St. Benedict still provided the most ample framework for a cultured life. By the 1120s, however, the Benedictine model (in its "reformed" Cluniac version) was under attack from apologists for newer orders. The Cistercian Bernard of Clairvaux, probably the best-known champion of a newer monasticism, mercilessly exposed the "corruption" of the Cluniacs, and was answered by an aggrieved Peter the Venerable, Abbot of Cluny (DOCUMENT 36). Their debate reflects one of the most important movements affecting twelfth-century life—the enormous recrudescence of lay piety, and the concomitant appearance of monastic orders that attracted adult recruits in large numbers.

This change in the pattern of Europe's ascetic life took place largely outside the formal hierarchy of the church. Indeed the church—and in particular the Roman curia—was preoccupied with constructing its own ideology to combat the recent *de jure* separation of the Eastern and Western churches (Leo of Ochrida's open letter, DOCUMENT 37, does no more than to articulate centuries-old grievances) and to support Gregory VII's all-out assault on the prevalent control of church offices by laymen. Wido's *Book of the Controversy Between Hildebrand and Henry* (DOCUMENT 38) is an attempt to counteract the Roman rhetoric and discredit the church's position by slandering its flamboyant head. At the same time, churchmen throughout the West were encouraging the unleashing of public religiosity by setting the thoughts of hundreds of feudal nobles and men of lesser rank on the reconquest of the Holy Land. The crusading mentality, consciously prepared by Urban II, Peter the Hermit and dozens of itinerant preachers, required a wrenching of the Christian teachings into a non-Christian militancy. Bernard of Clairvaux celebrated the new dialectic of the warrior monk in his treatise *In Praise of the New Militia of the Temple* (DOCUMENT 39), dedicated to the recently founded order of Knights Templars.

By the mid-twelfth century, the first two crusades had considerably advanced Europe's knowledge of geography; in the ninth-century *Book of the Measurement of the Earth* by the Irish monk Dicuil (DOCUMENT 40), who may have been a member of the circle of scholars at the court of Louis the Pious, the ancients' knowledge of geography was still prized equally with contemporary observations. In another area of speculation, Bishop Patrick's eleventh-century verses *On the Honor of the Human Condition* (DOCUMENT 41) exalted man to an extent incompatible with generalized statements about medieval "anti-humanism." Although his view of man embraces an Augustinian analysis of the mind, it also echoes the optimism of certain classical Roman writers.

Another sort of connection with the world of Rome was established in Geoffrey of Monmouth's *History of the Kings of Britain* (DOCUMENT 42), in which Julius Caesar was made to claim that he was distantly related to the Britons. Hoping at once to celebrate and buttress Norman rule in England, Geoffrey drew on the legend of the British chieftain Arthur. In the *History*, Arthur became a mighty conqueror and creator of a wonderfully cultured court; it has been suggested that this image was created to counter the fame of Roland, vassal of Charlemagne and victor over the Moors in the late eleventh-century *Song of Roland*. In addition, Geoffrey's descriptions of Caerleon foreshadowed the chivalrous pattern to be established at the courts of Henry II and Philip Augustus.

Well before 1150, several centers of learning were taking on the outlines of the great universities they were to become by the end of the century; Abelard's picaresque career was launched by his fame as a master on the hill of St. Geneviève in Paris, and the Camaldolese monk Gratian was helping to establish the reputation of Bologna's masters of the canon law. In his *Ethics* (DOCUMENT 43), Abelard attempted to isolate the components of sin, and ended by exonerating man for his propensities toward evil; sin itself, in his analysis, became an act of will. His effort to work out the logic of sin arose perhaps out of the twelfth-century masters' generally optimistic attitude toward the application of reason to many areas of belief and custom. Nowhere was the tool of reason more useful than in organizing the body of decrees and traditions making up the canon law. Gratian's *Decretum*, or *Concord of Discordant Canons* (DOCU-

MENT 44), arranged the often contradictory opinions of church authorities systematically to answer groups of questions under specific rubrics; scholasticism was in the ascendant.

In the popular mind, another sort of reasoning usually prevailed, particularly with respect to the Jews, the biblical murderers of Jesus. But the tenth-century gentile *Dispute of the Church and the Synagogue* (DOCUMENT 45) is surprisingly sensitive to the nobility of Jewish tradition and puts into the mouth of the synagogue remarkably sensible arguments against accepting Jesus as the Messiah. Itineraries of shrines of frequent pilgrimage were not uncommon in popular literature from the late eleventh century on. William of Malmesbury inserted one such guide, describing the gates of Rome and celebrating its vanished glories, into his *Chronicle of the Kings of England* (DOCUMENT 46) to relieve the tedium of his political narrative. Increased travel invariably brought increased knowledge of the non-Christian world. Peter the Venerable (DOCUMENT 47) took the lead in facilitating this knowledge by commissioning the translation of large quantities of Moslem literature into Latin. Unfortunately, broader acquaintance did not breed tolerance, but its opposite. The period from 1075 to 1150, so innovative and relatively free from dogmatism, could not in the end allow a heretical and subversive doctrine to go unchallenged.

PART THREE: THE HIGH MIDDLE AGES

In every area of life, Western Europe after 1150 exhibited an astonishing complexity of attitudes and undertakings. The High Middle Ages did not represent a static consolidation of older ideas and social practices, but a slow accretion of glosses to old custom which eventually made it new.

It has been said that during these years men were more and more inclined to view themselves as members of a group or groups rather than as individuals. It is undeniable that there were many more such groups, or corporations, as they were more commonly called, in the fourteenth century than there had been in the eleventh, and the range of their common interests was bewilderingly diverse. A group of craftsmen might petition jointly for the grant of a privilege or the removal of a grievance. A group of students and masters might declare themselves to be a university (from *universitas,* corporation). A group of lesser nobles and townsmen, summoned to accede to royal legislation, might feel their community of interest keenly enough to threaten a king.

Henry II's charter granted to the tanners of Rouen (DOCUMENT 48) is an illustration of royal recognition and exploitation of a corporation. In this instance, there was very little difference between the guild structure and collective vassalage (and most towns, at least in northern Europe, were, legally, collective vassals).

After 1150, it becomes more and more difficult to trace social change without finding the intentions of a ruler at its origin. The legal proceedings against the prior of Boxgrove (DOCUMENT 49) attest the deliberate process of royal justice in England, as well as the close connection between the king and his Jews; the order of postponement of the French *parlement* and the records of its proceedings (DOCUMENT 50) indicate the king's central position in that institution's maintenance; *The Chronicle of Bury St. Edmunds* (DOCUMENT 51) is little more than a royal itinerary; and the passage from Pierre Dubois' *On the Retaking of the Holy Land* (DOCUMENT 52) is part of an elaborate imperialistic scheme for French possession and exploitation of the Near East written for Philip IV, which gives full consideration to the remunerative potentiality of increased Western control of the Eastern trade. The time-honored rhetoric of conversion is there too, but to Dubois, secular control of even that process would be more effective than spiritual.

The later medieval university, itself not entirely exempt from the pressures of secular and spiritual powers, was in addition frequently embroiled in local unrest (DOCUMENT 58), and in 1229 the University of Paris dispersed itself as a protest against the mayor and his henchmen. The masters and students did not take advantage of Henry III's offer of England as an alternative place of settlement, but many of them helped to found another university at Toulouse.

The vast increase in commercial activity characteristic of the High Middle Ages produced a proliferation of documentary remains: records of loans (usually disguised as money changing, as in the Genoan contract of exchange, DOCUMENT 53); treatises on the merchants' profession, as the Florentine Pegolotti's *Practice of Commerce* (DOCUMENT 54); evidences of the undying traffic in slaves (DOCUMENT 57); and, occasionally, commercial agreements between a town and its overlord (DOCUMENT 56).

By the second half of the twelfth century, partly as a result of the crusades, the original ideal of military knighthood had been enlarged to include a cluster of social, humanitarian and spiritual responsibilities. It was this enlarged ideal that continued to justify the existence of the knightly class long after its functional usefulness waned. For as mercenary and even national armies came to replace the feudal cavalry on the medieval battlefield, the knightly elite became a military anachronism. The thirteenth-century Roman ritual of knighthood (DOCUMENT 59) used ceremony to reinforce this ideology. Even in economic terms, however, feudalism was undergoing an irreversible mutation; fiefs were commonly paid in money, and not to knights alone (DOCUMENT 62a), but even to craftsmen (DOCUMENT 62b).

Contending with the feudal elite for leadership in medieval society were the towns (and the congeries of self-regulating craft guilds), whose vigorous growth resulted in a celebration of the historical venerability of town life. Giovanni Villani's *Chronicle of Florence* (DOCUMENT 61) was one such glorification; in it he judged the powers of Europe according to their dealings with his city.

If townsmen and landed nobility had little reason for mutual assistance, a third segment of society—the peasantry—felt the weight of oppression and exploitation by the other two. Froissart's *Chronicles* (DOCUMENT 63) recount, with bitter bias, the pitiful risings of the peasantry in late fourteenth-century

England and France. These rebellions, though unsuccessful, were only the beginnings of the waves of violent protest against the social order that troubled the course of the 1300s and later centuries. Violence and its causes were to persist throughout the late Middle Ages, despite the contemporary rediscovery, on another social level, of the more hopeful view of man's potential embodied in humanism.

If the cenobitic monastic orders had been the normal framework for medieval man's piety and social concern, as well as his scholarship, during most of the period before 1150, after the early thirteenth century the mendicant orders had taken their place. The followers of the saintly Francis of Assisi (who so strikingly resembled Jesus in his radicalism, inconsistency and fanatic irrationality) sought to alleviate the world's ills by living in the world. Francis espoused mendicancy for himself and his friars as a preferable alternative to living in the secluded security habitual to monks, in which they lived on the rents from valuable lands. Ubertino da Casale, an early fourteenth-century Franciscan who expressed the vision of the order's most uncompromising sector, the Spirituals, saw Francis as a predestined image of Jesus, a model for sinful man to follow, who would usher in the "age of the Holy Spirit" (DOCUMENT 64). The apocalyptic strain in Franciscan thought tended to make the order more immediate in its devotion to man's physical problems and less inclined to obey an ecclesiastical hierarchy that spoke with the mouth of the past. This spirit of rebellion against outworn authority is reflected in a political pamphlet by the Franciscan William of Ockham (c. 1300–1349) (DOCUMENT 65), in which, by rigidly restricting ecclesiastical jurisdiction to the realm of the spiritual, he was able to argue that princes control all material possessions of the church. In the Prologue to the *Ordinatio*, Ockham's Franciscan contemporary John Duns Scotus (DOCUMENT 66) makes it clear however that the scholastics' art, the carefully balanced use of philosophy and theology to construct reason's monument to faith, was at best a fragile and impermanent one.

Bernard Gui's handbook for the inquisitor (DOCUMENT 67)

grew out of the church's most serious problem in the years following 1150: widespread popular piety, which often blossomed into heresy. His treatise embodies its most trenchant solution, the institutionalized inquisition. His formulas for the conducting of hearings and the handing down of sentences of condemnation indicate that heresy was a mundane vice and its uprooting a scientific virtue. Medieval heresy was largely a matter of numbers; only the views of the majority could be orthodox. Medieval government, however, operated on no such assumption, and Marsilius of Padua's democratic theories were not to become fashionable, at least in secular affairs, until the eighteenth century.

Within a century after *The Defender of Peace* (DOCUMENT 68) was written in 1324, Europe had experimented with a form of popular government within the church, and had found it productive only of schism and ill-feeling. Such was the current of dissatisfaction among the laity that the later thirteenth and fourteenth centuries witnessed a powerful resurgence of mysticism and anti-rationalism in religion. The distaste for all things worldly (including a conspicuously worldly church) produced, in Tauler's *Sermons* (DOCUMENT 69a), a vision of the "death of jubilation," a final severance from the burden of physical existence through an excess of divine ecstasy. The anonymous *Book of the Poor in Spirit* (DOCUMENT 69b), written probably by a member of the Third, or lay, Order among the Dominicans, advocated the abandonment of reason (which heightens man's awareness of multiplicity) altogether, as a hindrance to the attainment of the simple union with God. As the gulf between high cleric, theologian and lay believer widened, the church, as an institution, became increasingly diffuse in its agreed opinions and fragmented in its corporate authorities. More than ever, Christendom was becoming an area of several faiths.

The literature of the High Middle Ages continued to be preoccupied with "religious" themes. Nevertheless, the treatment of those themes became increasingly secular. The troubadours, trouvères and Minnesänger celebrated love in its varying degrees of passion and piety. Through the exaltation of Mary, already encouraged by Bernard of Clairvaux, and elaborated in the thirteenth century (often with less simple directness than in the poetry of Prince Wizlaw of Rügen, DOCUMENT 70), women were exalted and noble ladies became the objects of the distant worship and despair of poets. In *The Three Marys* (DOCUMENT 71), composed to be used as part of the Easter liturgy, the dramatist has glossed a few lines of the Easter sequence, introducing a conspicuously non-biblical character, the *unguentarius,* or unguent seller, and adding comic relief through his exploitation of his female customers. *The Romance of the Rose* (DOCUMENT 72) and *The Dance of Death* (DOCUMENT 73) allow of no frivolity. The former is an elaborate allegorical survey of the psychological ritual of courtly love, the latter a morbid celebration of the inescapable fate of all sorts and conditions of men who must "go upon this daunce."

By the mid-twelfth century, the university at Bologna had received the protection of the Emperor Frederick Barbarossa (DOCUMENT 74). Within a little over a hundred years, the universities were firmly in command of Europe's intellectual life, and had virtually completed their assimilation of the Aristotelian corpus, in its Moslem shroud (DOCUMENT 76). Giles of Rome's *On the Errors of the Philosophers* (DOCUMENT 75) was one of many thirteenth- and fourteenth-century attempts to purge the newly rediscovered texts of non-Christian thinkers of their anti-Christian premises, many of which were entering too familiarly into the works of "orthodox" theologians like Thomas Aquinas. At the same time, the Oxford friar Roger Bacon (DOCUMENT 77) was speaking boldly, if almost uniquely, against the dangers of excessive reliance on tradition to the exclusion of unshackled thought. The famed theologian Thomas Bradwardine, in his *Treatise on Proportions* (DOCUMENT 78), exposed a series of prevalent misinterpretations of Aristotle's theory of motion. Although the work served rather to buttress than to promote the abandonment of Aristotelian science, still it was important in the development of mathematical physics. That the university could also produce thoroughgoing skeptics is clear from Nicolaus of Autrecourt's *First Letter to Bernard of*

Arezzo (DOCUMENT 79). Nicolaus' skepticism is the counterpart, within the academic sphere, of the disillusionment and withdrawal that produced the resurgence of mysticism among his contemporaries.

Among the more popular manifestations of everyday belief, the wonder-stories in Caesarius of Heisterbach's *Dialogue on Miracles* (DOCUMENT 80) were meant only partially to edify; in large measure they were intended to entertain. The poignant *Letter to Blessed Queen Mary* (DOCUMENT 81) of the crusader Ricoldo de Monte-Croce—part of a series of letters, including one to God, another to the celestial curia, and a final one to Ricoldo's fellow soldiers who died in the siege of Acre in 1291 —is the honest expression of a naïve faith, severely tested by the irreversible Christian losses in the Holy Land. Henry of Lancaster's *Book of Holy Medicines* (DOCUMENT 82), a collection of private meditations in the form of a devotional treatise, was the work of a brilliant soldier, diplomat and man of affairs at the English court who died of plague in 1351. His powerful sensual imagery and intimate adoration of Jesus and Mary are characteristic of the personal piety of the later Middle Ages.

If it is difficult to trace the rise of distinctly medieval patterns of society and thought, it is nearly impossible to trace their decline. Perhaps "diffusion" more accurately describes the fate of medieval ideologies and their institutional embodiments. Many of the assumptions implicit in the feudal contract were embodied in the paternalistic monarchical theories of early modern states. The idea persisted long into the modern period that a knightly elite should function as the collective arbiter of chivalrous gentility. Finally, the recurrent attempts to reform Europe's medieval church (or to replace it with a more perfect version of itself, built afresh) prove the compelling power which that institution continued to exert over the minds of "modern" men. These documents, then, chronicle the development of a civilization that has determined the general outline of much of modern Europe's life and thought.

PART ONE

CHRISTIANITY AND THE EARLY MIDDLE AGES

THE CHANNELS OF PUBLIC LIFE

GOVERNMENT, COMMERCE AND
COMMUNICATIONS

1

DIO CASSIUS, *ANNALS OF ROME*

161 – 171

This passage from Dio's Annals *describes the philosopher-emperor Marcus Aurelius' (161–180) attempt to set the Germanic tribes against one another and so promote Rome's interests. The account makes it plain that by the late second century, diplomacy, backed up by evident military resources, was more important to an emperor's successful reign than far-sighted lawmaking or domestic statecraft.*

Marcus Antoninus, the philosopher, upon obtaining the sovereignty at the death of Antoninus, who adopted him, had immediately taken to share the authority with him the son of Lucius Commodus, Lucius Verus. He was personally weak in body and he devoted the greater part of his time to letters. It is told that even when he was emperor he showed no shame (or hesitation) at going to a teacher for instruction, but became a pupil of Sex-

SOURCE From *Dio's Annals of Rome*, trans. Herbert Baldwin Foster, Vol. V (Troy, New York: Pafraets Book Co., 1906), 247, 252–53.

tus, the Bœotian philosopher,[1] and did not hesitate to go to hear the lectures of Hermogenes on rhetoric. He was most inclined to the Stoic school.—Lucius, on the other hand, was strong and rather young, and better suited for military enterprises. Therefore, Marcus made him his son-in-law by marrying him to his daughter Lucilla, and sent him to the Parthian war. . . .

Marcus [Antoninus] remained in Pannonia in order to transact business with the embassies of the barbarians. Many came to him also at this time. Some promised an alliance: they were led by Battarius, a child twelve years old, and they received money and succeeded in restraining Tarbus, a neighboring potentate, who had come into Dacia, was demanding money, and threatening to make war if he should not get it. Others, like the Quadi, were asking for peace, and they obtained it, the emperor's purpose being to have them detached from the Marcomani. Another reason was that they gave horses and cattle, surrendered all the deserters and the captives at first to the number of thirteen thousand, though later they promised to restore the remainder as well. However, the right of free intercourse even at markets was not granted them, the intention being to prevent the Iazyges and the Marcomani, whom they had sworn not to receive nor let pass through their country, from either mingling with them or presenting themselves also in the guise of Quadi, —a plan which would enable them to reconnoitre the Roman position and to purchase provisions. Besides these who came to Marcus, many others despatched envoys, some by tribes and some by nations, offering to surrender themselves. . . . Others received land, in Dacia or in Pannonia or in Mœsia and Germany or in Italy itself. A few of them who settled at Ravenna made an uprising and even dared to take possession of the city: and for this reason he did not again bring any barbarian into Italy, but made even those who had previously come there find homes outside.

[1] Sextus of Chaeronea, grandson of Plutarch. (Ed.'s note)

ZOSIMUS, *THE HISTORY*

390 – 410

The Roman historian Zosimus' account of the reigns of Emperor Theodosius (379–395) and his sons Arcadius (Eastern Emperor, 395–408) and Honorius (Western Emperor, 395–423) attests to the enormous power and influence the barbarians had gained within the Empire. Their attacks threatened Rome's frontiers constantly, and it was barbarian military commanders in the imperial service who masterminded her defense. That the Germanic tribes were not incessantly bent on destruction of the Empire is apparent from the following description of the negotiations between imperial officials and Alaric the Visigoth that preceded his sack of Rome in 410.

During the stay of the new emperor, Theodosius, at Thessalonica, a great concourse arrived there from all parts of persons soliciting him on business, both public and private; who having obtained of him whatever he could conveniently grant, returned to their homes. As a great multitude of the Scythians beyond the Ister, the Gotthi, and the Taiphali, and other tribes that formerly dwelt among them, had crossed the river, and were driven to infest the Roman dominions, because the Huns had expelled them from their own country, the emperor Theodosius

SOURCE From *The History of Count Zosimus* (London: J. Davis, W. Green and T. Chaplin, 1814), 107–10, 124–27, 162–67, 171–72.

prepared for war with all his forces. All Thrace being now in the possession of the above mentioned tribes, and the garrisons of the towns and castles not daring to move out of their walls, much less to engage in the open field, Modares, who was of the royal family of the Scythians, and had not long before come over to the Romans, and for his fidelity had been made a general, placed his soldiers on the summit of a hill, which formed a spacious plain, and lay there unknown to the Barbarians. Learning from his scouts, that the enemy were in the fields below, luxuriously consuming the provisions they had plundered, by which they had intoxicated themselves, he commanded his soldiers to take with them only their swords and bucklers, and not their heavy armour as usual, and to attack the Barbarians while they were immersed in voluptuousness. This they performed, and destroyed in a very short space of time all the Barbarians, many of them dying insensibly, and others immediately on feeling their wounds. Having slain all they began to rifle the bodies, and from thence proceeded to the women and children. They took four thousand carriages, and as many captives as could be contained in them, besides many who usually walked, and only rode alternately when fatigued.

The army having made this good use of the occasion afforded by fortune, the affairs of Thrace, which had been on the brink of ruin, were now, the Barbarians being crushed beyond all hope, re-established in peace.

The eastern provinces were now in the most imminent danger, from the following causes. When the Huns, as I have related, had invaded the countries beyond the Ister, the Scythians, being unable to withstand their incursions, intreated the emperor Valens, who was then living, to admit them into Thrace, promising, in perfect submission to his commands, to perform the duty of faithful soldiers and subjects. By this promise Valens was induced to receive them; and imagining that it would be a surety of their fidelity to cause all their young children to be brought up in a different country, he sent a great number of infants into the east, and appointed Julius to superintend their maintenance and education, conceiving him to be a person of competent understanding for the fulfilment of both those offices. He, therefore, distributed them into various towns, to prevent them, when grown to manhood, from having an opportunity, by being collected in great numbers, of forming an insurrection. However, when they had attained maturity, the intelligence of what their countrymen had suffered in Thrace reached them in the different towns. This gave them much uneasiness; those of one city assembling together and sending private information to those in other places, that they intended to assault the Roman towns in revenge for the sufferings of their countrymen. Meantime Julius, discovering the design of the Barbarians, was in doubt how to act. At length he resolved not to give Theodosius information of the conspiracy, not only because he was then in Macedon, but that he had been appointed to that charge by Valens, and not by Theodosius, who scarcely knew him. He, therefore, privately sent letters to the senate of Constantinople. Being authorised by them to proceed as he deemed most conducive to the public good, he averted the danger with which the towns were menaced by the following measures. He sent for all the officers, and, before he disclosed to them his design, required them to take an oath of secresy. Being informed of it, and instructed how to act, they reported among the Barbarians of each town, that the emperor intended to bestow on them considerable presents, both in money and land, in order to bind them in gratitude to himself and the Roman people. For this purpose they were ordered to assemble on a particular day in the principal cities. This intelligence was so gratifying to the Barbarians, that their fury considerably abated. Upon the appointed day they all attended at the places at which they were desired to meet. When they were arrived, the soldiers, on the signal being made, mounted upon the roofs of the houses in the respective market-places in which they were stationed, and cast at the Barbarians such numbers of darts and stones, that they killed every man. Thus were the eastern cities delivered from their apprehensions, and, by the prudence of the officers, the disasters of the east and of Thrace were terminated.

Meanwhile, the emperor Theodosius, residing in Thessalonica, was easy of access to all who wished to see him. Having commenced his reign in luxury and indolence, he threw the magistracy into disorder, and increased the number of his military officers. There had previously been but one general or master of the horse, and one of the foot, but he now distributed those offices to more than five persons. Each of these was allowed the same stipend which either of the two had before enjoyed. It was likewise oppressive to the soldiers to be exposed to the avarice of so many commanders; for each of them endeavoured to extort from the allowance of the soldiers as much as one of the former two. He likewise increased the number of subaltern officers to more than double the original number, nor could the soldiers obtain the smallest part of their allowance. All this was occasioned by the negligence and excessive avarice of the emperor. He it was who introduced so vast an expence at the imperial table, that to serve it with such an extensive variety of dishes, whole legions of cooks, butlers, and other attendants, were employed. The number of eunuchs in the service of the emperor was immense, most of whom, and particularly those of handsome persons, disgraced at their pleasure any magistrate or officer. The whole government was, in effect, at their disposal; the emperor being guided by their pleasure, and changing his sentiments at their desire. As he squandered the public money without consideration, bestowing it on unworthy persons, he consequently impoverished himself. He therefore sold the government of provinces to any who would purchase them, without regard to the reputation or ability of the persons, esteeming him the best qualified who brought him the most gold or silver. Goldsmiths, bankers, and even the meanest professions, were therefore seen wearing the ensigns of magistracy, and selling the provinces to the best bidders.

A change so great and unfortunate having occurred in the state, the army became weak, and was soon annihilated. All the cities were likewise drained of money, partly by the excessive imposts and partly by the rapacity of the magistrates. For if any failed to appease their insatiable demands, they suborned villains to accuse them; thus acting as with the purpose of recovering what they had paid for their offices. The inhabitants of the towns lived in misery through their own poverty and the iniquity of the magistrates; their only resource being to intreat the gods to deliver them from such afflictions; for hitherto they were permitted to enter the temples, and to worship the gods in the manner of their country.

Theodosius, observing that the army was considerably diminished, permitted as many of the Barbarians beyond the Ister as were willing to enter his own army. Many of them were induced by his promises, and were embodied with the legions; conceiving that when more of them should be collected, they might attack the government, and without difficulty acquire possession of the sovereignty. . . .

Of the magistrates whom he had appointed, Rufinus was considered the chief, who was by birth a Celtic Gaul, and commanded the court guards. Upon him the emperor reposed the entire confidence of all his affairs, and held no other person in great estimation. This gave offence to Timasius and Promotus, who, after having subjected themselves to so many dangers for the public good, were placed only in the second rank of favourites. And Rufinus was by this rendered so haughty and assuming, that in a public assembly he uttered some very strong expressions against Promotus. Promotus, unable to endure these, struck Rufinus in the face with great violence and wounded him. On this Rufinus immediately repaired to the emperor, and shewing him his face, excited him to such rage, that he declared if their envy against Rufinus should not diminish, they should very shortly see him emperor. Rufinus, who for other reasons was an enemy to many other persons, through his excessive ambition of being superior to all, on hearing this, persuaded the emperor to send Promotus from the court to some place where he might exercise the soldiers. Having obtained his desire, he employed some Barbarians to wait in ambuscade as he was entering Thrace. These, as they were commanded, attacked him by surprize, and killed him. He was a man superior to the desire of wealth, and had behaved with sincerity both toward the commonwealth and the emperors; but was justly rewarded for his folly in serving those who conducted the public affairs with so much negligence and impiety.

When this action was rumoured abroad, and had become the theme of general conversation, every moderate and sober-minded person was displeased at such enormities; yet Rufinus, at the same time, as if in reward for some glorious deed, was made consul. Charges, without any reasonable foundation, were then alledged against Tatianus and his son Proculus, who had given no other offence to Rufinus, than that of having discharged without bribery, and as much as was possible according to their duty, their offices of prefect, the one of the court, and the other of the city. To effect what was designed against them, Tatianus, being first deprived of his office, was brought to trial, and Rufinus was appointed prefect of the imperial court. Although there were apparently other persons commissioned to sit as judges in this process besides Rufinus, yet he alone had authority to pronounce sentence. When Proculus discovered the plot, he effected his escape. Upon this Rufinus, who thought him an active person, and feared lest he should invent some mode of giving him uneasiness, went to his father Tatianus, and by deceitful oaths induced him to believe all that he said. He even persuaded the emperor to give both the father and son the most favourable hopes; until he had thus deluded Tatianus from a well-grounded suspicion into vain thoughts of security, and induced him by letters to recall his son. But as soon as Proculus arrived, he was seized and thrown into prison. Tatianus being sent to reside in his own country, they sat several times in judgment on Proculus, until at length the judges, as they had agreed with Rufinus, commanded him to be carried into the suburbs, called Sycæ, and there to suffer death. The emperor, on hearing this, sent to recall the sword from his throat; but the messenger of Rufinus proceeded so slowly, that before he arrived at the place, the head of Proculus was severed from his body.

During these occurrences, intelligence was brought that the emperor Valentinian was no more, and that his death happened in this manner: Arbogastes, a Frank, who was appointed by the emperor Gratian lieutenant to Baudo, at the death of Baudo, confiding in his own ability, assumed the command without the emperor's permission. Being thought proper for the station by all the soldiers under him, both for his valour and experience in military affairs, and for his disregard of riches, he attained great influence. He thus became so elevated, that he would speak without reserve to the emperor, and would blame any measure which he thought improper. This gave such umbrage to Valentinian, that he opposed him on several occasions, and would have done him injury had he known how to effect it. At length Valentinian, no longer able to submit to his correction, when Arbogastes was approaching him as he sat on the imperial throne, looked sternly upon him, and presented him with a writing, by which he dismissed him from his command. Arbogastes, having read it, replied, "You neither gave me the command, nor can deprive me of it;" and having said this, tore the writing to pieces, threw it down, and retired. From that period their hatred was no longer kept to themselves, but appeared in public. Valentinian sent frequent letters to the emperor Theodosius, acquainting him with the arrogant behaviour of Arbogastes towards the majesty of an emperor, and requesting him speedily to send assistance, or that he should suddenly make him a visit. Meantime Arbogastes, hesitating how to proceed, at length formed the following resolution:

There was in the court a person named Eugenius, a man of learning, who was a professor and teacher of rhetoric. He had been recommended to the notice of Arbogastes by Rictomeris as a person of a kind and obliging disposition, with a desire that he would make him his familiar friend, being one who would be serviceable to him in any circumstances where the assistance of a real friend would be needful. When Rictomeris was departed to the emperor Theodosius, by daily conversation Eugenius became the sincere friend of Arbogastes, who had no secret which he did not confide to him. Recollecting Eugenius, therefore, at this juncture, who by his extraordinary learning and the gravity of his conversation seemed well adapted for the management of an empire, he communicated to him his designs. But finding him not pleased with the proposals, he attempted to prevail on him by all the arts he could use, and entreated him not to reject what fortune so favourably offered. Having at length persuaded him, he deemed it advisable in the first place to remove Valentinian, and thus to deliver the sole authority to Eugenius. With this view he proceeded to Vienna, a town in Gaul, where the emperor resided; and as he was amusing himself near the town in some sports with the soldiers, apprehending no danger, Arbogastes gave him a mortal wound. To this audacious action the soldiers quietly submitted, not only because he was so brave and warlike a person, but because they were attached to him through his contempt of riches. As soon as he had performed this action, he declared Eugenius emperor, and infused into them the most favourable hopes that he would prove an excellent ruler, since he possessed such extraordinary qualifications.

When these events were related to Theodosius, his wife Galla filled the whole court with confusion by her lamentations for the death of her brother. The emperor likewise was overcome by grief and anxiety, having not only lost his associate in the empire, who was a young man and so nearly related to him, but the empire having fallen into the hands of men disaffected to himself, and likewise invincible; Arbogastes being brave and skilful, and Eugenius learned and virtuous. Although he made these reflections and frequently revolved them in his mind, yet he resolved at once as it were to throw the die for all that he possessed, and therefore made every preparation for war. In pursuance of his design he intended to make Rictomeris commander of the cavalry, having experienced his courage in many wars, and to appoint other officers over the legions. But Rictomeris dying of disease he was compelled to make a different choice. . . .

As affairs were thus ordered, Alaric began his expedition against Rome, and ridiculed the preparations made by Honorius. Being unwilling to enter on so important an affair with not more than nearly equal forces to his enemy, he sent for Ataulphus, his wife's brother, from the upper Pannonia, to share with him in the enterprize, he having under him a very considerable force of Goths and Huns. However, he did not wait for the arrival of his brother-in-law, but marching forward with expedition, passed by Aquileia and the other cities beyond the Po, namely Concordia, Altinum, and Cremona. When he had crossed that river, being as it were at some festival, and having no enemy to obstruct him, he arrived at a castle of Bononia, called Occuparia. From thence, passing through all Æmilia, and leaving Ravenna in his rear, he advanced to Ariminum, a great city of Flaminia. Moving by that likewise with haste, and by all the other towns of that province, he came to Picenum, which is situated at the extremity of the Ionian bay. From thence marching towards Rome, he sacked all the castles and towns in his way. Thus if Arsacius and Tarentius, the two eunuchs, had not hastened to bring Eucherius, the son of Stilico, from those quarters to Rome to be executed according to the command of the emperor, the youth would certainly have fallen into the hands of Alaric, and would have been saved. The eunuchs having fulfilled the injunctions laid on them to that effect, and having delivered Thermantia, the wife of Honorius, to her mother, went by sea to the emperor in Gallia Celtica, where he then resided, because they were not able to go to him by the same way they had come. For these reasons, the emperor conceiving that he should render good service to the commonwealth by rewarding these two eunuchs for their great exploits in restoring Thermantia to her mother, and in putting to death Eucherius, appointed Tarentius imperial chamberlain, and gave the next post under him to Arsacius. Having then cut off Bathanarius, who was commander of the troops in the greater Libya, and had married the sister of Stilico, he gave that command to Heraclianus, the person who had killed Stilico, and who received this honour as the recompense of his action.

When Alaric was near Rome, besieging its inhabitants, the senate suspected Serena of bringing the Barbarians against their city. The whole senate therefore, with Placidia, uterine sister to the emperor, thought it proper that she should suffer death, for being the cause of the present calamity. They observed, that "Alaric, upon Serena being removed, will retire from the city, because no person will remain by whom he can hope the town to be betrayed into his hands." This suspicion was in reality groundless, as Serena never had any such intentions. However she suffered justly for her impieties toward the gods, which I am now about to relate. When the elder Theodosius, after defeating the rebel Eugenius, arrived at Rome, and occasioned in all persons a contempt and neglect of divine worship, by refusing to defray the charge of the holy rites from the public funds, the priests of both sexes were dismissed and banished, and the temples were deprived of sacrifices. Serena, insulting the deities with derision, was determined to see the temple dedicated to the mother of the gods. In this perceiving some ornaments around the neck of the statue of Rhea, suitable to the divine worship that was paid to her, she took them off the statue, and placed them upon her own neck. An aged woman, who was the only one remaining of the vestal virgins, upbraided her severely for so impious an action. Serena not only returned very violent language, but commanded her attendants to drive or carry her away. Notwithstanding, the old woman, as she was leaving the place, prayed that whatever was due to such impiety might fall on Serena, her husband, and children. Serena did not notice what she had said, but left the temple pleased with the ornaments she had obtained. Yet afterwards she was frequently visited by an appearance, not only imaginary, in her dreams, but real, when she was awake, which predicted her death. Other persons likewise beheld the same appearance. So far did that just power of vengeance, whose office it is to punish the wicked, discharge its duty, that although Serena knew what would happen, she was without caution, and submitted that neck which she had decorated with the attire of the goddess, even to a halter. It is likewise said that Stilico, for an impiety not much unlike this of which Serena was guilty, did not escape the secret hand of vengeance. He is said to have commanded the doors of the capitol to be stripped of a large quantity of gold with which they were covered. They who were employed in that act found on some part of the doors this inscription, "These are reserved for a wretched prince." The veracity of the prediction contained in this inscription was proved, for he indeed died in the most wretched and miserable manner.

However, the death of Serena did not remove Alaric from the siege, but he blocked up the gates all round, and having possessed himself of the river Tiber, prevented the arrival of necessaries from the port to the city. The Romans, on perceiving this, still resolved to persevere in their defence, expecting daily to receive auxiliaries from Ravenna. But none coming to their assistance, and being disappointed in their hopes, they diminished the allowance of grain, and ordered that not more than half of the former quantity of provisions should be dressed each day; and afterwards when the scarcity increased, only a third part. Receiving no relief, and all their provisions being consumed, the famine, as might be expected, was succeeded by a pestilence, and all places were filled with dead bodies. As the dead could not be interred outside the city, for the enemy was in possession of all the avenues, the city was made their sepulchre. Thus it was in danger of being depopulated by an additional cause, and though no want of provisions had subsisted, yet the stench arising from the putrid corpses was sufficient to infect them with disease. . . . They tried all methods of support, which are abominable in the eyes of all mankind. They then resolved on sending an embassy to the enemy, to inform him that they were willing to accept any reasonable conditions of peace, and at the same time were ready for war, since the people of Rome had taken up arms, and by means of continual military exercise were become well disposed for action. Basilius was appointed their ambassador, who was a Spaniard, and governor of a province. Johannes, the chief of the imperial notaries, went with him, because he was acquainted with Alaric, and might be the means of effecting a reconciliation. The Romans did not certainly know whether Alaric himself was present or not, or whether it was he who besieged the city. For they were deluded by a report that it was another person, who had been a friend of Stilico, which had occasioned him to come against their city.

When the ambassadors came to him, they were ashamed of the ignorance in which the Romans had so long remained, but delivered the message of the senate. When Alaric heard it, and that the people having been exercised to arms were ready for war, he remarked, "The thickest grass is more easy to cut than the thinnest." Having said this, he laughed immoderately at the ambassadors. But when they spoke of peace, he used such expressions as were in the extreme of arrogance and presumption. He declared, that he would not relinquish the siege on any condition but that of receiving all the gold and silver in the city, all the household goods, and the Barbarian slaves. One of the ambassadors observing, "If you take all these, what will you leave for the citizens?" He replied, "Their Souls." When the ambassadors received this answer, they desired time to communicate it to the citizens, and to consult with them in what manner they should act. Having obtained that permission, they related all the conversation that had passed in their embassy. On this the Romans, being convinced that it was really Alaric who attacked them, and despairing therefore of all things that conduce to human strength, called to mind the aid which the city had formerly met with in emergencies; and that they, by transgressing their ancient institutions, were now left destitute of it.

While they were occupied in these reflections, Pompeianus,

the prefect of the city, accidentally met with some persons who were come to Rome from Tuscany, and related that a town called Neveia had delivered itself from extreme danger, the Barbarians having been repulsed from it by storms of thunder and lightning, which was caused by the devotion of its inhabitants to the gods, in the ancient mode of worship. Having discoursed with these men, he performed all that was in his power according to the books of the chief priests. Recollecting, however, the opinions that were then prevalent, he resolved to proceed with greater caution, and proposed the whole affair to the bishop of the city, whose name was Innocentius. Preferring the preservation of the city to his own private opinion, he gave them permission to do privately whatever they knew to be convenient. They declared however that what they were able to do would be of no utility, unless the public and customary sacrifices were performed, and unless the senate ascended to the capitol, performing there, and in the different markets of the city, all that was essential. But no person daring to join in the ancient religious ordinances, they dismissed the men who were come from Tuscany, and applied themselves to the endeavouring to appease the Barbarians in the best possible manner. With this design they again sent ambassadors. After long discussions on both sides, it was at length agreed, that the city should give five thousand pounds of gold, and thirty thousand of silver, four thousand silk robes, three thousand scarlet fleeces, and three thousand pounds of pepper. As the city possessed no public stock, it was necessary for the senators who had property, to undertake the collection by an assessment. Palladius was empowered to rate every person according to his estate, but was not able to complete the whole sum out of all, either because many persons concealed part of their property, or because the city was impoverished, through the avarice and unceasing exactions of the magistrates appointed by the emperor. The evil genius, who at that time presided over the human race, then incited the persons employed in this transaction to the highest pitch of wickedness. They resolved to supply the deficiency from the ornaments that

37

were about the statues of the gods. This was in effect only rendering inanimate and inefficacious those images, which had been fixed up, and dedicated to sacred rites and ceremonies, and were decorated with precious attire, for preserving the city in perpetual felicity. And since every thing then conspired to the ruin of the city, they not only robbed the statues of their ornaments, but also melted down some of them that were made of gold and silver. Among these was that of Valour or Fortitude, which the Romans call Virtus. This being destroyed, all that remained of the Roman valour and intrepidity was totally extinguished; according to the remarks of persons who were skilled in sacred rites and observances.

The money being thus raised, they thought it advisable to send an envoy to the emperor to confer with him concerning the ensuing treaty, and to inform him that Alaric required, not only money, but the sons of certain noblemen as hostages; being willing on these conditions to make peace, and likewise to enter into an alliance with the emperor, and to assist the Romans against all their enemies. The emperor resolving to conclude a peace, the money was paid to the Barbarians. This being done, Alaric gave the citizens a free market for three successive days, with permission to pass securely through certain gates of the city, and to bring corn from the port. By these means the citizens having a little recovered breath, by selling the remainder of their goods, or exchanging one article for another, to purchase necessaries; the Barbarians departed from Rome, and pitched their camps in several places in Tuscany. Almost all the slaves in Rome then fled from the city, and enrolled themselves among the Barbarians, to the number of forty thousand. . . .

Affairs having thus been concerted, the emperor called ten thousand Huns to his assistance in the war against Alaric. In order that he might have provisions ready for them on their arrival, he ordered the Dalmatians to bring corn, sheep, and oxen. He sent out scouts to gain information of the way by which Alaric intended to march to Rome. But Alaric, in the mean time, repented of his intention of proceeding against

Rome, and sent the bishops of each city, not only as ambassadors, but also to advise the emperor not to suffer so noble a city, which for more than a thousand years had ruled over great part of the world, to be seized and destroyed by the Barbarians, nor such magnificent edifices to be demolished by hostile flames, but to prefer entering into a peace on some reasonable conditions. He instructed them to state to the emperor, that the Barbarians wanted no preferments, nor did he now desire the provinces which he had previously chosen as his residence, but only the two Norica, which are situated on the extremity of the river Danube, are harassed by continual incursions, and yield to the treasury a very small revenue. Besides this he only demanded annually as much corn as the emperor should think proper to grant, and would remit the gold. And that a friendship and alliance should subsist between himself and the Romans, against every one that should rise to oppose the empire. When Alaric had made these extremely temperate propositions, his moderation being universally admired, Jovius, and the other ministers of the emperor, declared that his demands could not possibly be acceded to, since all persons, who held any commission, had sworn not to make peace with Alaric. For if their oath had been made to the diety, they might indeed probably have dispensed with it, and have relied on the divine goodness for pardon; but since they had sworn by the head of the emperor, it was by no means lawful for them to infringe so great a vow. So cautious were they who then held the chief management of affairs, as they were destitute of the care and protection of heaven.

Alaric, having thus received insult in return for his reasonable demands, hastened towards Rome with all his forces, designing closely to besiege that city.

IMPERIAL WEAPONS FACTORIES IN FIFTH-CENTURY GAUL

early fifth century

In addition to providing proof for continued Roman influence in what is now northeastern and southern France into the fifth century, this document attests to the strongly autarchic economy of the late Empire. By this period each region tended to produce the food and goods requisite for its own needs.

Under the jurisdiction of the illustrious master of the offices: Factories in the Gauls:

> At Argenton, all arms [are manufactured].
> At Mâcon, arrows.
> At Autun, weapons, missiles and body-armor.
> At Autun, shields. . . .
> At Reims, swords.
> At Trèves, shields.
> At Trèves, missiles.
> At Amiens, swords and shields.

SOURCE Translated from *Documents relatifs à l'histoire de l'industrie et du commerce en France,* ed. Gustave Fagniez, *Collection de textes pour servir à l'étude et à l'enseignement de l'histoire,* Vol. I (Paris: Alphonse Picard et Fils, 1898), 36.

4

THE THEODOSIAN CODE

438

*Compiled under Theodosius II (Eastern Emperor, 408–450)
and his cousin and co-ruler Valentinian III (Western Emperor,
425–454), the Theodosian Code is the earliest of the great
legal compilations of the late Empire. These passages reveal
serious weaknesses in the Roman governmental system in the
first half of the fifth century: abrogation of administrative responsibility by public officials of the curial class, the growth of
manorial counter-societies in rural areas run by large landowners
and, in general, pervasive disregard for civic loyalties.*

MINUTES OF THE SENATE OF THE CITY OF ROME

In the year of the 16th consulship of Our Lord Flavius Theodosius Augustus and the consulship of the Most Noble Acilius
Glabrio Faustus.—438.

When the Most Noble and Illustrious Anicius Acilius Glabrio
Faustus, thrice Ex-Prefect of the City, Praetorian Prefect, and
Consul Ordinary, in his home, which is at Palma, and the
Most Noble and Illustrious Flavius Paulus, Prefect of the City,
the Respectable Junius Pomponius Publianus, Vicar of the Eter-

SOURCE From *The Theodosian Code and Novels and the Sirmondian Constitutions*, trans. by Clyde Pharr (Princeton University
Press), Copyright 1952 by Clyde Pharr, pp. 3, 5–6, 427, 358, 353,
363. Reprinted by permission of Princeton University Press.

nal City, men of noble rank, and the Most August Order of the Senate, had assembled and had conferred together for a considerable time, and the Constitutionaries Anastasius and Martinus had entered pursuant to an order, the Most Noble and Illustrious Anicius Acilius Glabrio Faustus, thrice Ex-Prefect of the City, Praetorian Prefect, and Consul Ordinary, spoke as follows:

"The felicity that emanates from our immortal Emperors proceeds in its increase to the point that it arrays with the ornaments of peace those whom it defends in the fortunes of war. Last year when I attended, as a mark of devotion, the most felicitous union of all the sacred ceremonies, after the nuptials had been felicitously solemnized, the most sacred Emperor, Our Lord Theodosius, desired to add the following high honor also to His world, namely, that He should order to be established the regulations that must be observed throughout the world, in accordance with the precepts of the laws which had been gathered together in a compendium of sixteen books, and these books he had desired to be consecrated by His most sacred name. . . ."

The assembly shouted:

"Augustuses of Augustuses, the greatest of Augustuses!"

> Repeated eight times.

"God gave You to us! God save You for us!"

> Repeated twenty-seven times.

"As Roman Emperors, pious and felicitous, may You rule for many years!"

> Repeated twenty-two times.

"For the good of the human race, for the good of the Senate, for the good of the State, for the good of all!"

> Repeated twenty-four times.

"Our hope is in You, You are our salvation!"

> Repeated twenty-six times.

"May it please our Augustuses to live forever!"

> Repeated twenty-two times.

"Dearer than our children, dearer than our parents!"

> Repeated sixteen times. . . .

"In order that the established laws may not be falsified, let many copies be made!"

Repeated twenty-five times.

"In order that the established laws may not be falsified, let all copies be written in our letters!"

Repeated eighteen times.

"To this copy which will be made by the constitutionaries let no annotations upon the law be added!"

Repeated twelve times.

"We request that copies to be kept in the imperial bureaus shall be made at public expense!"

Repeated sixteen times.

"Hail! Faustus!"

Repeated seventeen times.

"A second term for you in the consulship!"

Repeated fifteen times.

"You regulate everything, you harm no man!"

Repeated thirteen times.

"Let copies be made and dispatched to the provinces!"

Repeated eleven times.

"Worthy purveyor of such great benefits!"

Repeated ten times.

"Hail! Paulus!"

Repeated twelve times.

"A consulship for you!"

Repeated eleven times.

"We request that the Codes be kept in the public bureaus!"

Repeated fifteen times. . . .

"Hail! Faustus!"

Repeated thirteen times.

"A second term for you in the consulship!"

Repeated ten times.

"We ask that you report to the Emperors the desires of the Senate!"

Repeated twenty times.

"Preserver of the laws, preserver of the decrees!"

Repeated sixteen times.

"All the rights of landholders are thrown into confusion by such surreptitious actions!"

Repeated seventeen times. . . .

Emperors Arcadius and Honorius Augustuses to Eusebius, Count of the Sacred Imperial Largesses.

In order that the splendid cities and towns may not fall into ruins through age, We assign a third part of the income from the farms belonging to a municipality to be used for the repair of public works and the heating of baths.

Given on the eleventh day before the kalends of July at Milan in the year of the consulship of Olybrius and Probinus. June 21, 395. . . .

The same Augustuses [Emperors Gratian, Valentinian and Theodosius] to Cynegius, Praetorian Prefect.

No apparitor shall be delivered to a municipal council under the guise and assessment of a penalty, except a person who, perhaps, flees the municipal council and begins to perform imperial service so that he may not have to perform the duties to which he was born. Therefore, you shall admonish all judges whatsoever who are subject to your jurisdiction that no one of them shall suppose that any person shall be assigned to a municipal council in lieu of a punishment, since, in any case, not an honor, but a penalty must accompany every criminal.

Given on the eighth day before the ides of November at Constantinople in the year of the consulship of Richomer and Clearchus. November 6, 384. . . .

The same Augustuses [Emperors Valentinian and Valens] to Modestus, Praetorian Prefect.

Persons who are of the birth status of decurions shall be led forth from all homes[1] and shall be dragged forth to undergo the

---

[1] of powerful men, their protectors. (Ed.'s note)

performances of their compulsory public services. Of course, the harborers of such persons shall be threatened with loss of their property as well as loss of status, if they should proceed farther and should esteem the public welfare less than their personal desires and their protection.

Given on the third day before the ides of July at Ancyra (Ankara) in the year of the second consulship of Gratian Augustus and the consulship of Probus. July 13, 371. . . .

The same Augustuses [Emperors Arcadius and Honorius] to Dexter, Praetorian Prefect.

We observe that many men are hiding under the shadow of powerful men, in order that they may defraud their municipalities of the services which they owe. Therefore, a fine must be established to the effect that if any man should violate the general rule of the prescribed law, he shall be forced to pay to Our fisc five pounds of gold for each decurion and one pound for each member of a guild. Therefore, they shall expel all such men whom they harbor, lest Our Clemency should be aroused to greater indignation on account of the contumacy of those who disregard Our law.

Given on the seventeenth day before the kalends of July at Milan in the year of the consulship of Olybrius and Probinus.

FRANKISH RULE: *THE CHRONICLE OF FREDEGAR*
588 – 597

The seventh-century Chronicle of Fredegar *is the only extant historical source for a fairly large segment of Merovingian history. The chronicler's account of the reigns of Clovis' successors describes a violent and unstable society. His own disconnected narrative betrays his ignorance of historical and even literary continuity, and reflects the cultural poverty of his age. Though Fredegar's acquaintance with the East is cast almost in the mold of legend, he does provide evidence for Western merchants' contact with non-Christian areas.*

[588] At this same time Rauching and Guntramn Boso, Ursio and Bertefred, great men of the following of King Childebert, were executed on the king's orders because they had planned to assassinate him. Leudefred, duke of the Alamans, had also incurred the same king's displeasure; but he escaped into hiding. Uncelen was made duke in his place.

In this year Reccared, king of the Goths, embraced the love of God, and was first baptized in private. Then he summoned before him at Toledo all Goths who were still Arians, and all Arian books were ordered to be surrendered to him. These books

SOURCE From *The Fourth Book of the Chronicle of Fredegar with its continuations*, ed. and trans. by J. M. Wallace-Hadrill (London: Thomas Nelson and Sons, Ltd., 1960), 7–9, 12, 15, 29–30, 41, 42–43, 96.

were collected together in one house and were burnt at his command. He compelled all the Goths to be baptized into the Christian faith.

In this year Caesara, wife of Anaulf, the Persian emperor, left her husband and came with four male and four female servants to the blessed John, bishop of Constantinople. She said she was a private person and besought the blessed John to baptize her. She was baptized by the bishop himself, and the illustrious wife of the Emperor Maurice stood godmother to her. Her husband, the Persian emperor, on several occasions sent ambassadors to seek his wife, though the Emperor Maurice had no idea that that wife was Caesara; but the empress then suspected that she could be the person the ambassadors were seeking, for she was very beautiful. So she said to them: 'A woman has arrived here from Persia, saying that she is a private person. There she is. Perhaps she is the person you want.' When the ambassadors saw her they prostrated themselves on the ground in adoration and declared her to be the mistress they sought. The empress said to her, 'Make some reply to them.' She replied: 'I shall not address these fellows. They live dogs' lives. I will answer them only if they will do as I have done, and become Christians.' The ambassadors received baptism with willing hearts; after which Caesara said to them, 'If my husband is willing to become a Christian and to receive the grace of baptism, I will gladly return to him; but I will return on no other condition.' The ambassadors reported these words to the Persian emperor, who at once sent a mission to the Emperor Maurice to request that the blessed John be despatched to Antioch, for he wished to be baptized by him. The Emperor Maurice thereupon ordered the most prodigious preparations to be made at Antioch. The Persian emperor was there baptized with sixty thousand of his subjects; and it took John and other bishops two weeks to deal with the total number of Persians. Bishop Gregory of Antioch stood godfather to the Persian emperor himself. The Emperor Anaulf begged the Emperor Maurice to give him bishops and sufficient clergy to be established in Persia, so that all Persians might receive the grace of baptism. Maurice gladly gave them; and all Persia was speedily converted to Christianity.

[596] In this year Fredegundis and her son, King Chlotar, took possession of Paris and other cities after the barbarian fashion. To deal with Theudebert and Theuderic, Childebert's sons, she despatched a force which reached a place called Laffaux. The forces camped facing each other. Chlotar and his men hurled themselves upon Theudebert and Theuderic and made great carnage among their forces.

[597] Fredegundis died in the second year of Theuderic's reign.

Duke Wintrio was assassinated at the instigation of Brunechildis in the third year of the reign of Theudebert.

In the fourth year of Theuderic's reign, Quolen, by birth a Frank, was made patrician. In this year Marseilles and other cities of Provence were devastated by plague; and in the same year the water of the Lake of Thun, into which flows the river Aar, became so hot that it boiled and cooked shoals of fish. Also in this year died Warnachar, mayor of the palace to Theuderic. He distributed all his goods in alms to the poor.

In this same fortieth year of Chlotar's reign, the Lombard ruler Adaloald who had succeeded to the kingdom of his father Agilulf, received with kindness a representative of the Emperor Maurice, named Eusebius, who cleverly approached him and persuaded him to be massaged in his bath with some sort of ointment which had the effect of subjecting him to Eusebius' will and to none other. He was prevailed upon by him to order the killing of all the great men and lords of the Lombard kingdom and, with them out of the way, to place himself and all the Lombard people under the Emperor. But when he had put to death twelve innocent magnates, the rest saw the danger that faced them. So all the Lombard lords unanimously chose as king the duke of Turin, Charoald, who had married Gundeberga, King Adaloald's sister.

The lovely Queen Gundeberga was in all things good-natured and full of Christian piety. She was generous in alms-

48

giving and universally loved for her bounty. A certain Lombard named Adalulf, who was constantly at court in the king's service, one day found himself in her presence. The queen was as well disposed to him as she was to all others and accordingly remarked what a fine upstanding man he was. Hearing this, he said quietly to the queen, 'You deign to like my looks; pray, then, bid me sleep with you.' But she violently refused and spat in his face to show her contempt for him. Adalulf saw that he had endangered his life and thereupon made haste to King Charoald, for whom he said he had secret information. An audience being granted, he said to the king: 'My lady Queen Gundeberga has for three days been scheming with Duke Taso. She wants to poison you and then marry him and place him on the throne.' King Charoald took these lies seriously. He sent the queen into exile to the fortress of Lomello, where she was shut up in a tower. Chlotar sent a deputation to Charoald to enquire why he had humiliated his kinswoman Queen Gundeberga, and sent her into exile. Charoald replied by reporting the above-mentioned lies as if they had been the truth, whereat Ansoald, one of the deputation, remarked to Charoald as if on his own account, without any authority: 'You could get out of this difficulty without loss of face by ordering your informer to arm himself and do single combat with a representative of the queen. By such combat the judgement of God would determine Gundeberga's innocence or—who can tell?—guilt.' King Charoald and all his magnates liked this advice. Adalulf was ordered to arm himself for the fight; while Gundeberga and her cousin Aripert arranged that a certain Pitto should be Adalulf's opponent in arms. They fought, and Pitto killed Adalulf. So Gundeberga was forthwith re-established as queen, after three years in exile.

At this time the blessed Pope Gregory twice sent an embassy from the seat of the holy apostle Peter at Rome to Prince Charles, with the keys of the tomb of the saint, a link from his chains and many rich presents. Such things had never been seen or heard of before. The pope proposed a bargain whereby he should desert the imperial cause and, with the approval of the Roman people, join that of the said Prince Charles. The prince received the embassy with extraordinary honours and made it costly gifts. He then sent Grimo, abbot of Corbie, Sigebert, a monk of the cloister of the holy martyr Denis and others of his entourage with fine presents to the threshold of Saint Peter and Saint Paul at Rome.

6

A MEROVINGIAN FAIR

July 30, 629

The fair of St. Denis, or Dionysius, described in this decree of Dagobert is unique; historians know of no others during the Merovingian period. Yet it is reasonable to infer from this document that the manorial economy of early medieval France was, at least in the first part of the seventh century, complemented by a certain amount of commercial exchange between districts carried on by men who made their living as traders. Dagobert's reference to "our lord and glorious patron Dionysius" testifies to the close symbolic associations between the saint and the French ruling house, associations that were to remain strong throughout the medieval period.

Dagobert, king of the Franks, to the illustrious Leutho, Vulfio, and Rauco, to the counts and all our agents, vicars, hundred-men, and other ministers of our republic. May your solicitude

SOURCE Translated from *Documents relatifs à l'histoire de l'industrie et du commerce en France*, ed. Gustave Fagniez, *Collection de textes pour servir à l'étude et à l'enseignement de l'histoire*, Vol. I (Paris: Alphonse Picard et Fils, 1898), 43–44.

and prudence know both how much we desire it and that we have set up a market in honor of our lord and glorious patron Dionysius, to be held on the [day of the] mass which occurs once a year on the seventh of the Ides of October [Oct. 9], consisting of all the tradesmen in our kingdom and those who come from across the sea, in that highway which leads to the city of Paris, in the place which is called the quarter of Saint Martin. We order, moreover, that the same market be extended throughout four weeks, so that traders from Lombardy or Spain or Provence or from other regions are able to come to it. And we wish and expressly command that no trader dare to do business in the district of Paris, unless it be in honor of Saint Dionysius; and if anyone defies this order, he shall pay the fine of our ban in deference to the saint. Finally, we command and expressly order you, and all of your agents or apprentices or successors present and to come, that there be no impediment of any kind, to this, Saint Dionysius', market, from us or from you, neither within the city of Paris, nor by the gates in the same district, from tolls or waterway-taxes, bridge-tolls, river-tolls, involuntary taxes, duties, navigational tolls, camp-tolls, military tolls, wine tolls, ground rents, praise-taxes,[1] or salt-taxes, levied anywhere or by anyone, except those that can be exacted on the merchandise of the fair on our behalf or for the public fisc. The share of Saint Dionysius and his agents they may hold temporarily through this our indulgence and authority. And so that our command concerning this holy place be upheld the more strongly in our time and in the future, we ordered it to be strengthened by the writing below in our hand, and we commanded that it be sealed with our ring. King Dagobert made his writing below. Dado offered [this document]. Dated on the third of the Kalends of August [July 30], in the second year of Dagobert's reign, prosperously despatched, in God's name. Amen.

[1] A formulistic phrase with no specific meaning, often included in French charters whose provisions concerned monastic lands or privileges. (Ed.'s note)

CHARLEMAGNE, *A CAPITULARY ON MILITARY SERVICE IN THE HOST*

812

A CAPITULARY ON THE CHURCH

789

The Capitulary on Military Service gives a good account of Charlemagne's techniques of controlling his host, or army. Fines are used to threaten both important royal vassals and their subordinate vassals; care is taken to prevent the accumulation of weapons by potential enemies of the king. In the Capitulary on the Church, Charles (who in 789 is only King of the Franks), hedges his laws with impressive-sounding decrees of church councils, and assumes the responsibility of regulating the procedures and even the morals of the clergy, in keeping with the contemporary theory of theocratic monarchy.

A CAPITULARY ON MILITARY SERVICE IN THE HOST

The Capitularies which the Lord Emperor constituted at Boulogne, which is at the sea's shore, in the forty-fourth year of his reign, in the month of October, the sixth indiction.

SOURCE Translated from *Sacrorum Conciliorum Nova et Amplissima Collectio*, ed. Joannes Dominicus Mansi *et alii*, Vol. XVII (Paris, 1902), 493–96, 213–17.

Of a free man summoned to the host

Any free man whatever, who should be summoned to the host, and who should refuse to come, shall pay the full army-tax [*heribannum*], that is, 60 *solidi*. And if he cannot pay, he shall place himself in the service of the Prince, with his own person as guarantor, until such time as he shall have paid off the debt [*bannus*]. And then he shall return again to his free status. And if that man who placed himself in [the royal] service because of the army-tax should die in that service, [nevertheless] his heirs shall not lose the inheritance which belongs to them, nor their liberty, nor shall they be liable to pay army-tax.

Of collecting the army-tax

Let no count presume to collect the army-tax for any cause whatever—neither for guard service, nor for cartage, watch and ward tax, nor for hospitality, nor for any other tax, and [let him not collect it] unless our envoy has first received our share of the army-tax on our behalf, and has given him his third from it. The same army-tax shall not be collected in land or slaves, but in gold and silver, silken cloaks or arms, animals or cattle, or in such coin as may be useful.

Of those who hold honors[1] of the crown and, summoned to the host, should not come to the agreed meeting, shall abstain, for as many days as he has come late, from meat and wine.

Of those who return from the host without leave

Concerning anyone who shall have returned from the host without leave or permission from the Prince, which act the Franks call *herifliz* [literally, fleeing the host], we wish that the ancient custom, that is, the capital sentence, be observed in his punishing. . . .

Prohibition of drinking challenges in the host

Let no one in the host challenge his equal or any other man to drink. Whoever shall be found drunken in the army shall be so ostracized that he shall drink only water, until he realizes the evil he has done.

[1] lands, fiefs. (Ed.'s note)

Of vassals now serving in the palace, and yet holding benefices

Concerning royal vassals who now serve within the palace, and yet are known to hold benefices, it is ordered that whichever of them shall remain in the palace with the Lord Emperor shall not bring their household vassals with them, but shall permit them to go to the count in whose districts they live.

Of those who remain in their lord's households without Imperial permission, and do not join the host

Any free man who shall be found, this year, not to have joined the host with his lord, shall be forced to pay the full army-tax. And if the lord or the count dismissed him from his palace, the same shall pay the debt for him; and as many army-taxes shall be extracted from him as there are men he has dismissed from his household. . . .

That no shields or swords may be given or sold to a stranger by anyone without royal permission

It is ordained that no bishops or abbots or abbesses or any rector of a church may either presume to give or sell shields or swords to any stranger whatever, without our permission, unless they are his vassals. And if it should happen that, in a church or holy place, more shields are found than are sufficient for the men of the said church, then the rector shall ask the Prince what he orders done with them. . . .

A CAPITULARY ON THE CHURCH

Of those who are excommunicated by their own bishop.
To all.

There are some who, having committed sins, are excommunicated by their own bishop, and are nevertheless presumptuously accepted into the fellowship or communion of other ecclesiastics or laymen: which situation the holy Nicene Council, and likewise that of Chalcedon, and even that of Antioch and Sardica, prohibited. . . .

[lengthy citations from these Councils follow]

Of fugitive and wandering clergy

To all.

Again in the same Council, and no less in that of Antioch, likewise in that of Chalcedon, [it is ordered] that fugitive and wandering clerks are not to be received by anyone nor ordained without letters of commendation, and the permission of their bishops or abbots. . . .

[More quotes from conciliar legislation occur here; these passages follow every section of the capitulary.]

Of priests, deacons, or those who are among the clergy.

To the priests alone.

Again, in the same synod, priests and deacons and all who are among the clergy are prohibited from having women in their dwellings because of the suspicion this would cause; unless they be either their mother, sister, or other such women who do not give rise to suspicions. . . .

Of priests who sing the mass yet do not take communion.

To the priests.

Rumor has it that certain priests celebrate the mass, and do not take communion: which, we read, is altogether prohibited in the laws of the Apostles. For how can the priest, if he has not communicated, truly say, "We accept, O Lord, the sacraments"? . . .

Of suffragan[1] bishops

To the bishops.

Again, in the same Council [of Antioch], it is ordered that suffragan bishops look to their metropolitans, and that they dare to do nothing in their parishes without the opinion and advice of their metropolitan; nor should the metropolitan act similarly without their consent. . . .

Of bishops or anyone whosoever from among the clergy.

To all clergy.

Again, in the same Council, it is ordered that no bishop nor

[1] subordinate. (Ed.'s note)

any cleric without consent or written authorization of the bishops or metropolitans, presume to demand that his legal cases be brought before the royal dignity, but they ought to be examined in the common council of the bishops. . . .

8

CAROLINGIAN MERCHANTS
805

This document describes a predetermined itinerary for merchants going into parts of central Europe still ruled by pagan tribes. The careful organization of the journey, and the emperor's interest both in protecting them and in regulating their merchandise, helps to prove the frequency of such trading expeditions.

The traders who go into the lands of the Slavs and Avars should proceed with their goods this far: into Saxon lands as far as Bardowiek, where Hredi should act as their protector; and to Schessel, where Madalgaud should perform this service; and to Magdebourg, where Aito should do the same. And as far as Erfurt, Madalgaud should watch over them, as he should also as far as Hallstadt. [When they proceed] to Forchheim, Breemberg, and Ratisbonne, Audulf should be in charge of their safety; if they go on to Lorsch, Warnar should do the same. And let

SOURCE   Translated from *Documents relatifs à l'histoire de l'industrie et du commerce en France*, ed. Gustave Fagniez, *Collection de textes pour servir à l'étude et à l'enseignement de l'histoire*, Vol. I (Paris: Alphonse Picard et Fils, 1898), 50.

them not carry arms or shields to sell. If they are found carrying these, let all their goods be taken away, half of them being apportioned to the palace, the other half divided equally between our envoy and the one who discovered them.

9

THE THEODOSIAN CODE

438

These sections of the Code reveal the particularly desperate problems of late Roman society: widespread attempts to avoid military service, attempts by the imperial government to lure slaves into the army, and the general breakdown of the police power of the state, which can no longer protect its citizens from its soldiers.

The same Augustuses [Emperors Arcadius and Honorius] to Hilarius, Prefect of the City.

If any member of the guild of swine collectors by a petition for assistance of any kind or by the attainment of high rank should be known to have evaded the compulsory public service

SOURCE From *The Theodosian Code and Novels and the Sirmondian Constitutions,* trans. by Clyde Pharr (Princeton University Press), Copyright 1952 by Clyde Pharr, pp. 411, 170, 236, 172–73. Reprinted by permission of Princeton University Press.

to which he was born or to have betaken himself to service on various office staffs by means of annotations or rescripts elicited from Our Serenity, he shall be recalled to his original public service, whether he is found obligated through his paternal or his maternal ancestry. For if by pretense any privileges have arisen to the detriment of the people, such privileges must be deprived of their force. No admission at all to any high office whatsoever or to any imperial service shall be granted to any such person, but if any such privileges henceforth should be elicited or impetrated from Our imperial altars through annotations or rescripts or in any manner whatsoever, they shall be annulled.

1. Also if any person has betaken himself to the privileges of the clergy, he must either assume his own compulsory obligation to the State, or he must cede his own patrimony to that guild which he deserts.

2. But if any person either by purchase or by gift or by any other title whatever holds landed estates obligated to a guild, he must either assume his proportional part of the compulsory public service or cede such possessions. 3. The same general rule of Our regulation shall be observed with reference to all other guilds which are recognized as sharing in the privileges of the City of Rome.

Given on the 18th day before the kalends of February at Rome in the year of the consulship of Bassus and Philippus. Jan. 15, 408.

The same Augustuses [Emperors Valentinian and Valens] to Magnus, Vicar of the City of Rome.

According to the decree of the sainted Constantine, Your Sincerity shall not permit those persons who avoid active military service by amputating their fingers to be protected from such service by this mutilation of their hands, since indeed, they may be of service in some part of the State, even though they have voluntarily mutilated themselves.

Given on the fifth day before the kalends of May in the

year of the consulship of Lupicinus and Jovinus.—April 27, 367. . . .

Emperors Valentinian, Theodosius, and Arcadius Augustuses to the Provincials.

We grant to all men the unrestricted right of resistance if any soldiers or private citizens should enter their fields as nocturnal ravagers or should beset frequented roads by attacks from ambush. This right is granted to everyone in order that whoever so deserves shall be subjected immediately to punishment, shall receive the death which he threatened, and shall incur that danger which he intended for another. For it is better for a man to fight back at the proper time than for him to be avenged after his death. Therefore, We entrust the right of vengeance to you, and what it is too late to punish by trial We repress by edict. Let no man spare a soldier who should be resisted with a weapon as a brigand.

Given on the kalends of July in the year of the consulship of Tatianus and Symmachus.—July 1, 391.

Emperors Arcadius, Honorius and Theodosius Augustuses to the Provincials.

In the matter of defence against hostile attacks, We order that consideration be given not only to the legal status of the soldiers but also to their physical strength. Although We believe that freeborn are aroused by love of country, We exhort slaves also, by authority of this edict, that as soon as possible they shall offer themselves for the labors of war, and if they receive their arms as men fit for military service, they shall retain the reward of freedom, and they shall also receive two solidi each for travel money. Especially, of course, do We urge this service upon the slaves of those persons who are retained in the armed imperial service, and likewise upon the slaves of federated allies and of the conquered peoples, since it is evident that they are making war also along with their masters.

Given on the fifteenth day before the kalends of May at Ravenna in the year of the sixth consulship of Arcadius Augustus and the consulship of the Most Noble Probus.—April 17 (Feb. 15), 406.

10

THE BURGUNDIAN CODE

483 – 532

Compiled between 483 and 532, The Burgundian Code was an important step in the Romanizing of a Germanic tribe. The Code attempts to mold Burgundian customary law, derived from the traditions of the folk and enforced by moral pressure alone, into Roman written law, enforced by political authority. Although the Code recognized the rights of Romans and those of their Germanic neighbors separately, it does indicate that intermarriage between Romans and Burgundians of similar social standing was common. Despite this, the strong Germanic traditions of the wergeld system (money payments made to compensate for an injury) and of compurgation (clearing oneself of a criminal accusation by means of a collective oath) remained in use among the Burgundians.

SOURCE From *The Burgundian Code. Liber Constitutionum sive lex Gundobada,* trans. by Katherine Fischer (Philadelphia: University of Pennsylvania Press; London: Geoffrey Cumberlege, Oxford University Press, 1949). *Translations and Reprints from the Original Sources of European History,* 3rd series, ed. John L. Lamonte (Philadelphia, 1949), Vol. V, 17, 29–31, 63, 85–86.

PREFACE

First Constitution

1. In the name of God in the second year of the reign of our lord the most glorious king Gundobad, this book concerning laws past and present, and to be preserved throughout all future time, has been issued on the fourth day before the kalends of April (March 29) at Lyons.

Of the Commission of Crimes Which Are Charged Against Native Freemen.

1. If a native freeman, either barbarian or Roman, is accused of a crime through suspicion, let him render oath, and let him swear with his wife and sons and twelve relatives: if indeed he does not have wife and sons and he has mother or father, let him complete the designated number with father and mother. But if he has neither father nor mother, let him complete the oath with twelve relatives.

2. But if he who must take oath wishes to take it with raised hand (*de manu*), and if those who are ordered to hear the oath —those three whom we always command to be delegated by the judges for hearing an oath—before they enter the church declare they do not wish to receive the oath, then he who was about to take oath is not permitted to do so after this statement, but they (the judges) are hereby directed by us to commit the matter to the judgment of God (i.e., to ordeal).

3. If however, having received permission, he has taken the oath, and if he has been convicted after the oath, let him know that he must make restitution by a ninefold payment (*in novigildo*) to those in whose presence the judge ordered him to give his oath.

4. But if they (those appointed to hear the oath) fail to come to the place on the appointed day, and if they shall not have been detained by any illness or public duty, let them pay a fine of six solidi. But if they were detained by any illness or duty, let them make this known to the judge or send other persons in their place whom they can trust to receive the oath for them.

5. If moreover he who is about to take the oath does not come to the place, let the other party wait until the sixth hour of the day; but if he has not come by the sixth hour, let the case be dismissed without delay.

6. But if the other (the accusing party) does not come, let him who was about to take the oath depart without loss. . . .

Let Burgundians and Romans Be Held Under the Same Condition in the Matter of Killing Slaves.

1. If anyone kills a slave, barbarian by birth, a trained (select) house servant or messenger, let him compound sixty solidi; moreover, let the amount of the fine be twelve solidi. If anyone kills another's slave, Roman or barbarian, either ploughman or swineherd, let him pay thirty solidi.

2. Whoever kills a skilled goldsmith, let him pay two hundred solidi.

3. Whoever kills a silversmith, let him pay one hundred solidi.

4. Whoever kills a blacksmith, let him pay fifty solidi.

5. Whoever kills a carpenter, let him pay forty solidi.

Of Inflicted Wounds.

1. Whoever cuts off with a blow the arm of a man, either a freeman or slave, let him compound half his wergeld; if he does not cut the arm off, let him be judged according to the nature of the wound.

2. If anyone inflicts a wound on another's face, we order him

to pay three times the price in fee simple established for wounds on a part which is protected by clothing. . . .

Of Excluding Barbarians Whenever Contention Arises Between Two Romans Concerning the Boundaries of Their Fields.

1. Inasmuch as it has been established under certain penalty that no barbarian should dare to involve himself in a suit which a Roman has brought against another Roman, we advocate a stricter handling of these cases, and command that the law remain just as we ordered it established in earlier times. . . .

Of Sales Which Are Made Without Witnesses.

1. If anyone has bought a bondservant, or field, or vineyard, or landsite and house built in any place, we order that if it has not been confirmed in writing or witnessed, he shall lose his payment; that is, provided that the writing has not been subscribed and sealed by seven or five witnesses dwelling in that place.

2. Indeed, if five witnesses are not found to be present, we order that it be signed by three suitable witnesses of blameless reputation from those dwelling in that place; but, if this is not done, we order the document to be invalid. . . .

Of the Marriage Price (Wittimon).

1. If any Burgundian of the highest (optimas) or middle class (mediocris) unites with the daughter of another (probably of the same class) without her father's consent, we order that such a noble make a triple payment of one hundred fifty solidi to the father whose daughter he took, if he took her without stating his intentions in advance or seeking his consent; and let the fine be thirty-six solidi.

2. Indeed if one of the lower class (leudes) has presumed

63

to do this (i.e., has married one of his own class without her father's consent), let him likewise make a triple payment, that is, forty-five solidi; and let the fine be twelve solidi.

Of Jews Who Presume to Raise Their Hands Against a Christian.

1. If any Jew presumes to raise a hand against a Christian with fist, shoe, club, whip, or stone, or has seized his hair, let him be condemned to the loss of a hand.

2. But if he wishes to redeem his hand, we order him to redeem it with seventy-five solidi; and let the fine be twelve solidi.

3. Besides this, we order that if he has presumed to raise a hand against a priest, let him be handed over to death, and let his property be given into our treasury.

THE ASCETIC LIFE

11

THE DEAD SEA SCRIPTURES: *THE MANUAL OF DISCIPLINE*

c. 170 B.C. — A.D. 68

The teachings of Jesus were rooted in Jewish ascetic tradition; the writings of the Essene sect, a semi-monastic community which had flourished for nearly two centuries before his birth, contain many teachings similar to those attributed to him in the Gospels. This passage from the Essene Manual of Discipline, *a treatise on the monastic life, instructs initiates to renounce the material world, follow the Prince of Lights rather than the Angel of Darkness (a dualist conception of deity that persisted into heterodox Christian thought), and share their goods communally. Like the Essenes, the earliest Christians seem to have been elitist; it was only later, under the influence of Pauline teachings, that they adopted an inclusive and widely evangelical attitude.*

Of the Commitment

Everyone who wishes to join the community must pledge himself to respect God and man; to live according to the com-

SOURCE From *The Dead Sea Scriptures*, trans. by Theodor H. Gaster, 39–40, 43–44, 58. Copyright © 1956 by Theodor H. Gaster. Reprinted by permission of Doubleday & Company, Inc.

munal rule; to seek God [   ]; to do what is good and
upright in His sight, in accordance with what He has commanded through Moses and through His servants the prophets;
to love all that He has chosen and hate all that He has rejected;
to keep far from all evil and to cling to all good works; to act
truthfully and righteously and justly on earth and to walk no
more in the stubbornness of a guilty heart and of lustful eyes,
doing all manner of evil; to bring into a bond of mutual love all
who have declared their willingness to carry out the statutes of
God; to join the formal community of God; to walk blamelessly
before Him in conformity with His various laws and dispositions;
to love all the children of light, each according to his stake in
the formal community of God; and to hate all the children of
darkness, each according to the measure of his guilt, which God
will ultimately requite.

All who declare their willingness to serve God's truth must
bring all of their mind, all of their strength, and all of their
wealth into the community of God, so that their minds may be
purified by the truth of His precepts, their strength controlled by
His perfect ways, and their wealth disposed in accordance with
His just design.

Of initiation

Moreover, all who would join the ranks of the community
must enter into a covenant in the presence of God to do according to all that He has commanded and not to turn away from
Him through any fear or terror or through any trial to which
they may be subjected through the domination of Belial.

Of the two spirits in man

All that is and ever was comes from a God of knowledge. Before things came into existence He determined the plan of them;
and when they fill their appointed roles, it is in accordance with

His glorious design that they discharge their functions. Nothing can be changed. In His hand lies the government of all things. God it is that sustains them in their needs.

Now, this God created man to rule the world, and appointed for him two spirits after whose direction he was to walk until the final Inquisition. They are the spirits of truth and of perversity.

The origin of truth lies in the Fountain of Light, and that of perversity in the Wellspring of Darkness. All who practice righteousness are under the domination of the Prince of Lights, and walk in ways of light; whereas all who practice perversity are under the domination of the Angel of Darkness and walk in ways of darkness.

Of the property of 'presbyters'

The property of the 'specially holy men'—that is, of 'the men that walk blamelessly'—is not to be put into a common pool with that of men who may still be addicted to deceit and may not yet have achieved that purity of conduct which leads them to keep apart from perversity and to walk in integrity.

Until the coming of the Prophet and of both the priestly and the lay Messiah, these men are not to depart from the clear intent of the Law to walk in any way in the stubbornness of their own hearts. They shall judge by the original laws in which the members of the community were schooled from the beginning.

12

THE NEW TESTAMENT: THE SERMON ON THE MOUNT

c. 75 – 80

Taken from the second-oldest of the Gospels, this account of Jesus' sayings outlines an inflexible moral code in which sin is very broadly defined to include not only wrong acts but wrong intentions. Christians are to make no compromise with human weakness, and must "be perfect." This burden of perfection necessarily led to radical internalizing of the focus of belief; forced to repress outward violence, the Christian was nevertheless urged to do violence to himself as punishment for his sinful instincts. Although these demanding standards were later softened by the church, they continued to influence movements of monastic foundation and reform throughout the medieval period.

1 And seeing the multitudes, he went up into a mountain: and when he was set, his disciples came unto him:
2 And he opened his mouth, and taught them, saying,
3 Blessed are the poor in spirit: for theirs is the kingdom of heaven.
4 Blessed are they that mourn: for they shall be comforted.
5 Blessed are the meek: for they shall inherit the earth.
6 Blessed are they which do hunger and thirst after righteousness: for they shall be filled.

SOURCE From *Matthew* 5, 1–12, 27–30, 38–44, 48.

7 Blessed are the merciful: for they shall obtain mercy.

8 Blessed are the pure in heart: for they shall see God.

9 Blessed are the peacemakers: for they shall be called the children of God.

10 Blessed are they which are persecuted for righteousness' sake: for theirs is the kingdom of heaven.

11 Blessed are ye, when men shall revile you, and persecute you, and shall say all manner of evil against you falsely, for my sake.

12 Rejoice, and be exceeding glad: for great is your reward in heaven: for so persecuted they the prophets which were before you.

27 Ye have heard that it was said by them of old time, Thou shalt not commit adultery:

28 But I say unto you, That whosoever looketh on a woman to lust after her hath committed adultery with her already in his heart.

29 And if thy right eye offend thee, pluck it out, and cast it from thee: for it is profitable for thee that one of thy members should perish, and not that thy whole body should be cast into hell.

30 And if thy right hand offend thee, cut it off, and cast it from thee: for it is profitable for thee that one of thy members should perish, and not that thy whole body should be cast into hell.

38 Ye have heard that it hath been said, An eye for an eye, and a tooth for a tooth:

39 But I say unto you, That ye resist not evil: but whosoever shall smite thee on thy right cheek, turn to him the other also.

40 And if any man will sue thee at the law, and take away thy coat, let him have thy cloke also.

41 And whosoever shall compel thee to go a mile, go with him twain.

42 Give to him that asketh thee, and from him that would bor-
row of thee turn not thou away.

43 Ye have heard that it hath been said, Thou shalt love thy
neighbor, and hate thine enemy.

44 But I say unto you, Love your enemies, bless them that
curse you, do good to them that hate you, and pray for
them which despitefully use you, and persecute you;

48 Be ye therefore perfect, even as your Father which is in
heaven is perfect.

13

PSEUDO-DIONYSIUS THE AREOPAGITE,
THE MYSTICAL THEOLOGY
AND *THE CELESTIAL HIERARCHIES*

mid-fifth century

*The author of these works, long assumed to be Dionysius the
Areopagite, or presbyter, spoken of in Acts 17, 34, was probably
a Syriac monk, writing in the fifth century. Because he was
presumed to have belonged to the apostolic age and because
his mystical works combined Neo-Platonic and Christian thought
into a harmonious blend, medieval theologians revered and borrowed extensively from his treatises, especially from the two
quoted here. From his Greek sources, however, the pseudo-
Dionysius inherited certain ideas inconsistent with Christian or-*

SOURCE From Dionysius the Areopagite, *The Mystical Theology*
and *The Celestial Hierarchies*, with commentaries by the editors of
the Shrine of Wisdom (Fintry, Brook, Nr. Godalming, Surrey: The
Shrine of Wisdom, n.d.), 9–10, 19, 37, 45–47, 51–52, 54–56, 58–59.

*thodoxy: the passages below verge dangerously on pantheism
(the belief that God is contained in all things—that he is not
separate from his creation, but an integral part of it), polytheism
(belief in multiple gods, or godlings) and the theory of eternal
continuing creation which denies the Judeo-Christian concept of
linear time, with a definite beginning and eventual final end.*

THE MYSTICAL THEOLOGY

CHAPTER I

What is the Divine Darkness?

Supernal Triad, Deity above all essence, knowledge, and
goodness; Guide of Christians to Divine Wisdom; direct our path
to the ultimate summit of Thy mystical Lore, most incomprehensible, most luminous, and most exalted, where the pure,
absolute, and immutable mysteries of theology are veiled in the
dazzling obscurity of the secret Silence, outshining all brilliance
with the intensity of their Darkness, and surcharging our blinded
intellects with the utterly impalpable and invisible fairness of
glories surpassing all beauty. . . .

But these things are not to be disclosed to the uninitiated, by
whom I mean those attached to the objects of human thought,
and who believe there is no superessential Reality beyond, and
who imagine that by their own understanding they know Him
Who has made Darkness His secret place. And if the principles
of the divine Mysteries are beyond the understanding of these,
what is to be said of others still more incapable thereof, who
describe the transcendental First Cause of all by characteristics
drawn from the lowest order of beings, while they deny that He
is in any way above the images which they fashion after various
designs; whereas, they should affirm that, while He possesses all
the positive attributes of the universe (being the Universal
Cause), yet, in a more strict sense, He does not possess them,
since He transcends them all; wherefore there is no contradic-

tion between the affirmations and the negations, inasmuch as He infinitely precedes all conceptions of deprivation, being beyond all positive and negative distinctions. . . .

> *That He Who is the pre-eminent Cause*
> *of all things intelligibly perceived*
> *is not Himself any of those things.*

Again, ascending yet higher, we maintain that He is neither soul nor intellect; nor has He imagination, opinion, reason, or understanding; nor can He be expressed or conceived, since He is neither number, nor order; nor greatness, nor smallness; nor equality, nor inequality; nor similarity, nor dissimilarity; neither is He standing, nor moving, nor at rest; neither has He power, nor is power, nor is light; neither does He live, nor is He life; neither is He essence, nor eternity, nor time; nor is He subject to intelligible contact; nor is He science, nor truth, nor kingship, nor wisdom; neither one, nor oneness; nor godhead, nor goodness; nor is He spirit according to our understanding, nor filiation, nor paternity; nor anything else known to us or to any other beings, of the things that are or the things that are not; neither does anything that is, know Him as He is; nor does He know existing things according to existing knowledge; neither can the reason attain to Him, nor name Him, nor know Him; neither is He darkness nor light, nor the false, nor the true; nor can any affirmation or negation be applied to Him, for although we may affirm or deny the things below Him, we can neither affirm nor deny Him, inasmuch as the all-perfect and unique Cause of all things transcends all affirmation, and the simple pre-eminence of His absolute nature is outside of every negation—free from every limitation and beyond them all. . . .

What is Hierarchy, and what the use of Hierarchy?

Hierarchy is, in my opinion, a holy order and knowledge and activity which, so far as is attainable, participates in the Divine

Likeness, and is lifted up to the illuminations given it from God, and correspondingly towards the imitation of God. . . .

The aim of Hierarchy is the greatest possible assimilation to and union with God, and by taking Him as leader in all holy wisdom, to become like Him, so far as is permitted, by contemplating intently His most Divine Beauty. . . .

Theology has given to the Celestial Beings nine interpretative names, and among these our divine initiator distinguishes three threefold Orders. In the first rank of all he places those who, as we are told, dwell eternally in the constant Presence of God, and cleave to Him, and above all others are immediately united to Him. And he says that the teachings of the holy Word testify that the most holy Thrones and many-eyed and many-winged Ones, named in the Hebrew tongue Cherubim and Seraphim, are established immediately about God and nearest to Him above all others. Our venerable hierarch describes this threefold Order as a co-equal unity, and truly the most exalted of the Hierarchies, the most fully Godlike, and the most closely and immediately united to the First Light of the Godhead.

The second, he says, contains the Powers, Virtues, and Dominions, and the last and lowest choirs of the Celestial Intelligences are called Angels, Archangels, and Principalities. . . .

The name Seraphim clearly indicates their ceaseless and eternal revolution about Divine Principles, their heat and keenness, the exuberance of their intense, perpetual, tireless activity, and their elevative and energetic assimilation of those below, kindling them and firing them to their own heat, and wholly purifying them by a burning and all-consuming flame; and by the unhidden, unquenchable, changeless, radiant, and enlightening power, dispelling and destroying the shadows of darkness.

The name Cherubim denotes their power of knowing and beholding God, their receptivity to the highest Gift of Light, their contemplation of the Beauty of the Godhead in Its First Manifestation, and that they are filled by participation in Divine Wisdom, and bounteously outpour to those below them from their own fount of wisdom.

73

The name of the most glorious and exalted Thrones denotes that which is exempt from and untainted by any base and earthly thing, and the supermundane ascent up the steep. For these have no part in that which is lowest, but dwell in fullest power, immovably and perfectly established in the Most High, and receive the Divine Immanence above all passion and matter, and manifest God, being attentively open to divine participations. . . .

Of the Dominions, Virtues, and Powers, and their middle Hierarchy.

Now we must pass on to the middle Order of the Celestial Intelligences, contemplating with supermundane sight, as far as we may, the Dominions and the truly majestic splendour of the Divine Virtues and Powers. For the names of these supernal Beings denote the divine characteristics of their likeness to God.

The name given to the holy Dominions signifies, I think, a certain unbounded elevation to that which is above, freedom from all that is of the earth, and from all inward inclination to the bondage of discord, a liberal superiority to harsh tyranny, an exemptness from degrading servility and from all that is low: for they are untouched by any inconsistency. They are true Lords, perpetually aspiring to true lordship, and to the Source of lordship, and they providentially fashion themselves and those below them, as far as possible, into the likeness of true lordship. They do not turn towards vain shadows, but wholly give themselves to that true Authority, forever one with the Godlike Source of lordship.

The name of the holy Virtues signifies a certain powerful and unshakable virility welling forth into all their Godlike energies; not being weak and feeble for any reception of the Divine Illuminations granted to it; mounting upwards in fullness of power to an assimilation with God; never falling away from the Divine Life through its own weakness, but ascending unwaveringly to the superessential Virtue Which is the Source of virtue:

74

fashioning itself, as far as it may, in virtue; perfectly turned towards the Source of virtue, and flowing forth providentially to those below it, abundantly filling them with virtue.

The name of the holy Powers, co-equal with the Divine Dominions and Virtues, signifies an orderly and unconfined order in the divine receptions, and the regulation of intellectual and supermundane power which never debases its authority by tyrranical force, but is irresistibly urged onward in due order to the Divine. It beneficently leads those below it, as far as possible, to the Supreme Power Which is the Source of Power, Which it manifests after the manner of Angels in the well-ordered ranks of its own authoritative power. . . .

Of the Principalities, Archangels, and Angels, and of their last Hierarchy.

There remains for us the reverent contemplation of that sacred Order which completes the Angelic Hierarchies, and is composed of the Divine Principalities, Archangels, and Angels. And first, I think, I ought to explain to the best of my ability the meanings of their holy names.

The name of the Celestial Principalities signifies their Godlike princeliness and authoritativeness in an Order which is holy and most fitting to the princely Powers, and that they are wholly turned towards the Prince of Princes, and lead others in princely fashion, and that they are formed, as far as possible, in the likeness of the Source of Principality, and reveal Its superessential order by the good Order of the princely Powers.

The choir of the holy Archangels is placed in the same threefold Order as the Celestial Principalities; for, as has been said, there is one Hierarchy and Order which includes these and the Angels. But since each Hierarchy has first, middle, and last ranks, the holy Order of Archangels, through its middle position, participates in the two extremes, being joined with the most holy Principalities and with the holy Angels. . . .

The highest Order, as we have said, being in the foremost

75

place near the Hidden One, must be regarded as hierarchically ordering in a hidden manner the second Order; and the second Order of Dominions, Virtues, and Powers, leads the Principalities, Archangels, and Angels more manifestly, indeed, than the first Hierarchy, but in a more hidden manner than the Order below it; and the revealing Order of the Principalities, Archangels, and Angels presides one through the other over the human hierarchies so that their elevation and turning to God and their communion and union with Him may be in order; and moreover, that the procession from God, beneficently granted to all the Hierarchies, and visiting them all in common, may be with the most holy order. . . .

Let us also remind you in connection with your knowledge of hierarchy that Pharaoh was shown through visions by the Angel who presided over the Egyptians, and the Prince of Babylon was shown by his own Angel, the watchful and overruling Power of Providence. And for those nations the servants of the true God were appointed as leaders, the interpretations of angelic visions having been revealed from God through Angels to holy men near to the Angels, like Daniel and Joseph.

For there is one Sovereign and Providence of all, and we must never suppose that God was Leader of the Jews by chance, nor that certain Angels, either independently, or with equal rank, or in opposition to one another, ruled over the other nations; but this teaching must be received according to the following holy intention, not as meaning that God had shared the sovereignty of mankind with other Gods, or with Angels, and had been chosen by chance as Ruler and Leader of Israel, but as showing that although one all-powerful Providence of the Most High consigned the whole of mankind to the care of their own Angels for their preservation, yet the Israelites, almost alone of them all, turned to the knowledge and light of the True God. . . .

This may fittingly be added, that each Celestial and human intelligence contains in itself its own first, middle, and last powers, which are manifested in a way analogous to the afore-

said ordination belonging to each of the Hierarchical Illuminations; and accordingly each intelligence, as far as is right and attainable to it, participates in the most spotless purity, the most
abundant light, and the most complete perfection. For nothing
is self-perfect nor absolutely unindigent of perfection, save only
That Which is truly self-perfect and above all perfection.

14

CELTIC MONASTICISM: ST. COLUMBAN,
THE COMMUNAL RULE AND PENITENTIAL

550–615

*Beginning in the late sixth century, St. Columban (d. 615)
and other Celtic missionaries carried their particular brand of
Christianity to the Continent and accomplished the conversion
of large parts of the population of northern Europe. Because
the Irish Church centered around monasteries rather than secular dioceses, Columban sought to stabilize the religious life of
the newly converted peoples by making a number of monastic
foundations; the* Communal Rule *exemplifies the life he envisioned for his monks. Unlike the* Rule *of St. Benedict, which
eventually superseded it on the Continent, Columban's* Rule
*paid scant attention to matters of administrative detail and the
external rhythm of the monks' daily lives; instead, as the listing
of chapters below indicates, it dwelt on punishment of moral in-
fractions and on the inward state of the brethren's minds. The*

SOURCE From St. Columban, *Communal Rule* and *Penitential*,
in *Sancti Columbani Opera, Scriptores Latini Hiberniae*, ed. G. S. M.
Walker (Dublin: Dublin Institute for Advanced Studies, 1957), 143,
145, 169, 171, 181.

Penitential *prescribes rather harsh penances for sins and, like the* Rule, *places the emphasis on the inward, spiritual well-being of the monks.*

Here begins the Communal Rule of the Fathers.

I. Of confession before meat or entering our beds, and of keeping grace at table, likewise also of silence.

II. That the lamp should be blessed, and of him who has called anything his own, and of the management of the knife at table, and of him who has lost anything in serving, and of prostration in the synaxis, and of him who has lost the crumbs.

III. Of him who has lost anything carelessly, and who has spilt anything on the table, and who on leaving the house has not bowed himself for prayer, and who forgets the prayer before work, and who eats without grace, and who on returning home has not bowed himself, and of him who has confessed all this.

IIII. He who at the beginning of a psalm has not chanted well, and who has bitten the Lord's chalice with his teeth, and who has not kept his place, and who has laughed in the synaxis, and who receives blessed bread, and who forgets to make the offering. Of idle tales and of self-excuse, and of setting counsel against counsel, and of striking the altar.

V. Of him who utters a loud speech, and who excuses himself, and who contradicts a brother in pointing something out, and that those who excuse themselves are not the sons of God.

VI. Of him who has said a proud word, and who utters a loud speech, and who conceals someone's fault until he may utter it for a bad end, and who censures another's works, and who utters reproof against reproof.

VII. Of him who slanders another, and of the argumentative, and him who censures his superior, and of him who has been melancholy, and who entices his brother to evil, and who condemns another's obedience.

VIII. Of him who instructs his brother against his own senior, and who gainsays his case to his prior, and who does not ask pardon when reproved, and who wishes to be the visitor of others, and those who visit the kitchen without orders, and who go outside the bounds, and who speak together when forbidden, and who say that they are not permitted to do what they are asked, and of those who say We are doing what you tell us, and who knowingly transgress, and of him whose chrismal has fallen off.

VIIII. Of him who utters an idle word, and of brethren doing penance, and of minor penances.

X. Of a brother who has been disobedient, and who says and does not, and who murmurs, and who fails to seek pardon or excuses himself, and who provokes two brethren to anger, and of lying, and of him who contradicts a brother, and who breaks a commandment, and who does the work enjoined him with negligence, and who slanders his abbot, and who forgets or loses something out of doors.

XI. Of him who speaks with a lay person, and who completes his work and then does something without orders, and of him who is double-tongued, and who eats in a strange house, and who tells a past sin, and who on returning from the world tells also of worldly things, and of him who is the accomplice of one who does something contrary to the injunction of the rule.

XII. Of him who excites wrath in his brother, and of him who does not come to grace at table, and who sleeps at prayer, and who does not respond Amen, and who neglects an hour-office, and who does not hear the call to prayer, and who communicates in his night-garment.

XIII. Of him who on the fourth and sixth day eats before nones, and who tells a lie, and who sleeps in the same house as a woman, and who does not close the church behind him, and who spits in church, and who is forgetful of psalmody.

XIV. Of him who comes too slowly to some signal, and who

makes a sound after the peace, and who enters with his head covered, and who does not ask a prayer, and who eats without praying, and who makes a noise during prayers, and who retains anger or melancholy.

XV. Of neglect in the offerings. Here end the chapters.

Here begins the actual Communal Rule of the Brethren.

[A diversity of faults should be cured by the application of a diversity of penance. Therefore, my dearest brethren] I. It has been ordained, my dearest brethren, by the holy fathers that we make confession before meat or before entering our beds or whenever it is opportune [of all failings, not only mortal ones, but also of minor omissions] since confession and penance free from death. . . .

[In every place and occupation the rule of silence is determined to be strictly kept, so that we may be cleansed from every vice as far as human weakness is able, which usually rushes into vices with a precipitate course of speech, and that we may utter with the mouth some edification for our neighbours, for whom our Saviour Jesus shed His holy blood, rather than abuse of the absent conceived in our heart, and altogether idle words, for which we shall render an account to a just Avenger.

[These things have seemed good to be ordained for those who wish to take the high road to the topmost peaks of heaven, and who, while the sins of savage men surround them in the darkness, wish to cleave to the One God, sent upon this earth. They shall doubtless receive immortal rewards with the highest joy, which never declines for ever.

[Here ends the Communal Rule of St. Columban the Abbot. Thanks be to God.]

PENITENTIAL

Of Penance here begins.

1. True penance is not to commit things worthy of repentance but to lament what has been committed. But since this is an-

nulled by the weakness of many, not to say of all, the measures of penance must be known. And thus a scheme of these has been handed down by the holy fathers, so that in accordance with the greatness of the offences the length also of the penances should be ordained.

2. Therefore, if any has sinned in thought, that is, has desired to kill a man, or to commit fornication, or to steal, or to feast in secret and be drunken, or indeed to strike someone, or to desert, or to do anything else like this, and has been ready in his heart to carry out these sins; let him do penance for the greater in half a year, for the less in forty days on bread and water. . . .

12. The talkative is to be punished with silence, the restless with the practice of gentleness, the gluttonous with fasting, the sleepy with watching, the proud with imprisonment, the deserter with expulsion; let each suffer exactly in accordance with his deserts, that the just may justly live. . . .

27. If any, desiring a bath, has washed quite alone, let him do penance with an imposition. But if any, while washing lawfully in presence of his brethren, has done this standing, unless through the need for cleansing dirt more fully, let him be corrected with twenty-four strokes.

28. But if any, even while sitting in the bath, has uncovered his knees or arms, without the need for washing dirt, let him not wash for six days, that is, let that immodest bather not wash his feet until the following Lord's Day. Yet a monk, when standing privately alone, is permitted to wash his feet; while a senior even publicly, but with another washing his feet,[1] is permitted to be washed standing.

29. But before sermon on the Lord's Day let all, except for fixed requirements, be gathered together, so that none is lacking to the number of those who hear the exhortation, except for the cook and porter, who themselves also, if they can, are to try hard to be present when the gospel bell is heard.

30. It is ordained that confessions be made carefully, especially of mental disturbances, before going to Mass, lest per-

---

[1] Such assistance would be needed by the very old.

haps any should approach the altar unworthily, that is, if he
does not have a clean heart. For it is better to wait until the
heart is healed, and becomes a stranger to offence and envy,
than rashly to approach the judgement of the throne. For
Christ's throne is the altar, and His Body there with the Blood
judges those who approach unworthily. Therefore, just as we
must beware of mortal and fleshly sins before we communicate,
so we must refrain and cleanse ourselves from interior vices and
the sicknesses of a drooping spirit, before the covenant of true
peace and the bond of eternal salvation.

THE SECULAR CLERGY

15
_____

CLEMENT OF ALEXANDRIA,
EXHORTATION TO THE GREEKS

c. 180 – 215

The Greek Father Clement, who studied in Alexandria and even-
tually in about 200 founded a Christian catechetical school
there, was concerned to fight paganism with its own weapons.
His Exhortation to the Greeks *represents an abandonment of the*
older Christian idea of avoiding pagan learning altogether and
the growth of a different attitude among Christian intellectuals,
which encouraged familiarity with pagan authors and techniques

SOURCE From [Clement of Alexandria], *Exhortation to the*
Greeks, trans. by Thomas B. Falls (New York: Christian Heritage,
Inc., 1949), *The Fathers of the Church,* Vol. VI, 373, 377–80, 397.

of argument. Clement used his knowledge to point out what he saw as the contradictions and inconclusiveness of Greek thought, hoping to lure the disillusioned Greeks to Christianity.

I beseech God, at the beginning of this my plea to you Greeks, that I may know the words which I ought to address to you, and that, after you have restrained your usual fondness for polemics and have been freed of your fathers' error, you may prefer to accept what is for your own good. And if what at first seemed useless to you now appears to be useful, do not think that you thereby offend your ancestors. A thorough examination often shows that things which had appeared to be of great value proved to be otherwise when subjected to close scrutiny. Now, since we intend to discuss the true religion (and it is my studied opinion that they who wish to pass their lives in safety consider nothing more important than true religion, because of the judgment which awaits us at the end of this life, and which is proclaimed not only by our ancestors in God, namely, the prophets and lawgivers, but also by those men from your midst whom you consider wise, not only poets, but also philosophers, who proclaimed among you that they had reached the true knowledge of God), I deem it advisable that we first examine the teachers of religion, both our teachers and yours, in order to determine who they were, when they lived, and how great a reputation they enjoy. Thus, they who inherited a false religion from their ancestors may, on perceiving the truths, be freed from their old error. While we, by this means, may make manifest that we practice the religion of our forefathers in God. . . .

Now, if you refrain from quoting the poets, because you claim that poetic license permits them to fabricate myths and, under the guise of mythology, to attribute many false things to the gods, what other teachers of religion would you have, and where would you say they acquired such knowledge of your religion? (For it is impossible to gain a knowledge of such great and divine matters, unless from those who were already ac-

83

quainted with these matters.) Undoubtedly, you will reply: the sages and philosophers. For it is your custom to run to them, as to a fortified wall, whenever your poets' opinions of the gods are quoted. Therefore, since we should proceed in chronological order, I shall cite the opinions of your wise men in that order, and you will see that their theology is much more ridiculous than that of your poets. First of all, Thales of Miletus, that pioneer student of natural philosophy, claimed that the first principle of all things was water, for he taught that all things came from water and that eventually all things returned to water. Another native of Miletus, Anaximander, later held that the first principle of all things was the infinite, from which everything sprang and into which all things fell back. A third Miletan, Anaximenes, thought that air was the first principle from which all things originated and into which they all resolved. All these men, forming a succession from Thales on, followed what they called a natural philosophy.

Tracing another school of thought, we see that Pythagoras of Samos, son of Mnesarchus, considers numbers, with their proportion and harmony, and their resultant elements, as the basis of things. In his system he also includes the unity and infinite duality of numbers. . . .

You can readily perceive the confusion that exists among those who you say are your wise men—whom you call your teachers of religion. Some of them affirm that water is the first principle of all things; others say that air is; still others, fire; and others claim that some other of the above-mentioned elements were the first causes. These men actually said these things; furthermore, all of them used specious arguments to prove their unsound teachings, and each one endeavored to show that his own doctrine was more acceptable than the next. Can you tell me, therefore, my dear Greek friends, how they who look for salvation could safely approach these philosophers to learn from them the true religion, when the philosophers themselves cannot agree among themselves, but in their philosophical disputes contradict one another's opinions?

Perhaps they who refuse to abandon their ancient and anti-quated error will insist that they did not receive their religious instruction from the above-mentioned persons, but from those two whom they consider the most noted and accomplished philosophers, namely, Plato and Aristotle. Indeed, they think that these two have assimilated a knowledge of the true and perfect religion. But I would first like to inquire of those who make such a claim: From whom have Plato and Aristotle acquired such knowledge? It would not be possible for them to either have such knowledge or be able to transmit it accurately to others, unless they learned such great and divine matters from someone who knew them. Secondly, it is my opinion that the teachings of those two philosophers should be submitted to a close examination, in order to determine whether they openly contradict each other.

If we discover that they do not agree with each other, we should easily conclude that they also are ignorant. For Plato, acting as though he had just descended from Heaven and had accurately learned and witnessed all celestial matters, states that the Most High God exists in a fiery substance. Yet Aristotle, in explaining at length his own system of philosophy in a book addressed to Alexander the Macedonian, openly and expertly refutes Plato's opinion, claiming that God does not exist in a fiery substance. Instead, he said that God exists in a mysterious sort of ethereal and immutable body, a kind of fifth substance which he himself invented. Here are his words: 'It is not true, as some have erroneously stated of the Divinity, that God exists in a fiery substance.' Furthermore, as if not satisfied with this defamation of Plato, he quotes as a witness to the truth of this theory of an ethereal body, one whom Plato had expelled from his republic, after branding him a liar and a third imitator of the images of truth (for that is what Plato calls Homer). Aristotle wrote: 'Thus states Homer: Jupiter obtained the broad heaven in the air and the clouds.' In this way, he hoped to give further weight to his opinion by the authority of Homer's testimony, not realizing that, if he used Homer to prove the truth of his state-

85

ments, many of his doctrines would, on the contrary, be proved false. . . .

Although Plato very probably approved of the teaching of Moses and the other Prophets concerning the One and Only God, which he had learned during his visit to Egypt, yet he was afraid to say so, lest, after what had happened to Socrates, he might cause some Anytus or Meletus to come forward and accuse him before the Athenians in these words: 'Plato is a meddling fool who does much harm, for he does not accept the gods which the state recognizes.' Thus, in fear of the hemlock, Plato composed an artfully ambiguous dissertation on the gods, in which he admitted gods for those who desired them, and denied their existence for the benefit of those who professed no deity.

16

AUGUSTINE, ON CONTINENCE

c. 395

Written probably in about 395 (paradoxically, at the peak of his denunciations of the dualist Manicheans), Augustine's treatise On Continence *insisted that the celibate life was the ideal for all Christians. Labeling marriage as a compromise with the sinful flesh, Augustine's theology buttressed the concept that communities of religious, because of their vow of chastity, were "more Christian" than laymen, and that they existed in part to purify lay society vicariously.*

SOURCE From Augustine, *On Continence*, trans. by Sister Mary Francis MacDonald, *The Fathers of the Church*, Vol. XVI (New York: The Fathers of the Church, Inc., 1952), 189, 211–12.

We first declare and prove, namely, that continence is a gift of God. In the Book of Wisdom we have it written that, unless God give it, it is possible for no one to be continent. The Lord, moreover, concerning that major and also more renowned continence by which anyone refrains from marriage, says: 'Not all can accept this teaching, but those to whom it has been given.' And because, too, conjugal chastity even cannot be guarded, unless there be restraint from unlawful intercourse, the Apostle has proclaimed that each is the gift of God. When he spoke of the two types of life, the married life and that outside of marriage, he said: 'For I would that all men were as I am myself, but each one has his own gift from God, one in this way, and another in that.' . . .

Now, the flesh desires nothing except through the soul, but the flesh is said to lust against the spirit when the soul through carnal concupiscence wrestles with the spirit. We make up this whole: the flesh itself, which dies when the soul departs, is our weak part, and is not dismissed as to be fled from, but is placed aside to be received again, and, when it is received, it will be abandoned no more. 'What is sown,' indeed, 'a natural body rises a spiritual body. Then, at last, the flesh will desire nothing against the spirit when itself also will be called spiritual, since it will be fitted to live eternally, not only without any repugnance to the spirit, but even without any need of corporal nourishment. These two, therefore, which now struggle against each other within us, since we consist of both, let us pray and endeavor that they may be in accord. For, we ought not to consider one of them an enemy, but an imperfection whereby the flesh lusts against the spirit, and, when this is healed, it will not exist as itself. Both substances will be saved, nor will there be any battle in either. Let us listen to the Apostle: 'I know,' he says, 'that in me, that is, in my flesh, no good dwells.' . . .

And in another place he says: 'Therefore I myself, with my mind, serve the law of God, but with my flesh the law of sin.' Let those who have ears hear: 'Therefore I myself,' I being of mind and I being also of flesh; but 'with the mind I serve the law of God, with the flesh, however, the law of sin.' How did he mean that he served the law of sin by the flesh? Was it by consenting to carnal concupiscence? By no means! It was by having there the movements of the desires which he was unwilling to have—yet he had them. But, by not consenting to these desires with the mind, he served the law of God and restrained his members from becoming the instruments of sin.

17

AUGUSTINE, ON THE CITY OF GOD, AGAINST THE PAGANS

Augustine's most remarkable work, On the City of God, *was written on several levels and dealt in depth with history, philosophy and theology. Perceiving, in the early years of the fifth century, that Rome's culture as well as her remaining political strength were disintegrating under the increased pressure of barbarian attacks, Augustine determined to immortalize what he saw as the imperishable component of the Empire. Purged of her sordid pagan associations, Rome became for him the eternal City of God, existing in heaven and on earth simultaneously, dwelling place of all Christians who loved God more than earthly things.*

In the absence of justice, what is sovereignty but organized brigandage? For, what are bands of brigands but petty kingdoms? They also are groups of men, under the rule of a leader, bound

SOURCE From Augustine, *The City of God,* ed. Vernon J. Bourke, trans. by Gerald G. Walsh (Garden City, N.Y.: Image Books, 1958), 88–89, 99, 321, 325, 326, 328, 494, 502, 507.

together by a common agreement, dividing their booty according to a settled principle. If this band of criminals, by recruiting more criminals, acquires enough power to occupy regions, to capture cities, and to subdue whole populations, then it can with fuller right assume the title of kingdom, which in the public estimation is conferred upon it, not by the renunciation of greed, but by the increase of impunity.

The answer which a captured pirate gave to the celebrated Alexander the Great was perfectly accurate and correct. When that king asked the man what he meant by infesting the sea, he boldly replied: 'What you mean by warring on the whole world. I do my fighting on a tiny ship, and they call me a pirate; you do yours with a large fleet, and they call you Commander.' . . .

The cause, then, of the greatness of the Roman Empire was neither fortune nor fate. (I am using these words in the sense of those who say or think that fortune, or chance, is what happens without cause or rational explanation, and that fate is what is bound to happen, in spite even of the will of God or of men.) On the contrary, Divine Providence alone explains the establishment of kingdoms among men. As for those who speak of fate, but mean by fate the will and power of God, they should keep their conception but change their expression. . . .

What we see, then, is that two societies have issued from two kinds of love. Worldly society has flowered from a selfish love which dared to despise even God, whereas the communion of saints is rooted in a love of God that is ready to trample on self. In a word, this latter relies on the Lord, whereas the other boasts that it can get along by itself. The city of man seeks the praise of men, whereas the height of glory for the other is to hear God in the witness of conscience. The one lifts up its head in its own boasting; the other says to God: 'Thou art my glory, thou liftest up my head.'

In the city of the world both the rulers themselves and the people they dominate are dominated by the lust for domination; whereas in the City of God all citizens serve one another in charity, whether they serve by the responsibilities of office or by the duties of obedience. . . .

A shadow, as it were, of this eternal City has been cast on earth, a prophetic representation of something to come rather than a real presentation in time. Yet this shadow, merely symbolic as it is and not the reality that is to be, is properly called the holy City. . . .

In the world community, then, we find two forms, one being the visible appearance of the earthly city and another whose presence serves as a shadow of the heavenly City. . . .

Now, the city of man was first founded by a fratricide who was moved by envy to kill his brother, a man who, in his pilgrimage on earth, was a citizen of the City of God. It need not surprise us, then, that long afterwards, in the founding of that city which was to dominate so many peoples and become the capital of that earthly city with which I am dealing, the copy, so to speak, corresponded to the original—to what the Greeks call the archetype. For, in both cases, we have the same crime. As one of the poets puts it: 'With brother's blood the earliest walls were wet.' For Rome began, as Roman history records, when Remus was killed by Romulus, his brother. However, in this case, both men were citizens of the earthly city. It was the ambition of both of them to have the honor of founding the Roman republic, but that was an honor that could not be shared; it had to belong to one or the other. . . .

The two cities, of God and of the Devil, are to reach their appointed ends when the sentences of destiny and doom are passed by our Lord Jesus Christ, the Judge of the living and the dead. . . .

One thing that will happen, and most certainly happen, is what God, through His Prophet, said concerning the punishment of hell being eternal: 'Their worm shall not die, and their fire shall not be quenched.' And it was to emphasize this further that, when the Lord Jesus was counseling us to cut off members that scandalize us (meaning that we should cut off people whom we love as we love our right hand), He said: 'It is better for thee to enter into life maimed, than, having two hands, to go into hell, into the unquenchable fire, where their worm dies not, and the fire is not quenched. . . .

As I mentioned in the preceding Book, the present one is to be the last of the whole work, and is to deal with the eternal blessedness of the City of God. The word 'eternal' as here used means more than any period, however long, of centuries upon centuries which, ultimately, must have an end. It means 'everlasting' in the sense of the text which runs: 'Of His kingdom there shall be no end.' It does not mean the kind of apparent perpetuity produced by successive generations which come and go by births and deaths. Such a perpetuity is merely perennial like the color of an evergreen that seems to continue forever because the new leaves, sprouting while the old ones wither and fall, maintain an unchanging density of foliage. On the contrary, in the eternal City of God, each and all of the citizens are personally immortal with an immortality which the holy angels never lost and which even human beings can come to share. This is to be achieved by the supreme omnipotence of the Creator, the Founder of the City. . . .

18

VINCENT OF LÉRINS, *AGAINST HERESY*

c. 431 – 450

*This passage from the fifth-century theologian Vincent of
Lérins' treatise* Against Heresy *seeks to arrive at a logical determination of what constitutes heresy and, by the same means, to
achieve the more difficult aim of defining orthodoxy. The heretical doctrines outlined in this passage summarize the most serious
theological problems Christian thinkers had had to face in the
church's formative centuries.*

[4.] I have often then inquired earnestly and attentively of
very many men eminent for sanctity and learning, how and by
what sure and so to speak universal rule I may be able to distinguish the truth of Catholic faith from the falsehood of heretical pravity; and I have always, and in almost every instance,
received an answer to this effect: That whether I or any one
else should wish to detect the frauds and avoid the snares of
heretics as they rise, and to continue sound and complete in the
Catholic faith, we must, the Lord helping, fortify our own
belief in two ways; first, by the authority of the Divine Law,
and then, by the Tradition of the Catholic Church.

SOURCE From Vincent of Lérins, *Against Heresy, A Select Li-
brary of Nicene and Post-Nicene Fathers of the Christian Church,*
Second series, trans. by Philip Schaff and Henry Wace, Vol. XI
(New York: The Christian Literature Society; Oxford and London:
Parker & Co., 1894), 132, 139, 140, 141, 154.

[5.] But here some one perhaps will ask, Since the canon of Scripture is complete, and sufficient of itself for everything, and more than sufficient, what need is there to join with it the authority of the Church's interpretation? For this reason,—because, owing to the depth of Holy Scripture, all do not accept it in one and the same sense, but one understands its words in one way, another in another; so that it seems to be capable of as many interpretations as there are interpreters. . . .

[7.] What then will a Catholic Christian do, if a small portion of the Church have cut itself off from the communion of the universal faith? What, surely, but prefer the soundness of the whole body to the unsoundness of a pestilent and corrupt member? What if some novel contagion seek to infect not merely an insignificant portion of the Church, but the whole? Then it will be his care to cleave to antiquity, which at this day cannot possibly be seduced by any fraud of novelty.

[8.] But what, if in antiquity itself there be found error on the part of two or three men, or at any rate of a city or even of a province? Then it will be his care by all means, to prefer the decrees, if such there be, of an ancient General Council to the rashness and ignorance of a few. . . .

[33.] The heresy of Photinus, then, is as follows: He says that God is singular and sole, and is to be regarded as the Jews regarded Him. He denies the completeness of the Trinity, and does not believe that there is any Person of God the Word, or any Person of the Holy Ghost. Christ he affirms to be a mere man, whose original was from Mary. Hence he insists with the utmost obstinacy that we are to render worship only to the Person of God the Father, and that we are to honour Christ as man only. This is the doctrine of Photinus.

[34.] Apollinaris, affecting to agree with the Church as to the unity of the Trinity, though not this even with entire soundness of belief, as to the Incarnation of the Lord, blasphemes openly. For he says that the flesh of our Saviour was either altogether devoid of a human soul, or, at all events, was devoid of a rational soul. Moreover, he says that this same flesh of the

93

Lord was not received from the flesh of the holy Virgin Mary, but came down from heaven into the Virgin; and, ever wavering and undecided, he preaches one while that it was co-eternal with God the Word, another that it was made of the divine nature of the Word. For, denying that there are two substances in Christ, one divine, the other human, one from the Father, the other from his mother, he holds that the very nature of the Word was divided, as though one part of it remained in God, the other was converted into flesh: so that whereas the truth says that of two substances there is one Christ, he affirms, contrary to the truth, that of the one divinity of Christ there are become two substances. This, then, is the doctrine of Apollinaris.

[35.] Nestorius, whose disease is of an opposite kind, while pretending that he holds two distinct substances in Christ, brings in of a sudden two Persons, and with unheard of wickedness would have two sons of God, two Christs,—one, God, the other, man, one, begotten of his Father, the other, born of his mother. . . . Either, I say, he craftily affects in some places in his writings to believe one Christ and one Person of Christ, or else he says that after the Virgin had brought forth, the two Persons were united into one Christ, though at the time of her conception or parturition, and for some short time afterwards, there were two Christs; so that forsooth, though Christ was born at first an ordinary man and nothing more, and not as yet associated in unity of Person with the Word of God, yet afterwards the Person of the Word assuming descended upon Him; and though now the Person assumed remains in the glory of God, yet once there would seem to have been no difference between Him and all other men. . . .

[36.] In these ways then do these rabid dogs, Nestorius, Apollinaris, and Photinus, bark against the Catholic faith: Photinus, by denying the Trinity; Apollinaris, by teaching that the nature of the Word is mutable, and refusing to acknowledge that there are two substances in Christ, denying moreover either that Christ had a soul at all, or, at all events, that he had a rational soul, and asserting that the Word of God supplied the place of the rational soul; Nestorius, by affirming that there were always or at any rate that once there were two Christs. But the Catholic Church, holding the right faith both concerning God and concerning our Saviour, is guilty of blasphemy neither in the mystery of the Trinity, nor in that of the Incarnation of Christ. . . .

[37.] But it will be well to unfold this same doctrine more distinctly and explicitly again and again.

In God there is one substance, but three Persons; in Christ two substances, but one Person. In the Trinity, another and another Person, not another and another substance (distinct Persons, not distinct substances); in the Saviour another and another substance, not another and another Person, (distinct substances, not distinct Persons). How in the Trinity another and another Person (distinct Persons) not another and another substance (distinct substances)? Because there is one Person of the Father, another of the Son, another of the Holy Ghost; but yet there is not another and another nature (distinct natures) but one and the same nature. How in the Saviour another and another substance, not another and another Person (two distinct substances, not two distinct Persons)? Because there is one substance of the Godhead, another of the manhood. But yet the Godhead and the manhood are not another and another Person (two distinct Persons), but one and the same Christ, one and the same Son of God, and one and the same Person of one and the same Christ and Son of God, in like manner as in man the flesh is one thing and the soul another, but one and the same man, both soul and flesh. . . .

[38.] But when we use the word "Person," and say that God became man by means of a Person, there is reason to fear that our meaning may be taken to be, that God the Word assumed our nature merely in imitation, and performed the actions of man, being man not in reality, but only in semblance, just as in a theatre, one man within a brief space represents several persons, not one of whom himself is. For when one undertakes to sustain the part of another, he performs the offices, or does the acts, of the person whose part he sustains, but he is not himself that person. So, to take an illustration from secular life and one in high favour with the Manichees, when a tragedian represents a priest or a king, he is not really a priest or a king. For, as soon as the play is over, the person or character whom he represented ceases to be. God forbid that we should have anything to do with such nefarious and wicked mockery. Be it the infatuation of the Manichees, those preachers of hallucination, who say that the Son of God, God, was not a human person really and truly, but that He counterfeited the person of a man in feigned conversation and manner of life.

[39.] But the Catholic Faith teaches that the Word of God became man in such wise, that He took upon Him our nature. . . .

[79.] These then are the men whose writings, whether as judges or as witnesses, were recited in the Council: St. Peter, bishop of Alexandria, a most excellent Doctor and most blessed martyr, Saint Athanasius, bishop of the same city, a most faithful Teacher, and most eminent Confessor, Saint Theophilus, also bishop of the same city, a man illustrious for his faith, his life, his knowledge, whose successor, the revered Cyril now adorns the Alexandrian Church. And lest perchance the doctrine ratified by the Council should be thought peculiar to one city and province, there were added also those lights of Cappadocia, St. Gregory of Nazianzus, bishop and Confessor, St. Basil of Cæsarea in Cappadocia, bishop and Confessor, and the other St. Gregory, St. Gregory of Nyssa, for his faith, his conversation, his integrity, and his wisdom, most worthy to be the brother of Basil. And lest Greece or the East should seem to stand alone, to prove that the Western and Latin world also have always held the same belief, there were read in the Council certain Epistles of St. Felix, martyr, and St. Julius, both bishops of Rome. And that not only the Head, but the other parts, of the world also might bear witness to the judgment of the council, there was added from the South the most blessed Cyprian, bishop of Carthage and martyr, and from the North St. Ambrose, bishop of Milan.

19

A MEROVINGIAN SAINT'S LIFE:
THE LIFE OF BONITUS, BISHOP OF AUVERGNE

eighth century

*The Life of Bonitus is cast in a literary form that became highly
developed in the Middle Ages—the saint's life. Bonitus, from an
important noble family, rose through the secular ranks of government service to earn his elevation to the episcopacy. The hagi-
ographer, writing in the eighth century about seventh-century
events, relies on miracles to substantiate Bonitus' holiness.
Though his piety may indeed have been genuine, it seems evident that his high ecclesiastical position and eventual canoniza-
tion were based on noble birth and court preferment.*

Here begins the Prologue to the life of Blessed Bonitus, Bishop
and Confessor

The feast of the holy Theophania was drawing near, and the
ceremonies of the watching were already being celebrated when
your imperial powers, O most blessed fathers Adelfi and Euteri,
belatedly inquired why the neglected works of the blessed
priest and confessor Bonitus are not brought out more clearly
into the light, since the lives of the priests and confessors of this

SOURCE Translated from *Vita Boniti Episcopi Arverni*, in *Pas-
siones Vitaeque Sanctorum aevi Merovingici*, ed. B. Krusch and W.
Levison, *Monumenta Germaniae Historica, Scriptorum Rerum Mero-
vingicarum*, VI (Hanover and Leipzig, 1913).

see, Elidius and Gallus, have been related in splendid style;
and saying this, you ordered me to set forth something [about
Bonitus] in simple and rude language. . . .
Here Ends the Prologue.

Here Begins the Life of Saint Bonitus, Bishop and Confessor
   The illustrious Bonitus was descended from Arvernian lineage. His father was called Theodatus, his mother Syagria; they
were at least of senatorial rank, and from noble stock. Bonitus,
then, before he was born, was held to have received a significant presage of devotion [*salutatio*] from a certain holy priest
named Frigio. When this priest came to the paternal household
he was received by Bonitus' mother-to-be with great joy, and
when she, as was customary, asked for his blessing, she is said
to have heard this reply given as a devotion: "Thou holy to God
and venerable lord", he said, "give me your blessing". When
the mother had grasped the meaning of what he had said, and
silently weighing it, was pondering it in her heart, nonetheless
inquiring of the servant of God, she spoke saying: "What is
this you say, father?" . . . And he said: "I did not ask a blessing, as you think, from you, but from him who is in your womb,
since I perceive him to be a most high priest, chosen by God".
And she, praying, said: "I ask, O father, that that which you
have spoken shall, through your prayers, come to pass".
   Afterwards, when the child had become a boy and was settled with his parents in the forenamed city, he was trained in
the rudiments of grammar, instructed in the Theodosian decrees, and excelling in related studies also, he was examined by
his instructors, and advanced. When he was of the age of pu-
berty, his father being dead, with God as his guide he went to
the royal palace and put himself in the hands of Sigebert, a
minister of the king. Because Sigebert had grown very fond of
him, he was chosen to be the royal cup-bearer. Not long after
this, he gained the office of master of requests, accepting the
ring from the king's own hand; he fulfilled it so nobly that he
gained the affections of the prince and all the nobles, all the

duties having been handed over to him by the ministers of the palace. For he had, to be sure, bodily beauty, but was more beautiful in the mind and in the strength of his chastity.

Soon after this, he gratefully accepted a great honor from the prince. Then the prince died, and, his son being dead, his great-grandson succeeded him. So pleasing was Bonitus in his sight that he chose him to be prefect of Marseille, the first province, but he insisted to the suitors brought before him that he would rather be considered a priest than a judge. . . .

[Bonitus is raised to the episcopacy by the king]

Having thus accepted the bishopric, he considered himself to have accepted not an honor, but a burden, and he augmented the labor of his daily obligations by his fasts and vigils, which he kept throughout the night, and by silent reading in private, most especially during the Lenten season; in all, he was so zealous that you would think him not only most worthy of the priesthood, but worthy to live the monastic life as well. He bore two- and three-day fasts; indeed, we know him to have fasted for as many as four days. . . .

Now I shall relate how the Lord worked miracles by his virtue. When the day of the Lord's resurrection dawned, the brothers begged him to perform the solemnities of the mass for them. But, when, as was his custom, he washed his hands at the altar . . . a certain incapacitated brother named Auderamnus came and asked for the *levita*,[1] so that he might drink water from the priestly hands.

Having done so, he was restored to his former health, and immediately overjoyed, sat down to table with the brothers.

And another brother in the same monastery named Natholenum, when he took some of the same water, was, according to many, relieved of a fever by its virtue [alone]. These things which are related above were told us by the venerable father Adelfius. . . .

[1] A small vessel used in priestly ablutions. (Ed.'s note)

When the man of God, returning from Rome, came into the city of Chiusi in Tuscany, a certain blind woman begged his servants to give her the water in which he had washed his hands as a remedy to bathe her eyes. Although they were anxious to fulfil her request, the man of God, having washed his hands, ordered that the water be poured on the ground, as was his custom, so that they were able to steal hardly a drop of it; and giving it to the woman, they said: "Go and keep vigil tonight with this water in the basilica of the blessed Peter, which is in this city, and in the morning touch it to your eyes, as you have asked, according to your faith; we believe it will bring deliverance to you". The woman did as they said, and having fulfilled all, her eyesight restored, she beheld the light which she had sought with all her heart's desire. . . .

Now at that time nothing remained to him that he could give away as alms, and so as the gospel says he was naked, and did not even have two tunics to put on, and following the example of the blessed apostle Peter he had no gold or silver; but, restored by his divine virtues, he expended the treasure of health, which is more precious. Behold what the word of truth has said in the gospel: "He who hath forsaken all for my name's sake, shall receive a hundredfold, and shall inherit everlasting life. He receives a hundredfold who is established in the holiness and grace of God".[1] As blessed Paul said: "Our conversation is in heaven".[2] . . . Just so the blessed priest, who left much behind in this world, neither sought nor deserved anything earthly afterwards; but he received a hundredfold, since he shone with the grace of perfection, and now possesses eternal life with the saints in glory.

Then returning after this to Loudun, he remained there for four years, and continuing until the end, with God's aid, to do the good he had always done, he closed his days.

Here Ends the Life of Saint Bonitus, Bishop and Confessor.

[1] Mark 10, 29–30.   [2] Phil. 3, 20.

20

THE LETTERS OF ST. COLUMBAN

550 – 615

This letter of Columban to the pope clearly indicates the nominal connections between the Celtic Church and the Roman See in the sixth and earlier seventh centuries. Columban asks advice in dealing with bishops who ordained "for hire"—i.e., who were guilty of the sin of simony, yet it is evident that they have not been subject to papal control. Similarly, Columban laments the vexing problem of itinerant monks, a common phenomenon in Ireland although virtually unknown in continental areas. The bulk of the letter is devoted to the most serious point of dispute between the Roman and Celtic Churches—the accurate determination of the date of Easter, which was not finally settled until 664, when the Synod of Whitby finally settled the issues separating the two churches.

LETTER I

1. To the Holy Lord and Father in Christ, the fairest Ornament of the Roman Church, as it were a most honored Flower of all Europe in her decay, to the distinguished Bishop, who is

SOURCE   From St. Columban, *Letters,* in *Sancti Columbani Opera,* ed. G. S. M. Walker, *Scriptores Latini Hiberniae,* II (Dublin: The Dublin Institute for Advanced Studies, 1957), 3, 5, 9.

skilled in the Meditation of divine Eloquence, I, Bar-Jonah[1] (a poor Dove), send Greeting in Christ.

2. Grace and peace to thee from God our Father and from our Lord Jesus Christ. It is my desire, Holy Father, (let it not be extravagant in your sight) to ask about Easter, in accordance with that canticle, Ask thy father and he will show thee, thy elders and they will tell thee. For although, considering my insignificance, when my poverty writes to your distinction, I might be branded with that unusual remark of a certain philosopher, which he is said once to have made at the sight of a painted harlot, 'I do not admire the art, but I admire the cheek'; yet trusting in the faith of your evangelical humility I dare to write to you, and subjoin the matter of my grief. For there is no pride in writing when necessity demands a letter, though it be addressed to one's superiors.

3. What then do you say about an Easter on the twenty-first or twenty-second moon, which already (yet let it be said without offense to you) is proved to be no Easter, considering its darkness, by many laborious scholars? For as I believe, it does not escape your diligence, how scathingly Anatolius, 'a man of curious learning' as St. Jerome says, excerpts from whose writings Eusebius, bishop of Caesarea, inserted in his ecclesiastical history, and St. Jerome praised this same work on Easter in his catalogue—how scathingly Anatolius reasons about this period of the moon; who recorded a terrible judgment against the Gallican authorities in their error, as he maintains, concerning Easter, saying 'Certainly if the moon's rising shall have delayed until the end of two watches, which marks the middle of the night, light does not prevail over darkness, but darkness over light; which is certain to be impossible at Easter, so that some part of darkness should rule over the light, since the festival of the Lord's resurrection is light, and there is no communication of light with darkness. And if the moon has begun to shine in the

---

[1] Jonah is the Hebrew equivalent of "Columba," or "dove." (Ed.'s note)

third watch, there is no doubt that the twenty-first or twenty-second moon has arisen, on which it is impossible for the true Easter to be offered. For those who determine that Easter can be celebrated at this period of the moon, not only cannot maintain this on the authority of holy scripture, but also incur the charge of sacrilege and contumacy, together with the peril of their souls, when they maintain that the true light, which rules over all darkness, can be offered under conditions where darkness rules to some extent.' And we also read in the book of sacred dogma: 'Easter, that is the festival of the Lord's resurrection, cannot be celebrated before the passing of the Spring equinox, the beginning of the fourteenth moon', namely to avoid its preceding the equinox. Victorius has certainly broken this rule in his cycle, and thus has long since introduced error into Gaul, or to speak more humbly, has strengthened its growth. For on what principle can either practice stand, namely that the Lord's resurrection should be celebrated prior to His passion, which is ridiculous even to be thought of, or that the seven days ordained by the Lord's bidding in the law, on which alone the Lord's Passover is commanded to be eaten legally, which are to be reckoned from the fourteenth moon up to the twentieth, should be exceeded contrary to law and right? For the twenty-first or twenty-second moon is outwith the jurisdiction of light, since at that point of time it has arisen after the middle of the night, and with darkness prevailing over light it is illegal, as they say, for the festival of light to be held.

4. Why then, with all your learning, when indeed the streams of your holy wisdom are, as of old, shed abroad over the earth with great brightness, do you favor a dark Easter? I am surprised, I must confess, that this error of Gaul has not long since been scraped away by you, as if it were a warty growth; unless perhaps I am to think, what I can scarce believe, that while it is patent that this has not been righted by you, it has met with approval in your eyes. Yet your statesmanship can be excused in another and more honorable way; perhaps while you fear to be stamped as an innovator like Hermagoras, you are content

with your predecessors' authority, and especially with that of Pope Leo. . . . But in this matter you should not pay so much attention to my insignificant person, as to the many dead and living teachers who maintain these same conclusions I have noted, and you should imagine yourself to be prolonging the debate with them; for you must know that I am opening my voluble mouth from pious motives, though it be out of turn and out of measure. . . .

6. Concerning those bishops, however, who ordain uncanonically, that is for hire, I ask what you decree; Gildas the writer set them down as simoniacs and plagues. Are we really to communicate with them? For many, which is too serious a matter, are known to be such in this province. Or concerning others who, defiled as deacons, are later elected to the rank of bishops? For some exist, whose confessions I have heard on this, and who, discussing the matter with my poor self, wished to know for certain, whether after this they could without peril be bishops, that is to say, after buying orders for money, or after a secret adultery as deacons—yet I mean adultery committed with their wives; which among our teachers is reckoned to be of no less guilt.

7. In the third part of my inquiry, please tell me now, if it is not troublesome, what is to be done about those monks who, for the sake of God, and inflamed by the desire for a more perfect life, impugn their vows, leave the places of their first profession, and against their abbots' will, impelled by monastic fervor, either relapse or flee to the deserts. . . .

21

PLOTINUS, *THE ENNEADS*

c. 301

The Enneads *of the Neo-Platonist thinker Plotinus (205–270) represent his philosophy in the last decade of his life. Porphyry, Plotinus' pupil from about 262 to 268, edited and published them in 301. Plotinus' association of God with the Platonic idea of the Good and his description of the physical world as a dynamic hierarchy of levels of being were absorbed into the theology of Augustine and other early Christian thinkers.*

II. 9. AGAINST THE GNOSTICS

1. Since, then, the simple nature of the Good appeared to us as also primal (for all that is not primal is not simple), and as something which has nothing in itself, but is some one thing; and since the nature of what is called the One is the same (for this is not some other thing first and then one, nor is the Good something else first, and then good), whenever we say "the

SOURCE Reprinted by permission of the publishers and THE LOEB CLASSICAL LIBRARY from A. H. Armstrong, translator, Plotinus, *Enneads,* Vols. II and III, Cambridge, Mass.: Harvard University Press, Copyright, Vol. II, 1966, III, 1967, by the President and Fellows of Harvard College.

One" and whenever we say "the Good," we must think that the nature we are speaking of is the same nature, and call it "one" not as predicating anything of it but as making it clear to ourselves as far as we can. And we call it the First in the sense that it is simplest, and the Self-Sufficient, because it is not composed of a number of parts; for if it were, it would be dependent upon the things of which it was composed; and we say that it is not in something else, because everything which is in something else also comes from something else. If, then, it is not from something else or in something else or any kind of compound, it is necessary that there should be nothing above it. So we must not go after other first principles but put this first, and then after it Intellect, that which primally thinks, and then Soul after Intellect (for this is the order which corresponds to the nature of things): and we must not posit more principles than these in the intelligible world, or fewer. For if people posit fewer, they will either assert that Soul and Intellect are the same, or Intellect and the First; but it has been shown in many places that they are different from each other. It remains to investigate in our present discussion, if we are to posit more than these three, whatever other natures there could be beside them. . . . Intellect is as it is, always the same, resting in a static activity. Movement towards it and around it is already the work of Soul, and a rational principle proceeding from Intellect to Soul and making Soul intellectual, not making another nature between Intellect and Soul. Again, the supposition that one intellect thinks and the other thinks that it thinks, is certainly not a reason for making several intellects. For even if on our level it is one thing for an intellect to think and another for it to think that it thinks, yet all the same its thinking is a single application of the mind not unaware of its own activities; but it would be absurd to suppose this duality to exist in the case of the true Intellect, but the intellect which thinks that it thinks will be altogether the same as the intellect which did the thinking. Otherwise one intellect will be only thinking, and the other will be thinking

106

that it thinks, but the thinking subject will be another, and not itself. . . .

2. One must not, then, posit more beings than these, nor make superfluous distinctions in the realities of the intelligible world which the nature of these realities does not admit: we must lay down that there is one intellect, unchangeably the same, without any sort of decline, imitating the Father as far as is possible to it: and that one part of our soul is always directed to the intelligible realities, one to the things of this world, and one is in the middle between these; for since the soul is one nature in many powers, sometimes the whole of it is carried along with the best of itself and of real being, sometimes the worse part is dragged down and drags the middle with it; for it is not lawful for it to drag down the whole. This misfortune befalls it because it does not remain in the noblest, where the soul remains which is not a part—and at that stage we, too, are not a part of it—and grants to the whole of body to hold whatever it can hold from it, but remains itself untroubled, not managing body as a result of discursive thinking, nor setting anything right, but ordering it with a wonderful power by its contemplation of that which is before it. The more it is directed to that contemplation, the fairer and more powerful it is. It receives from there and gives to what comes after it, and is always illuminated as it illuminates.

3. Since, therefore, it is always illuminated and continually holds the light, it gives it to what comes next after it, and this is held together and fertilised by this light and enjoys its share of life as far as it can; as if there was a fire placed somewhere in the middle and those who were capable of it were warmed. . . . Of necessity, then, all things must exist for ever in ordered dependence upon each other: those other than the First have come into being in the sense that they are derived from other, higher, principles. Things that are said to have come into being did not just come into being [at a particular moment] but always were and always will be in process of becoming: nor will anything be dissolved except those things which have some-

thing to be dissolved into; that which has nothing into which it can be dissolved will not perish. . . .

7. It has been said already that this universe did not begin and will not come to an end but exists always as long as the intelligible realities exist. And it has been said before the Gnostics that the association of our soul with body is not to the advantage of the soul. But to apply conclusions drawn from our soul to the Soul of the All is as if somebody were to take the tribe of potters or smiths in a well-ordered city and make them a reason for blaming the whole. But one must take into account the differences between the universal soul and ours, in its management of body; it does not direct it in the same way, and is not bound to it. For, as well as all the other differences (of which we have mentioned a vast number elsewhere) this ought to have been taken into consideration, that we are bound by a body which has already become a bond. For the nature of body is already bound in the universal soul and binds whatever it grasps; but the Soul of the All could not be bound by the things it binds itself: for it is the ruler. Therefore it is unaffected by them, but we are not their masters; but that part of the universal which is directed to the divine above it remains pure, and is not hindered, but that part which gives life to the body takes no addition from it. For in general anything which is in something else is affected by what happens to it, but it does not itself give of its own to that other which has its own life. For instance, if a shoot of one tree is grafted on another, when anything happens to the stock the shoot is affected with it, but if the shoot is withered up it leaves the stock to live its own life. So also, if the fire in you is quenched, the universal fire is not quenched as well: since even if the universal fire were destroyed, the soul there in the universe would not be in any way affected, but only the structure of its body, and, provided that the other elements made it possible for some sort of universe to exist, it would not in any way concern the soul there. . . .

Our enquiry concerns love, whether it is a god or a spirit or an affection of the soul, or whether one kind is a god or spirit and another also an affection, and what sort of god or spirit or affection each of these is; it is worth while considering the ideas about it which have occurred to the rest of mankind and all the teachings of philosophy on this subject, and in particular all the opinions of that godlike man Plato, who has, of course, written much about love in many places in his works. He has said that love is not only an affection occurring in souls but asserts that it is also a spirit, and has described its origin, how and from what source it came to be. Now about the affection of soul for which we make love responsible,[1] there is no one, I suppose, who does not know that it occurs in souls which desire to embrace some beauty, and that this desire has two forms, one which comes from the chaste who are akin to absolute beauty, and one which wants to find its fulfilment in the doing of some ugly act; but it is appropriate to go on from there to a philosophical consideration of the source from which each of them originates. And if someone assumed that the origin of love was the longing for beauty itself which was there before in men's souls, and their recognition of it and kinship with it and unreasoned awareness that it is something of their own, he would hit, I think, on the truth about its cause. For the ugly is opposed to nature and to God. . . . It is true, certainly, that those who are moved to generation here below are content to have the beauty here below, the beauty which is present in images and bodies, since the archetype is not present to them which is responsible for their loving even this beauty here below. And if they come from this beauty here to the recollection of that archetype, this earthly beauty still satisfies them as an image; but if they do not recollect, then, because they do not know what is happening to them, they fancy this is the true beauty. If they remain chaste there is no error in their intimacy with the beauty here below, but it is error to fall away into sexual intercourse. And the man whose love of the beautiful is pure will be satis-

[1] That is Love as a substantial superhuman reality, a god or a spirit, who is responsible for producing the affection of love in the human soul.

fied with beauty alone, if he recollects the archetype or even if he does not, but the man whose love is mixed with another desire of "being immortal as far as a mortal may," seeks the beautiful in that which is everlasting and eternal; and as he goes the way of nature he sows and generates in beauty, sowing for perpetuity, and in beauty because of the kinship of perpetuity and beauty. . . . But some lovers even worship earthly beauty, and it is enough for them, but others, those who have recollected the archetype, venerate that higher beauty too, and do not treat this earthly beauty, either, with disrespect, since they see in it the creation and plaything of that other. These lovers, then, are concerned about beauty without any ugliness, but there are others who fall into ugliness and they too do so because of beauty; for in fact the desire of good often involves the fall into evil. So much, then, for the affections of the soul [produced by love].

But the Love whom we ought to make the main object of our philosophical discourse is the one whom not only the rest of mankind but those also who give accounts of the gods, and especially Plato, make a god; Plato in many places speaks of "Love son of Aphrodite," and says that his work is to be "guardian of beautiful boys" and mover of the soul towards the beauty of the higher world, or also to increase the impulse towards that world which is already there.

22

THE VENERATION OF ROME:
RUTILIUS NAMATIANUS, *THE HOMECOMING*

416

Rutilius Namatianus, a native of Gaul, spent much time in Rome and held the honorable posts of master of the offices and prefect of the city under Honorius. Rutilius' poem expresses the nostalgic fondness for Rome that survived, particularly among her upper-class subjects, well into the Christian era. Writing in 416, Rutilius felt keenly the threatened and actual devastation of the barbarian tribes, and was able to assess the effects of Alaric's sack of the city in 410; nevertheless he continues to speak of a Rome essentially untouched by physical destruction. Unlike his contemporary Augustine, Rutilius does not attribute Rome's greatness and longevity to divine favor, nor does he transmute the tangible city into an intangible theological concept.

> With many a kiss we print the gates we leave
> And loth our feet the sacred threshold cross.
> With tears we beg forgiveness, offer praise,
> As far as tears permit our words to run.

SOURCE   From *Rutilii Claudii Namatiani De Reditu Suo. The Homecoming of Rutilius Claudius Namatianus to Gaul in the Year 416 A.D.*, ed. Charles Haines Keene, trans. by George F. Savage-Armstrong (London: George Bell, 1907), 113, 115, 117, 119.

"HEAR, loveliest Queen of all the world, thy world,
O Rome, translated to the starry skies!
Hear, Mother of Men, and Mother of the Gods!
We, through thy temples, dwell not far from heaven.
Thee sing we, and, long as Fate allows, will sing;
None can forget thee while he lives and breathes.
Sooner shall we be guilty of the crime
Of burying in oblivion the sun
Than from our heart shall fade thy meed of love.
Thy gifts thou spreadest wide as the sun's rays,
As far as earth-encircling ocean heaves.
Phoebus, embracing all things, rolls for thee;
His steeds both rise and sink in thy domains.
Thee not with burning sands could Libya stay,
Nor thee did Ursa armed with frost repel.
Far as the habitable climes extend
Toward either pole thy valour finds its path.
Thou hast made of alien realms one fatherland;
The lawless found their gain beneath thy sway;
Sharing thy laws with them thou hast subdued,
Thou hast made a city of the once wide world.

"Venus and Mars the authors of our stock
We own,—She, mother of Aeneas' race,
He, father of the breed of Romulus;
Mercy in victory tempers strength in arms,
And in thy nature both the Gods unite.
Hence thy keen joy to strive and yet to spare
Quells whom it feared and loves whom it has quelled.
She who the olive made, the vine's revealer,
The boy who into earth first drove the plough,
Are worshipped; medicine won, through Paeon's art,
Honour of altars; for loftiness of soul
Alcides was made God. Thou, too, who hold'st
The world by triumphs bringing righteous law,
Mak'st all things live under a common bond.

"Thee, Goddess, thee each Roman nook remote
Doth celebrate in worship, and, with neck
Free, doth endure thy peace-creating yoke.
The orbs which all observe their ceaseless course
Have nowhere any fairer empire seen.
What empire like it did Assyria weld?
The Medes but their own borderers subdued;
The Parthian chiefs, the Kings of Macedon,
With varying fortune gave each other laws.
Yet not more life and force at birth were thine,
But more of prudence and deliberate mind.
Ennobled by just wars and modest peace
Thy glory to the utmost height has risen.
It is a smaller thing that thou dost reign
Than that thou dost deserve to reign; by deeds
Thou dost transcend thy glorious destiny.

"To tell the trophies of thy victories
Were task as hard as numbering the stars.
Thy glittering temples daze the wandering eyes;
I could believe the Gods themselves so housed.
Why tell of thine aërial aqueducts
Lofty as Iris could uprear her bow?
Say rather mountains lifted to the heavens!
Let Greece of such a work of giants boast,
If boast she can! The intercepted streams
Are stored within thy walls; thy lofty baths
Absorb whole lakes; and with the dashing spray
Of their own fountains are thy walls refreshed,
And echo to the voice of their own springs.
Hence a cool breeze tempers the summer's heat,
And purer draughts innocuous quench the thirst.
'Tis true for thee a sudden boiling flood
Rent the Tarpeian paths by foes assailed;
If it endured I might believe it chance;
Doomed to retire, it sprang to succour thee.

Why tell of groves with fretted porches girt
Where sports the native bird with varied song?
The year throughout is mellowed by thy spring,
And vanquished winter shelters thy delights.

"Rear high thy laurelled locks, renew, O Rome,
Youth's vernal tresses on thy reverend brow;
Let thy gold crown flash with embattled round,
And thy gold shield ray forth perpetual fires;
Let thy dire woe be blotted and forgot;
Let thy contempt for suffering heal thy wounds.
It is thy wont in woe to hope for weal,
And, like the heavens, bear wanings crowned with gain.
The flaming stars set but to rise once more;
The moon thou seest wanes—to wax again.
The victory at Allia kept not back
The punishment to conquering Brennus due;
The Samnites by their servitude repaid
The price of the hard terms they offered thee;
After full many a slaughter thou, subdued,
Drov'st Pyrrhus in full flight; and Hannibal
His own successes lived at last to mourn.
Things that refuse to sink, still stronger rise,
And higher from the lowest depths rebound;
And, as the torch reversed new strength attains,
Thou, brighter from thy fall, to heaven aspirest!
Spread far the laws through all Rome's length of years
Destined to last, and fear not—thou alone—
The distaff of the Fates, though even now,
Thy thousand years and sixteen decades ended,
Thy ninth new year beyond them rolls away.
The years to come are bounded by no bourne
While earth abides, while heaven sustains the stars.

23

THE CHRISTIAN APOCALYPSE:
THE REVELATION OF ST. JOHN THE DIVINE

c. 90–95

The vision of the end of time and government embodied in the powerful Revelation of John of Patmos continued to terrify as well as comfort Christians throughout the Middle Ages. It was ambiguous enough to be applied to many different historical circumstances, and it promised an eternally imminent end to unbearable human conditions. Christian sects labeled as heretical often associated the institutionalized church with the powers whose destruction the Revelation prophesied.

CHAPTER 6, 1–17

And I saw when the Lamb opened one of the seals, and I heard, as it were the noise of thunder, one of the four beasts saying, Come and see.

 And I saw, and behold a white horse: and he that sat on him had a bow; and a crown was given unto him: and he went forth conquering, and to conquer.

And when he had opened the second seal, I heard the second beast say, Come and see.

SOURCE From *Revelation* 6, 1–17; 7, 1–4; 17, 3–6.

And there went out another horse that was red: and power was given to him that sat thereon to take peace from the earth, and that they should kill one another: and there was given unto him a great sword.

And when he had opened the third seal, I heard the third beast say, Come and see. And I beheld, and lo a black horse; and he that sat on him had a pair of balances in his hand.

And I heard a voice in the midst of the four beasts say, A measure of wheat for a penny, and three measures of barley for a penny; and see thou hurt not the oil and the wine.

And when he had opened the fourth seal, I heard the voice of the fourth beast say, Come and see.

And I looked, and behold a pale horse: and his name that sat on him was Death, and Hell followed with him. And power was given unto them over the fourth part of the earth, to kill with sword, and with hunger, and with death, and with the beasts of the earth.

And when he had opened the fifth seal, I saw under the altar the souls of them that were slain for the word of God, and for the testimony which they held:

And they cried with a loud voice, saying, How long, O Lord, holy and true, dost thou not judge and avenge our blood on them that dwell on the earth?

And white robes were given unto every one of them; and it was said unto them, that they should rest yet for a little season, until their fellowservants also and their brethren, that should be killed as they were, should be fulfilled.

And I beheld when he had opened the sixth seal, and, lo, there was a great earthquake; and the sun became black as sackcloth of hair, and the moon became as blood;

And the stars of heaven fell unto the earth, even as a fig tree casteth her untimely figs, when she is shaken of a mighty wind.

And the heaven departed as a scroll when it is rolled together; and every mountain and island were moved out of their places.

And the kings of the earth, and the great men, and the
rich men, and the chief captains, and the mighty men, and every
bondman, and every free man, hid themselves in the dens and
in the rocks of the mountains;

And said to the mountains and rocks, Fall on us, and hide
us from the face of him that sitteth on the throne, and
from the wrath of the Lamb:

For the great day of his wrath is come; and who shall be
able to stand?

CHAPTER 7, 1 – 4

And after these things I saw four angels standing on the four
corners of the earth, holding the four winds of the earth, that
the wind should not blow on the earth, nor on the sea, nor on
any tree.

And I saw another angel ascending from the east, having
the seal of the living God: and he cried with a loud voice
to the four angels, to whom it was given to hurt the earth
and the sea,

Saying, Hurt not the earth, neither the sea, nor the trees, till we
have sealed the servants of our God in their foreheads.

And I heard the number of them which were sealed: and
there were sealed an hundred and forty and four thousand of all the tribes of the children of Israel.

CHAPTER 17, 3 – 6

So he carried me away in the spirit into the wilderness: and
I saw a woman sit upon a scarlet coloured beast, full of names
of blasphemy, having seven heads and ten horns.

And the woman was arrayed in purple and scarlet colour,
and decked with gold and precious stones and pearls, having a golden cup in her hand full of abominations and
filthiness of her fornication:

And upon her forehead was a name written, MYSTERY, BABYLON

THE GREAT, THE MOTHER OF HARLOTS AND ABOMINATIONS OF THE EARTH.

And I saw the woman drunken with the blood of the saints, and with the blood of the martyrs of Jesus: and when I saw her, I wondered with great admiration.

24

THE LEGEND OF SIMON MAGUS

c. 180 – 220

This fictitious account of an encounter between the magician Simon, mentioned in the book of Acts, and the first pope, Peter, shows the way in which papal powers were understood by the average unlettered Christian in the early centuries of the church. The legend survived well into the medieval period.

THE ACTS OF PETER WITH SIMON

[Paul in Rome has a vision bidding him go to Spain. During his absence, Simon Magus enters the city, flying over the gate.] . . . And the brethren in turn were greatly perturbed because Paul was not at Rome, nor Timothy nor Barnabas, for they had been sent by Paul into Macedonia, and there was no one to hearten them save such as had recently been catechumens. And Simon vaunted himself increasingly with his deeds

SOURCE From *The Acts of Peter with Simon*, trans. by James T. Shotwell and Louise Ropes Loomis, in *The See of Peter*, ed. James T. Shotwell and Louise Ropes Loomis (New York: Columbia University Press, 1927), 136–41, 148–49.

and some men in their daily talk called Paul a sorcerer, some even openly. And all the vast multitude which had been grounded in the faith abandoned it, except Narcissus; the presbyter, and two women in the hospice of the Bithynians and four who were no longer able to leave their homes but remained shut up day and night, giving themselves to prayer and beseeching the Lord that Paul might quickly return or that some other one might visit his servants, seeing that the devil with his wickedness had destroyed them.

And while they mourned and fasted, God instructed Peter in Jerusalem. For twelve years being now fulfilled since the Lord had called him, Christ revealed to him a vision, saying to him: "Peter, that Simon whom thou didst proclaim a sorcerer and didst drive out from Judaea has again forestalled thee at Rome. And shortly thou shalt hear of it, for Satan, whose power Simon claims to be, has by his craft and energy destroyed all who believed in me. But do not delay; tomorrow go [to Caesarea] and there thou shalt find a ship in readiness, sailing to Italy; and within a few days I shall impart to thee my grace, which has no bitterness." Then Peter, admonished by this vision, related it straightway to the brethren, saying: "It is needful for me to journey to Rome to expel the foe and adversary of the Lord and of our brethren." And he went down to Caesarea and immediately embarked upon a ship. . . .

And the rumor spread through the city to the dispersed brethren that it was reported that Peter had come to Rome on account of Simon, that he might prove him a seducer and persecutor of the good. Then the whole multitude gathered together, that they might see the apostle of the Lord laying the foundation in Christ. And on the first Sabbath, when the multitude had assembled to see Peter, Peter began to speak in a loud voice: . . . [Exhortation to repent.]

And the brethren repented and implored Peter to drive out Simon, who said he was the power of God and who was staying in the house of Marcellus, the senator, whom he had beguiled with his enchantments. And they said: "Believe us, brother

Peter; no man was nobler among men than this Marcellus. All the widows who hoped in Christ had him for refuge; all the orphans were fed by him. Nay more, brother, all the poor called Marcellus their patron and his house was named the house of the strangers and the poor. . . . Now this Marcellus is enraged and repents of his charity, saying: 'So much wealth wasted for so long a time and I in my folly believed that God knew of it and so I spent it!' Thus if any stranger comes to the door of his house he will beat him with a lash and order him driven away, saying: 'Would I had never spent so much money on the impostors!' And he utters other blasphemies. . . ."

. . . And the brethren asked Peter to contend with Simon and not to suffer him longer to delude the people. And Peter without delay left the synagogue and went to the house of Marcellus, where Simon was staying. And great throngs followed him. When he came to the house, he called the porter and said to him: "Go, say to Simon: 'Peter, through whom you fled from Judaea, awaits you at the door.'"

And Peter turned to the people who followed him and said: "You shall now behold a great and wonderful portent." And observing a large dog fastened with a heavy chain, Peter drew near and released him. And the dog, being released, assumed the voice of a man and said to Peter: "What will you bid me do, servant of the ineffable and living God?" And Peter said to him: "Go in and say to Simon, in the midst of his companions: 'Peter says to you: "Come out into an open place, since for your sake have I come to Rome, you wicked man and deceiver of simple souls."'" And the dog bounded from the spot and into the house and sprang into the midst of those who were with Simon and lifting up his forepaws, said with a loud voice: "Simon! Peter, the servant of Christ, who stands at the door, says to you, 'Come out into an open place, for on your account have I come to Rome, most wicked of men and seducer of simple souls.'" And when Simon heard this and saw the incredible sight, he paused in the words with which he was seducing his companions and they were all amazed. . . . And hearing this, the young man rushed into the atrium of the house and shouted aloud and cast himself against the wall and said: "Peter, there is a great struggle between Simon and the dog that you sent to him, for Simon is saying to the dog: 'Tell him that I am not here.' And the dog is saying to him more than you charged him and after he has performed the mystery with which you charged him, he will die at your feet." Then Peter said: "Demon, whoever thou art, in the name of our Lord Jesus Christ come out of the youth and do him no harm; show thyself to all who stand here." And hearing this, the young man rushed forward and, laying hold of a great marble statue that stood in the atrium of the house, shattered it with kicks. And it was a statue of Caesar. At that sight Marcellus beat his forehead and said to Peter: "A great crime has been committed and if it be reported to Caesar by a spy, he will punish us heavily." But Peter said to him: "I see you are not in the state in which you were a short time since, for you said you were ready to spend the whole of your substance to save your soul. But if you are truly penitent and believe in Christ with all your heart, take flowing water in your hands and pray the Lord and in his name sprinkle the fragments of the statue and it will be restored as before." Then Marcellus, nothing doubting but believing with all his heart, before he took the water lifted up his hands and said: "I believe in thee, Lord Jesus Christ, . . ." And he sprinkled water upon the stones and the statue became whole. . . .

The dog returned to Peter, who was seated with the multitude that they might look upon his face, and the dog told what it had done with Simon. And the dog said to the messenger and apostle of the true God: "Peter, you shall have a great struggle against Simon, the enemy of Christ, and of his servants; but many whom he has seduced you shall restore to the faith. Therefore you shall receive from God the recompense of your labor." And when the dog had said this, it fell down at the feet of the apostle Peter and gave up the ghost. And the throng beheld with great amazement the dog speaking and some threw themselves at Peter's feet, but others said: "Show us another sign that we may believe in you as a minister of the living God; for Simon did many signs in our presence and for that reason we followed after him."

. . . [Peter makes a smoked fish swim like one alive.] Then many followed him for that sight and believed on the Lord and they met day and night in the house of Narcissus, the presbyter. And Peter expounded to them the writings of the prophets and the words and deeds of our Lord Jesus Christ. . . .

. . . And Simon Magus after a few days promised the multitude to convict Peter of believing not on a true god but on a false. Therefore he performed many feats of magic, but the disciples, who were now steadfast, laughed at him. For in the dining-halls he made spirits return to their bodies, yet only in a fantasy, for in reality they did not. And what more is there to tell? He was extolled by many for his sorcery and he made the lame appear whole for a short time and the blind likewise and the dead he seemed to bring to life and awaken for a moment, even as he did Stratonicus. And Peter followed him everywhere and exposed him to those who looked on. So, when he was continually shamed and ridiculed by the Roman crowd and disbelieved for not achieving what he promised to do, he said to them: "Men of Rome, do you now think that Peter has vanquished me by his superior power and are you following after him? You have been deceived. Tomorrow I will leave you, godless and irreligious people, and fly to God, whose power I am even in my affliction. Though you have fallen, lo, I am the Standing One; and I shall ascend to my Father and say to him: 'Even me, the Standing One, thy son, they have endeavored to overthrow; but I did not yield to them and escaped to myself.'"

And the next day a vast multitude gathered in the Via Sacra, that they might behold his flight. And Peter came thither to see the spectacle, that he might expose him even in this, since, when Simon entered Rome, he had amazed the people by flying. For Peter, who exposed him, was not then at Rome and he had deluded the city with his wiles, so that some clave to him. And now, taking his stand upon a high place and seeing Peter, he began to speak: "Peter, now that I am about to ascend in the sight of all these people, I say to you: 'If your god has power, whom the Jews slew, stoning you whom he had chosen, let him show that his faith is of God and let it appear forthwith if it is worthy of God. For I shall ascend and reveal myself to all this multitude as I am.'" And lo, he rose on high over all Rome, while everyone beheld him soaring even over the temples and the hills, and the faithful bent their eyes upon Peter. And Peter, perceiving the marvel of the sight, cried to the Lord Jesus Christ: "If thou sufferest him to accomplish what he has begun, now all who have trusted in thee will be put to shame and the signs and wonders which thou gavest them through me will be vain. Hasten thy grace, Lord, I pray, and let him fall from high and be wounded but not killed; let him be made impotent and let his leg be broken in three places." And he fell from high and broke his leg in three places. Then they stoned him and went every man to his own house and everyone thereafter believed upon Peter. . . .

GERMANIC CHRISTIANITY: *THE HELIAND*

c. 830

*The anonymous Old Saxon verse epic to which a modern editor
has given the title* Heliand *(healer) was written in about 830.
Its ultimate source was Tatian's* Harmony of the Gospels, *a
blending of the four New Testament accounts of Jesus' life
into a single sequential narrative. Although* The Heliand *remains basically Christian, it represents an attempt to make the
gospel figures culturally intelligible to a Germanic people.*

There came from Rome-burg   from the mighty man
Over the earth-folk,   from Octavian himself,
Ban and bidding   over his broad fealty;
This was come from Caesar   unto every king:
To the home-sitting ones   as far as the war-lords
Wielded their power   o'er the people and land.
'Twas hight that all men   habited outside their own
                     boroughs
Should seek now their homeland,   all heroes their heritage,
To bide their lord's heralds;   each landsman should go
Quickly to the clan   of his kinsmen,
To the burg of his birth.   The ban was proclaimed

SOURCE From *The Heliand,* trans. from the Old Saxon by Mari-
ana Scott, *University of North Carolina Studies in the Germanic
Languages and Literatures,* No. 52 (Chapel Hill: The University of
North Carolina Press, 1966), 11–14, 154–72.

Over this wide, wide world.   And the world-folk did
                              gather,
In every bastion the men all.   The messengers fared
                              forth,
Those come from Caesar,   book-learned thanes.
And neatly they wrote   each name on a scroll,
Both land and the man,   so that no lord could avoid it,
No man his tax;   but all must pay tribute,
The heroes each for his head.   So to his homeland
Came Joseph, the good man,   as God the Almighty,
The Wielder had willed it;   with his family he came,
Sought his shining castle,   his lordly seat,
The bastion at Bethlehem,   where they both did dwell,
Hero and holy maid,   Mary the good.
There stood in earlier days   the shining throne
Of the high-born king,   of the earl of the Hebrews,
Of David the good,   as long as he governed
And kept lofty seat.   They were his kith,
Were come from his clan,   were of good kin all,
Both through their birth.   Then I heard that the bright
                              tidings
Admonished Mary,   and the might of God:
That on this site   a Son should be hers,
Born here in Bethlehem,   the Mightiest of Bairns,
The Strongest of Kings.   Come was the Shining One,
Mighty here to man's light,   as for many a day
Pictures of Him   and tokens aplenty
Had foretold in this world.   So all had turned true,
As the sages had spoken it   in the long, long ago.
Through His Own Self's strength,   how most surely He would
                              come
To this earth-realm here —   with humility — He,
Protector to many.   Then His mother did take Him,
And she swaddled Him well,   the fairest of women,
With garments and goodly gems.   With her two gracious
                              hands

She lovingly laid Him,   the Little Man,
The Child in the crib,   though He had God's strength,
The Master of Men.   There His mother sat by Him,
The woman there waking;   she herself warded Him,
Held there the Holy Bairn;   and her heart doubted not —
The mind of the maid.   It became known to the many
Over this wide, wide world.   The warders did hear it:
Grooms were they there,   keeping guard outside,
Were war-men on watch;   with the horses they were,
With the beasts in the field.   And lo: before them they
                    saw
The darkness divide in the air.   Down came God's light —
Through the clouds came shining,   surrounding the grooms
Afar in the fields.   And sorely they feared,
These men, in their minds.   Then God's mighty angel
They saw coming afar.   To them together he spoke,
Hight that the grooms   not dread any grief
From the light. "For lo!"   quoth he, "A glad thing
I tell you and truly,   long longed-for tidings
Bespeaking great power: for in this selfsame night
Christ, Blessed Bairn of our own God,   is born in the
                    bastion of David,
He — our Master All Good.   That is joy to mankind,
The weal of all folk.   So that ye may find
The Mightiest of Babes   in Bethlehem-burg,
Take this as a token   that I now tell unto you
With soothy words: that He lieth swaddled,
A Child in a crib,   though He be King
Over earth and heaven   and the children of men,
All-Wielder o'er World."   Verily as he spoke this word,
There was come with   this single one of the angels
A multitude down   from the meadows of Heaven —
A holy host,   the fair folk of God.
They spoke, lauded greatly   the Lord of Mankind.
They raised holy song,   as they returned through the
                    clouds

126

To the meadows of Heaven.   And the warders did hear
How the great host of angels   gave praise unto Almighty
God
With these words most reverently: "Honor be" quoth
they,
"To our Lord Himself in the highest,   to the King of
Heaven —
And on earth be peace   to all children of men,
To folk of good will   who accept their God
With hearts ever pure."   The herdsmen understood
That a mighty thing   had admonished them:
Blithe tidings there.   They turned back to Bethlehem
That selfsame night,   for their spirits longed
Most greatly to see   Christ Himself.
The angel of God had shown   unto them the shining token,
So that they themselves —   they could wander forth
To the Bairn of God.   Straightway they found Him, the
Babe,
The Lord of Mankind,   the Master of Peoples.
They praised God the Wielder,   and with their words
They made known far and wide   in the shining castle
What tokens holy they had seen indeed   from the meadows
of Heaven,
What signs there, fair in the field.   The woman full well
Kept these things in her heart,   the holy virgin,
The maid in her mind: whatever she heard the men there
saying.
Fittingly she reared Him,   the fairest of women;
With her love the mother   did raise the Master of Men,
The Holy Heavenly Bairn. . . .

The Holy Christ   was come to the house
Where they should accomplish   the custom there of the
land,
Following the bidding of God,   as it was for the Jewish
folk

Ancient custom and law   from time immemorial.
On the evening   All-Wielding Christ did go
To take His seat in the hall;   and He bade His disciples
Come unto Him, the twelve   who were truest to Him,
These men most loyal   to Him in their minds
Both in words and in ways.   Well did He know
The thoughts in their hearts,   our Holy Lord —
He greeted them over the banquet.   "I yearn indeed,"
He said, "to sit   together with you
And partake of the feast,   share the Passover
Of Jews with you, My beloved.   Now must I tell unto you
The will of the Lord,   that in this world no longer
May I enjoy meat with mankind   before it must be fulfilled,
The kingdom of Heaven.   For Me there is at hand
Both torment and torture,   which I must truly endure
For the people, this land-folk here."   So did He speak to
                              His thanes,
The Holy Lord,   and His heart was grieved,
His spirit darkend with sorrow,   and to His disciples
                              He spoke,
The Good Man to His faithful: "Why, I give unto you the
                              kingdom of God,
Give you the light of Heaven,   and ye give unto Me
Most sweetly your thaneship.   But now ye wish not to ful-
                              fill this,
But waver far from the word.   Now verily I say unto you
That one of your twelve   will become untrue,
One will sell Me   among the kinship of Jews,
Will sell Me for silver,   and will take such riches,
Such precious treasure;   and give his Lord in return,
His sweet, his beloved Liege.   But great sorrow shall come
                              unto him
From that deed, and much pain.   For he shall perceive them,
The Weird Sisters,   and shall see the end of his care.
He shall know most truly   that it would be a far sweeter
                              thing,

128

A far better one,   if he had never been born
To live in this light,   than that he take pay
For evil deeds   and wrongful advise."
Then each earl began   to look around at the others,
To gaze about sorrowfully,   for they were sore of soul
And troubled indeed of heart;   they heard their Lord there
Speaking words of lament.   They were worried
To which of the twelve   He would now tell
That he was the miscreant,   the man who had bargained
With the people for the pieces of silver.   Nor was it
                    simple for any person,
For any thane to confess   such a crime,
Such a sinful mind;   but each man denied it —
And all became fearful   and dared not ask
Until Simon Peter,   though he himself dared not speak —
This worthy man   did make motion
To John the good: to the Bairn of God
He was in these days   the dearest one,
The one most beloved,   and Holy Christ gave him leave
To rest in His lap,   to lie against His breast,
And on it to lean his head;   there heard he so many a
                    holy mystery,
So many deep thoughts;   and to his dear Lord he did speak
And began to question Him.   "Who shall that be, my Liege?"
Quoth he, "Who would sell Thee,   the Richest of Kings,
To the folk of the foe?   Full anxious we are,
O Wielder, to know."   He had ready His words,
The Holy Christ: "See thou into whose hands I here
Give of My meat before these men: he hath most wicked
                    thoughts,
Beareth great bitterness of mind: he shall deliver Me
                    into bonds,
Into the power of the foe,   where they shall deprive Me
                    of My age,
Shall destroy My life."   Thereafter He did take

The meat before the men and gave of the meat unto that
mean scoundrel,
Into Judas' hand, and He spoke unto him,
He Himself before His disciples, and He straightway com-
manded
That he fare far away from the folk. "Do as thou thinkest,"
quoth He,
"Do as thou needst must do; no longer mayest thou
Hide thy will and intent — thy Weird is at hand,
Thy time draweth near." When the troth-breaker
Did take of the meat and with his mouth did eat thereof,
The power of God did forsake him, and the Fiend did enter
Into his body then, that loathsome wight;
And Satan was bound more sorely to him,
Bound hard 'round his heart, since the help of God
Had left him here in this light. To those who change lords
Under this heaven: to such woe will indeed come.
Then setting out from there and thinking up evil,
Judas did leave; against his Liege this thane
Harbored great grimness of heart. It had grown very dark,
It was deep in the night. Now the Son of the Lord
Tarried still at the feast; and for His disciples there
The Wielder did bless both the wine and the bread,
The Holy King of the Heavens; and with His hands He did
break it
And gave it to His disciples and gave thanks unto God,
Grateful unto Him, who created all that was there,
The world and its winsomeness; and He spoke many a word:
"Believe ye this clearly," quoth He, "that this is My
body
And My blood as well. I give both unto you
To eat and to drink. This I shall give on earth,
Shall spill and spread onto it, and shall ransom you
To the realms of the Lord and to life everlasting
In the light of Heaven. Remember ye ever
And follow ye that which I give unto you at this feast.

Make it known unto the many,   for this is a mighty thing.
With it ye shall honor Him,   who is your Lord.
Hold this to My memory as a holy token,
So that the children of men   will cherish and keep it,
All men in this mid-world: that through My love I have
                                        done so,
Through the grace of the Lord.   And think ye ever
How I have bidden you   to keep firm this brotherhood,
To have fastness of mind, much love in your hearts,   so
                that the children of men
Over the whole of the earth   will all understand
That ye are most truly   the disciples Mine.
I shall also make known unto you   how a fierce, wily
                                        Fiend,
A sword-strong foe   shall tempt your spirits,
Satan himself.   He cometh to ensnare
Your souls most boldly.   Straightway must ye make stead-
                                        fast
The thoughts in your breasts. . . .
                        Judas rightly did lead them,
Man hate-filled of heart.   After him the Jews did go
                                        marching,
The folk-clans of the foe.   In their midst they carried
                                        fire,
Lights in lamp-vessels;   and they led forth torches,
Bright burning down from the city,   as they began most
                                        eagerly
To stride up the mountain.   This spot Judas knew well,
The one to which he should lead   the land-folk all.
As they now fared to the spot   in front of the folk,
He said unto them as a sign,   lest they seize by mistake
Some other man: "I shall first go to Him," quoth he,
"Shall kiss Him and say: that is Christ Himself!
Then shall ye seize Him   with the strength of the crowd;
Shall bind Him up there on the mount   and bring Him
                        down to the bastion,

131

Lead Him down 'mid the land-folk: His life hath he for-
                              feited
With His words full well."   And the people went,
Until they were come   to the Christ Himself —
The grim folk of the Jews,   to where He stood with His
                              followers,
The Lord Most Glorious,   biding his god-sent fate,
The wonderous time.   Then Judas went toward Him,
Man without troth,   and unto God's Bairn
He nodded His head   and here spoke to his Lord,
Kissed Him, Mighty Christ,   carried out his word,
Pointed Him out to the people,   as he had promised before.
The Lord of All Peoples   bore all with His patience,
The Wielder of World;   and with His words He did speak
                              unto him,
Asked him most boldly: "Why hast thou come to Me with
                              this host?
Why dost thou lead this land-folk to Me?   And to this
                              loathesome crowd
Thou sellest Me with thy kiss,   among the clans of the Jews
Betrayest Me to these many?"   He went to speak to the many,
To the other people,   and to ask with His words
Why they were come to seek Him   so zealously here
With their thralls in the night.   "To whom do you wish to
                              bring need and distress,
To some one of mankind?" . . .
Then the angry folk of the Jews   did become insolent,
The host most haughty,   since they had Holy Christ
And could lead Him away   in limb-bondage,
Take Him forth in their fetters.   And the foe went again
From the mount to the town.   And God's Mighty Bairn
Did go 'mid the host   with His hands all bound,
Drear and sad, down to the dale.   For His dearest thanes
Had broken their troth,   as He Himself had foretold.
But it was not for fear   that they forsook Him,

132

God's Bairn, their Beloved,   but so long before there had
                                been
The word of the prophet,   that it would indeed be thus.
Therefore they could not avoid their own deeds.   And after
                                the crowd
Went Peter and John,   those two men well-known,
And followed from afar.   Full anxious were they
To know what the grim-minded Jews   meant to do with God's
                                Bairn,
To their Lord most Dear.

PART TWO

THE CENTRAL MIDDLE AGES

THE CHANNELS OF PUBLIC LIFE

GOVERNMENT, COMMERCE AND
COMMUNICATIONS

26

REGULATIONS OF THE ROYAL COURT AT PAVIA

between c. 1010 and c. 1020, based on tenth-century sources

*The well-ordered taxation of goods passing in and out of the
Lombard kingdom described in this document broke down under
the weight of the commercial expansion of the eleventh and
twelfth centuries. The authority exercised by officials of the
central government at Pavia in the tenth century gradually
passed into the hands of the northern Italian communes themselves, once their wealth and influence had secured them their
political freedom.*

. . . Merchants entering the kingdom [of Italy] were
wont to pay *decima*[1] on all merchandise at the customs
houses at [the beginning of] the roads appertaining to the king. And
the [customs houses] are these: the first is Susa, the second
Bard, the third Bellinzona, the fourth Chiavenna, the fifth Bol-
zano, the sixth Volargne, the seventh Trevile, the eighth San

SOURCE From Robert S. Lopez and Irving W. Raymond, *Medieval Trade in the Mediterranean World*, Columbia University Records of Civilization, (New York: Columbia University Press, 1955),
56–58.

[1] a 10-per cent tax.

Pietro di Zuglio on the Monte Croce road, the ninth near Aquileia, the tenth Cividale del Friuli. All persons coming from beyond the mountains into Lombardy are obligated to pay the *decima* on horses, male and female slaves, woolen, linen and hemp cloth, tin, and swords. And at the gate they are obligated to pay the *decima* on all merchandise to the delegate of the treasurer. But everything that [pilgrims] bound for Rome to Saint Peter's take with them for expenses is to be passed without payment of the *decima*. No one ought to exact the *decima* from the pilgrims themselves bound for Rome or to hinder them in any way. And if anyone does so, let him be anathema.

As for the nation of the Angles and Saxons, they have come and were wont to come with their merchandise and wares. And [formerly], when they saw their trunks and sacks being emptied at the gates, they grew angry and started rows with the employees of the treasury. The [parties] were wont to hurl abusive words and in addition very often inflicted wounds upon one another. But in order to cut short such great evils and to remove danger [of conflicts], the king of the Angles and Saxons and the king of the Lombards agreed together as follows: The nation of the Angles and Saxons is no longer to be subject to the *decima*. And in return for this the king of the Angles and Saxons and their nation are bound and are obligated to send to the [king's] palace in Pavia and to the king's treasury, every third year, fifty pounds of refined silver, two large, handsome greyhounds, hairy or furred, in chains, with collars covered with gilded plates sealed or enameled with the arms of the king, two excellent embossed shields, two excellent lances, and two excellent swords wrought and tested. . . .

27

THE DECLINE AND FALL OF THE CAROLINGIAN EMPIRE: NITHARD, *HISTORY OF THE SONS OF LOUIS THE PIOUS*

841 – 844

This contemporary account of the feuding between Charlemagne's grandsons describes a frightened populace waiting out the indecisive period of civil war and trying to ally itself with the strongest contender. The fragmentation of Carolingian power is given formal sanction by the agreement in 842 to divide the imperial territory into three parts.

[840] Learning of his father's death, Lothar sent out messengers everywhere as soon as he could, especially throughout France [*Francia*], to say that he was about to come to take possession of the empire he had been given earlier, and to promise those who held benefices of his father, that he would grant them too, and, moreover, that he wished to enlarge them. He also ordered that men of dubious fidelity reaffirm their loyalty by oath; what is more, he ordered them to go to meet him [in France] as quickly as possible, threatening those who refused with death. As for Lothar himself, he advanced slowly, waiting to see how things would turn out before he crossed the Alps.

SOURCE Translated from Nithard, *Histoire des Fils de Louis le Pieux,* ed. and trans. by Ph. Lauer, Vol. VII: *Les Classiques de l'histoire de France au Moyen âge* (Paris: Librairie Ancienne Honoré Champion, 1926), 36, 38, 40, 42, 44, 58, 60, 130.

Attracted by greed and terror, men poured in from everywhere at his approach; perceiving this, he became puffed up by the numbers of his troops and began to devise a strategy by which he could easily invade the entire empire. Since he knew also that his route was near Louis, he decided to send out a force against him first, and turned all his energies to crushing him with his men. Meanwhile, by messengers, he shrewdly assured Charles in Aquitaine that he was on his side, as his father had appointed him to be and as befitted a godfather towards his godson. . . . And, having done that, he turned his course toward Worms.

At the same time Louis left part of his army there to guard the city and then went off to put down the rebellious Saxons. Because of this, Lothar was able to compel the guard to flee after a small skirmish, and, crossing the Rhine with his entire army, he turned toward Frankfurt. There he unexpectedly met Louis, and, having concluded a truce toward nightfall, they made their camps, one there, the other at the place where the Main and Rhine join—hardly a brotherly arrangement. Since Louis was offering a manly resistance, and Lothar was distrustful of his ability to overcome him without a battle and hoping to defeat Charles more easily, he delayed battle by [making] an agreement to meet again in the same place on the third of the Ides of November [November 11] and, if no treaty had been agreed to before that date, they would determine what [inheritance] was rightfully due to each by force of arms. Then, putting off [these] matters, he turned his energies to defeating Charles.

At about the same time, Charles had come to Bourges. . . . Hearing the news widespread by rumor, he chose Nithard and Augier as his messengers, and sent them as soon as he could to Lothar, asking and pleading with him to remember the oaths they swore to one another, and that he preserve that which his father had established among them; what is more, he reminded him of their status as brothers, and that he was Lothar's younger brother, [and said that] if each of them retained what was his own, and if Lothar would allow him to keep that which his father conceded to him, without conflict, he would promise to be his vassal and subject, as was fitting toward a first-born brother. . . .

Lothar, for his part, pretending to be well-disposed toward the messengers, sent them back with his greetings alone, and replied that he was about to answer concerning other matters through his own messengers. Moreover, because they had been unwilling to break their oaths in order to join his party, he took away the benefices his father had given them. In doing so he unwittingly revealed how he was planning to treat his brother.

Meanwhile all those between the Meuse and Seine sent to Charles, asking him to come before they were conquered by Lothar, promising to await in readiness his coming. Charles, leaving Aquitaine quickly with a very few men, came to Querzy and received kindly all those who came to him from the forest of Charbonnière and the surrounding area. . . .

At the same time that all this was happening to Charles, Lothar was devoting all his thought to subduing Louis, or, if you prefer, to destroying him utterly, by trickery or by force. To this end he was easily able to bring in Ottokar, Archbishop of Mainz, and Count Adalbert of Metz; both of them had a mortal hatred for Louis.

For Adalbert had recovered from the illness under which he had lain for almost a year just in time to help in the fratricide; and he was at that time so skilled in giving advice that no one was willing to depart from his advice, once given. At his insistence, Lothar crossed the Rhine, having collected an innumerable multitude of men behind him, sending ahead, as usual, agents to tempt or threaten the wavering populace into submission. But those who were on Louis' side, fearing that they could not endure such a large army, went over to Lothar, or fled, leaving Louis defenseless; and he, totally lacking support, retreated with a very few men and went into Bavaria. . . .

An amazing thing, worthy of mention, happened to Charles

on Holy Saturday. Now, neither he nor anyone in his army had with him more than the clothes he wore and his arms and horse; as Charles was getting out of the bath and preparing to put on the same clothes he had taken off, suddenly messengers from Aquitaine appeared at the doors, bearing the crown, the regalia, and all that pertained to the divine cult.

Who would have believed that so few men, with so little information, could cross so much territory unharmed (with the danger of robbery everywhere), bearing many talents of gold and an infinite multitude of jewels? And, what is much more remarkable, they were able to arrive at a definite place at the stated day and hour, even though Charles himself couldn't have predicted where he might be at that time. This could hardly have happened without divine aid or command. . . .

[842] Then, in mid-June, on a Thursday, Lothar, Louis, and Charles met, each one accompanied by an equal number of lords, on an island near the city of Mâcon, called Ansilla, and each swore this oath to the others: that they would keep peace from that day on, and that they would divide the empire (all but Lombardy, Bavaria and Aquitaine) into three parts, as equally as they could, by an agreement arranged by their vassals; and the choice of the three parts was to go to Lothar. Each of the three brothers was to guarantee to the others the parts he had accepted, during his lifetime, provided the others did the same for him. With that done, and after words of peace had been exchanged, they separated peacefully, and returned to their camps, to deliberate further on other matters the next day.

28

THE DEEDS OF CONRAD II

1046–47

*This account of the election, consecration and imperial corona-
tion of Conrad II (1024–1039), written by one of his chaplains,
Wipo, shows the continued strength of the idea of elective monarchy in the Empire. Wipo's insistence on the spiritual character of the imperial office and the divine origin of kingly
power was not coincidental—it was intended to buttress the
court's claim that the emperor could invest bishops with their
offices, and so control the church in his territories. Beneath the
formal rhetoric of the verse epitaph, a large measure of genuine
devotion to the emperor is apparent, as are the various images
a medieval king presented to his subjects.*

While all the magnates, and, so to say, the valor and the vitals
of the kingdom, had convened there, they pitched camps on
this side and in the region about the Rhine. . . . For there was
to be deliberation, not about a middling matter, but about one
which, unless considered with very great zeal in a fervent breast,
might be terminated to the ruin of the whole body of the kingdom. . . .

Two Conrads were there, of whom one, since he was of the
greater age, was named Cuono the Elder; but the other was

SOURCE From *Imperial Lives and Letters of the Eleventh Century*, trans. by T. E. Mommsen and Karl F. Morrison (New York and
London: Columbia University Press, 1962), 60–62, 65–67, 79, 99.

143

called Cuono the Younger. Both were very noble men in German Francia, born of two brothers, one of whom was called Hezil and the other Cuono. We learn that these [latter] were born of Otto, duke of the Franks, with two others, Bruno and William. Of these, Bruno, become pope of the Apostolic See of the Roman Church, was called by a changed name Gregory [V]; and William, made bishop of the Strassburg church, exalted it in a wondrous way. Although the two aforesaid Cuonos were, as has been said, very noble on their fathers' parts, they were not at all less outstanding on their mothers' sides. Mathilda, the mother of Cuono the Younger, was born of the daughter of Conrad, King of Burgundy. Adelheid, mother of Cuono the Elder, sprang from a very noble family of the Lotharingians. . . .

The Archbishop of Mainz, whose opinion had to be taken before all, asked by the people what was seemly to him, with a full heart and a happy voice, acclaimed and elected the elder Cuono as his lord and king, and rector and defender of the fatherland. The other archbishops and the remaining men of holy orders unhesitatingly followed him in this vote. The younger Cuono, who had been negotiating for a short time with the Lotharingians, returned suddenly and elected him as lord and king with the greatest good will. The King, taking him by the hand, made him sit beside him.

Then, one by one, men from each of the several realms repeated the same words of election again and again; there was a shout of acclamation by the people; all consented unanimously with the princes in the election of the King; all eagerly desired the elder Cuono. On him they insisted; him they placed without any hesitation before all the mighty lords; him they judged to be most worthy of the regal power; and they demanded that there be no delay of his consecration. . . .

III. *On the Consecration of the King*

When the election was over, everyone, with the greatest eagerness, hastened to follow the King to Mainz, where he was to receive the most holy unction. They went rejoicing; the clergy chanted psalms, the layfolk sang, each in his own fashion. At no time have I found that God received such great praises from men on one day in one place.

If Charlemagne had been present, alive, with his scepter, the people would not have been more eager, nor could they have rejoiced more at the return of so great a man than at the first coming of this King. The King arrived at Mainz. And there, received with due honor, he waited devoutly for his consecration, [as one] desirable to all. When the Archbishop of Mainz and all the clergy solemnly prepared themselves to bless him on the day of the birth of St. Mary, the Archbishop delivered this sermon to the King during the sacred offices of regal unction:

"All power of this transient age is derived from one most pure font. It is usually the case, however, that when several rivulets spring forth from the same source, at one time they are turbulent, at another, clear, while at their head, the font stays fast in its purity. In the same way, inasmuch as the human state dares to set Creator and creation side by side for comparison, we have the power to conjecture in a similar way about God the Immortal King and about earthly kings. For it has been written: 'All power is of God.' When this Omnipotent King of kings, the author and the beginning of all honor, pours the grace of some dignity upon princes of the earth, insofar as it is in accord with the nature of its origin, it is pure and unstained. When, however, it has come to those who wield this dignity unworthily and pollute it with pride, malice, lust, avarice, wrath, impatient willfulness, and cruelty, they will serve the perilous potion of iniquity to themselves and to all subject to them, unless they purge themselves by doing penance. O let the whole Church of the Saints pray and intercede before God that the dignity which is offered pure today by God to our present lord and King, Conrad, be preserved inviolate by him as far as is humanly possible. . . .

You have come to the highest dignity: you are the vicar of Christ.

"No one but his imitator is a true ruler. It is necessary that in this 'throne of the kingdom' you reflect on the perpetual honor.

It is great felicity to rule in the world, but the greatest is to triumph in Heaven. Although God requires many things of you, He wishes most of all that you render judgment and justice, and peace for the fatherland, which always looks to you; and [He wishes] that you be the defender of churches and clerics, the guardian of widows and orphans. With these and other good [works] your throne will be firmly established here and forever. . . ."

xvi. *That King Conrad was made Emperor at Rome*

Therefore, King Conrad, having entered Rome in the same year as above—that is, 1027 from the nativity of the Savior, in the tenth indiction—was wondrously received by Pope John [XIX] and all the Romans with royal honor. And on the holy day of Easter, which fell that year on the VII of the kalends of April, he was elected emperor by the Romans, and he received the imperial benediction from the Pope. . . .

xl. *Verses on the Death of the Emperor Conrad*

Let him who has a serene voice proffer this canticle
Of the lamentable year and the ineffable hurt
For which every man grieves publicly and in his home.
The populace sighs for [its] lord in vigils and through [its]
    sleep:
"O King God, guard the living and have mercy upon the dead!"

In the year one thousand nine and thirty,
From the nativity of Christ, nobility fell prostrate on all sides.
Caesar fell, the head of the world, and with him many of the
    greatest,
The Emperor succumbed, Conrad, lover of law.
"O King God, guard the living and have mercy upon the
    dead!" . . .

Born of the blood of kings, he excelled all by far.
Glorious in person, handsome under his crown,
The scepter, the kingdom, the Empire, to none were more be-
 coming.
He adorned the commonwealth with honor—he labored to this
 end.
"O King God, guard the living and have mercy upon the dead!"

After he replenished Franconia with the abundance of peace,
He tamed the Alamanni and all the tyrants of the kingdom.
He imposed the bit of the law upon the Saxons and Bavarians.
Laudable Italy saw his mighty deeds.
"O King God, guard the living and have mercy upon the dead!"

29

_____

THE INVESTITURE CONTROVERSY:
LETTERS OF HENRY IV TO POPE GREGORY

1073

*In 1073 the leading princes of Saxony led a conspiracy against
the Emperor, Henry IV. As part of his plan for defeating the
rebels Henry dispatched this ingratiating letter to Pope Gregory
VII, hoping to secure his support.*

To the most watchful and zealous Lord Pope, Gregory, distinguished by heaven with the apostolic dignity, Henry, by the

SOURCE   From "Letters of Henry IV," *Imperial Lives and Letters
of the Eleventh Century,* trans. by T. E. Mommsen and Karl F.
Morrison (New York and London: Columbia University Press,
1962), 141–42, 147–49, 156.

grace of God King of the Romans, sends the most faithful expression of due subservience.

Since, in order to continue rightly administered in Christ, the kingship and the priesthood are always in need of the strength which He delegates, it is surely fitting for them, my lord and most loving father, not to disagree with one another, but rather to cleave to each other, inseparably joined with the bond of Christ. Thus and in no other way, the concord of Christian unity and the condition of the Church's religious life are preserved in the bond of perfect charity and peace.

With God's consent we have held the office of kingship for some time now, but we have not shown to the priesthood the proper justice and honor in all things. To be sure, we have not borne in vain the avenging sword of the power given us by God; yet we have not always unsheathed it justly in judicial punishment against wrongdoers. Now, however, through divine mercy, we have been stung in some measure by remorse, and having turned against ourself in self-accusation, we confess our former sins to you, Most Indulgent Father, placing our hopes in the Lord that absolved by your apostolic authority we may be worthy of forgiveness. . . .

For not only have we usurped ecclesiastical properties, but we have also sold the churches themselves to unworthy men—men embittered with the gall of simony—who entered not by the door but by some other way; nor have we defended the churches as we should have. . . .

RENUNCIATION OF GREGORY VII
BY THE GERMAN BISHOPS[1]

1076

Two years after the above letter was written, Gregory issued a proclamation banning lay investiture of bishops, an act that cut deeply into Henry's political power. In the next letter the German bishops indicate their preferred allegiance to the king by repudiating their loyalty to Gregory.

Siegfried, archbishop of Mainz, Udo of Trier, William of Utrecht, Herman of Metz, Henry of Liége, Ricbert of Verden, Bido of Toul, Hozeman of Speier, Burchard of Halberstadt, Werner of Strassburg, Burchard of Basel, Otto of Constance, Adalbero of Würzburg, Rupert of Bamberg, Otto of Regensburg, Egilbert of Freising, Ulric of Eichstätt, Frederick of Münster, Eilbert of Minden, Hezilo of Hildesheim, Benno of Osnabrück, Eppo of Naumburg, Imadus of Paderborn, Tiedo of Brandenburg, Burchard of Lausanne, and Bruno of Verona, to Brother Hildebrand:

When you had first usurped the government of the Church, we knew well how, with your accustomed arrogance, you had presumed to enter so illicit and nefarious an undertaking against human and divine law. We thought, nevertheless, that the pernicious beginnings of your administration ought to be left unnoticed in prudent silence. We did this specifically in the hope that such criminal beginnings would be emended and wiped away somewhat by the probity and industry of your later rule. But now, just as the deplorable state of the universal Church

---

[1] The renunciation is part of a manuscript collection of Henry's letters which includes answers and other miscellaneous documents. (Ed.'s note.)

cries out and laments, through the increasing wickedness of your actions and decrees, you are woefully and stubbornly in step with your evil beginnings. . . .

Through you, all administration of ecclesiastical affairs has been assigned to popular madness. Since some now consider no one a bishop or priest save the man who begs that office of Your Arrogance with a most unworthy servility, you have shaken into pitiable disorder the whole strength of the apostolic institution and that most comely distribution of the limbs of Christ, which the Doctor of the Gentiles so often commends and teaches.[2] And so through these boastful decrees of yours—and this cannot be said without tears—the name of Christ has all but perished. Who, however, is not struck dumb by the baseness of your arrogant usurpation of new power, power not due you, to the end that you may destroy the rights due the whole brotherhood?[3] For you assert that if any sin of one of our parishioners comes to your notice, even if only by rumor, none of us has any further power to bind or to loose the party involved, for you alone may do it, or one whom you delegate especially for this purpose. Can anyone schooled in sacred learning fail to see how this assertion exceeds all madness? . . . since the Church of God is imperiled by so great a tempest arising from abuse born of your innovations, and since you have degraded your life and conduct by such multifarious infamy, we declare that in the future we shall observe no longer the obedience which we have not promised to you. And since none of us, as you have publicly declared, has hitherto been a bishop to you, you also will now be pope to none of us. . . .

THE VOW OF HENRY IV TO GREGORY AT CANOSSA

Henry's defiance of Gregory's radical reform also took the form of a letter, which was swiftly followed, however, by the em-

[2] Romans 12, 5; I Corinthians 12, 2. [3] Cf. I Peter 2, 17.

peror's excommunication. Henry outmaneuvered the pope's reprisal in 1077 by dashing in the middle of winter to Canossa (where Gregory had halted in his journey into the Empire to preside over Henry's deposition) to ask for absolution. Gregory was bound to absolve him even though Henry's sincerity was questionable. This selection records the latter's promise of non-reprisal.

Before the date the Lord Pope Gregory is to set, I, King Henry, shall bring about justice according to his judgment or harmony according to his counsel with regard to the complaint and objection now being made against me by archbishops, bishops, dukes, counts, the other princes in the realm of the Germans, and those who follow them by reason of the same objection. If a concrete obstacle hinder me or him, I shall be ready to do the same when that hindrance has been overcome. Also, if the same Lord Pope Gregory should wish to go beyond the mountains to other lands, he, those who are among his retainers or guards, and those who are sent by him or come to him from any region, will be safe in coming, staying, and going thence, from any harm to life and limb and from capture by me and by those whom I can control. Moreover, no other difficulty prejudicial to his honor will occur with my assent; and should any person create one for him, I shall help him [Gregory] in good faith, according to my ability.

Done at Canossa, 28 January, the fifteenth Indiction.

30

THE MAKING OF A TOWN:
NINTH-CENTURY BRUGES

latter ninth century

This account of how the town of Bruges came into existence documents the growth of a commercial center dependent on the needs of courtiers and suitors of the court; it implies that, at least in this case, geographical features and broad social changes affected the rapid development of the town far less than the circumstantial needs of the castle-dwellers.

After this, because of the work or needs of those living in the château,[1] there began to stream in merchants—that is, dealers in precious goods—who set themselves up in front of the gate, at the château's bridge; then there followed tavern-keepers, then inn-keepers to provide the food and lodging for those who came to do business in the presence of the prince, who was often

---

SOURCE   Translated from: *Documents relatifs à l'histoire de l'industrie et du commerce en France,* ed. Gustave Fagniez, *Collection de textes pour servir à l'étude et à l'enseignement de l'histoire,* Vol. I (Paris: Alphonse Picard et Fils, 1898), 54–55.

[1] The château of Bruges, built by Baldwin Iron Arm, Count of Flanders, who married Charles the Bald's daughter Judith in 862.

there. Houses began to be built and inns to be made ready, where those were to be lodged who could not be put up inside the château; and they were accustomed to use this phrase: "Let us go to the bridge." So many dwellings accumulated there that right away it became a large town [*villa magna*] which to this day bears the name "Brugghe," which, in their tongue, means "bridge."

31

───────

MANORIAL RECORDS
OF THE TENTH AND ELEVENTH CENTURIES

These documents testify, among other things, to the total integration of churchmen into manorial society; the imputation of the church's power over the countryside is, however, somewhat exaggerated by the fact that most extant manorial records were kept by monastic and episcopal landlords. The tenth-century charter from Stavelot enumerates the mutual advantages accruing to laymen and the church that could result from a pious donation of lands. Rainulf and his family, assured of a "heavenly reward," enjoy the use of extra lands while they live; the monks of Stavelot acquire all of their possessions upon their deaths. An even greater boon to a monastery was a noble or royal foundation, such as the one described in the founding charter of Boxgrove Priory. The first late eleventh-century document describes a property dispute among vassals of the Count of Blois, who makes a judgment in an impromptu court session. If the lands of a monastery were not sufficiently increased by gifts, they could be augmented by outright purchase, as the next document illustrates. Finally, the census of Chaumousey provides a systematic listing of the produce and services due from a manse, or farmlet, under the abbey's control.

April 25, 943

Whoever should donate something from among his chattel to those who live in community for God's church, can be certain of receiving a heavenly reward. Therefore I, Rainulf, and my wife Huoda, donate jointly our personal possessions to the church of Saint Peter in the monastery of Stavelot, where the body of lord Remaclus lies, whereof the venerable Odilo is both Abbot and guardian, two manses in the village of Navaugle, which lie between [the lands of] Saint Remaclus and Saint Lambert, between the Iwoine and the Vachaux. In return for which we accept from the monastery, with the consent of the aforesaid abbot and all the brethren, boon service in the above-mentioned village of Navaugle and [four manses] in the village of Orgoni. Our agreement is that for as long as we live, I, Rainulf and my wife Huoda and our son Godfrey will pay twelve pennies every year at the feast of Saint Remaclus: so that if we fail to pay or if we should be late in paying, we shall try to collect it as the law provides. And we are not, under this agreement, empowered to sell or trade this property, but are rather to increase it, and after all our deaths both pieces of land, together with all that has accrued to it and all the above-mentioned appurtenances, shall revert to the church of Stavelot without any opposition. In order that this boon-service remain a firm and unchanging agreement, it is supported by this contract.

Done publicly at the monastery of Stavelot on the 17th of the Kalends of May [April 25], in the seventh year of the reign of

SOURCE Translated from *Recueil des Chartes de l'Abbaye de Stavelot-Malmedy*, ed. Joseph Halkin and C. G. Roland, Vol. I (Brussels: Kiessling et Cie. P. Imbreghts, 1909), 152–53.

glorious King Otto. The seal of Abbot Odilo who had this charter drawn up. The seal of Odilardo, his advocate. The seals of Everard Aricus, Engonus, Mannonus, Ermenfindus, Therdericus, Asculfrus, Aricus.

1105

Charter of Robert de Haia, son of Ranulf the seneschal of Robert Count of Mortain, nephew of Eudo the steward of King William [I], giving notice that in this year 1105—being 13 of the Indiction, Henry being king in England, with his wife Matilda similarly sprung of royal stock, Ralf being bishop of Chichester, Philip king in France—he has given, with his wife's approval, to the abbey of the Holy Trinity, l'Essay, for his soul and those of King Henry and the queen his wife, these churches of the fee of Hannac, which the king gave him, with their lands and tithes; the church of St. Mary of Boxgrove in the diocese of Chichester, and two and a half hides of land round about it, and the whole tithe of that parish and of his Christmas rents there and the tithe of his wood, from pannage and sale, with firing and timber for their buildings and pannage for their swine and pasture for all their stock. . . . Of this gift the witnesses were on the part of the said Robert, Humfrey de Sartelleio, Ralph de Carrou, Ranulf de Sancto Georgio, on the part of the church, Robert nephew and William his son, Rainfred de Sancta Oportuna, Aufrid, Rainald Magnus, Robert Cook, and Anschetil son of Robert Baker.

SOURCE From *The Chartulary of Boxgrove Priory,* trans. and ed. by Lindsay Fleming, Publications of the Sussex Record Society, LIX (Cambridge: 1960), 14–15.

After lord Abbot Bernard acquired the territory Rosdonium from Hugh, ruler of Blois, who laid false charge against us about it, in the same plea Erchenbald Pejor Lupo accused us about it in our presence, saying that although Hugh was said to have held the property from him, he alienated it, but he was himself unwilling to sanction any alienation. Both parties agreed to determine the accuracy of the allegation in court. Court was called into session at the oak-tree; Count Stephen and his court judged that the lord abbot did not have to answer in any way concerning that holding which lord Abbot Bartholomew held for so long, and lord Abbot Bernard held after him without any objections from him. These were the witnesses: from among the monks, the lord abbot, Drogo his bailiff, Henry the steward, Bernard the cellarer, Ivo, prior of the same obedience [order], and Odo, who was then prior [at Bernard's monastery], and Matthew; from among the laity, Lancelin of Balgentiac, Henry his seneschal, Rainald Meingot, Guicher of Chastel, Rainald, Hugh of Gualardonio, Berner the vice-count, Hugh the cup-bearer . . . from among the servants, Vuinebald the chamberlain of the lord abbot, John and Otger, stewards, Hilduin our cellarer of Castro novo. Done at the Suevrum, where Count Stephen was at the time encamped, in the year 1092 after the incarnation of the Lord, in the time of Philip, king of the French.

SOURCE Translated from *Cartulaire de Marmoutier pour le Dunois,* ed. Emile Mabille (Châteaudun: n.d.), 134–35.

1092

We wish it known to all, both present and to come, that when Gaufredus and Hato, monks of the Greater Monastery [of Dunois], were at the town of Méry-sur-Seine, they bought one carrucate of land from the boy Fulcher, at the place which is called Bad Neighbor. The price was one horse and half a measure of oats. Nivelo, from whose fief the land came, allowed this sale, as did Hemelin his brother and Richilda his mother and his two sisters, Melisande and Sizilia, who were given half a measure of grain and twelve pennies from the sale. These also witnessed it: Archer the prefect, Gerard Holdland, the servant Garin, Rainald of Aeneto, William his squire, Stephen Bursard; from among the monks, Clement and Geoffrey, and Hato. Be it known also that this purchase of land at Bad Neighbor, made by the boy Fulcher of Merliaco, was approved by Nivelo and Hamelin his brother. Done in this 1092nd year after the Lord's incarnation, in the reign of King Philip.

SOURCE Translated from *Cartulaire de Marmoutier pour le Dunois,* ed. Emile Mabille (Châteaudun: n.d.), 135.

GENERAL CENSUS OF THE ABBEY OF CHAUMOUSEY IN THE FORM OF A CHARTER PROMULGATED BY THE ABBOT SEHIER

1109 – 28

Sehier, principal provider for the church of Chaumousey, to our brothers now living and to come, perpetual greeting in the Lord. Because I have entrusted to the memory of our successors the allods which have been donated to our church in my time through the oblations of the faithful, in two little volumes, I judged it most useful to include in this charter the rents from single allods, so that, having been informed by it, future brothers may know what they ought to exact from each of our possessions at various times during the year.

CHAPTER I

First therefore, I shall speak briefly of those things about which we made inquiry under oath, and which we discovered by investigation concerning our allods at Masnile and Ravrum. . . . §1. Information was given us of eight and one-half quarter allods and fourteen manses, which came from the patrimony of Lady Bertha at Mérul-en-Xaintois, each of which should owe a quarter-rent. At the Lord's Nativity, each owes three loaves and three capons and three pennies and an

SOURCE Translated from Charles-Edmond Perrin, *Recherches sur la Seigneurie Rurale en Lorraine d'après les plus anciens censiers* (*IXe–XII siècle*), Publications de la Faculté des lettres de l'université de Strasbourg, Fascicule 71 (Paris: Les Belles Lettres, 1935), 711–13, 715–16.

obol for wood. Each owes also in the month of March fifteen feet of hedge and at Easter a cock with five eggs. Each owes also in June and in autumn and in March a *crovatam*. Also in July, reaping and hay-storing and five shingles for the roof of our barn, and at the first cleaning of that barn and manure-spreading, they owe manure-carrying and the yearly tax. In August each owes two measures of the autumnal tax and two quarterly taxes. At the feast of St. Remi each owes two pennies and an obol for meat and at the feast of St. Martin two pennies and a hen. Each also owes one quarter of threshing five measures of grain in our barn at the court's measure and must plough *ascengias* in June, before the feast of St. Peter and in autumn before the feast of St. Adelphus, and in March each ought to sow his own *ascengiam*; in autumn he must sow ours. . . .

CHAPTER III

The same Bertha gave us eight quarter-allods with the same number of manses in Noncourt. Each quarter-allod owes: at the feast of the Nativity four loaves and three pennies and a pig worth a dozen pennies and in March fifteen feet of hedge and in July two rakes; in July also each owes reaping and hay-storage and, at the first cleaning of the barn and manure-spreading, each owes manure-carrying and the yearly rent and five shingles per year for the roof of our barn. And now that I have begun to speak of the barn, I shall add briefly how our barn is to be built and repaired in each allod by those who hold quarter-allods from us. If our barn is to be built or repaired, whoever holds our quarter-allods shall aid us for one day, without our providing food or pay; on the remaining days, until the work is finished, they shall carry it through for us, accepting food from us, but no pay of any kind. In the same way they shall aid us in building or repairing a mill. . . .

We own five quarter-allods at Housséville, of which three owe us: at Easter a cock with ten eggs, and in mid-May two pennies and an obol and in July reaping and at the feast of

St. Remi two pennies and an obol and at the Nativity three pennies. They owe threshing of a measure of grain and ploughing of a measure of ground for sowing. The other two quarter-allods owe, beyond these things, at the Nativity three more pennies, a pig worth twelve pennies, and one of them ploughs. . . . . .[1] owes three torches at the Nativity to work the *tostrinam* for one year [he] owes two shingles for the barn, the next year three shingles plus cleaning the barn and spreading manure. Each quarter-allod owes at the Nativity three loaves and three capons and three pennies. In March each owes fifteen feet of hedge and at Easter two cocks with thirty eggs and in May of one year three pennies and alternate years six pennies. Each owes in June and in autumn and in March a *crovatam*. . . .

[1] The rest of this chapter is missing from the manuscript. (Ed.'s note.)

32

———

THE BLOOD FEUD: RAOUL GLABER, *HISTORIES*

888

Among the more hazardous obligations of noble birth was protecting family honor; once a relative's blood had been shed, a knight was obligated to avenge the victim. Systems of compensatory payment for wounds and even for murder were imposed by medieval governments in an attempt to prevent the sort of wasteful feuding described in this passage.

SOURCE Translated from Raoul Glaber, *Les Cinq Livres de ses Histoires* (900–1044), ed. Marcel Prou (Paris: 1886), 48.

[A certain] man and his wife were sprung from very noble families; because of this, [after their deaths] no small amount of litigation arose among their sons and grandsons concerning the paternal estates and surrounding villages. It happened that by chance, not long afterward, a certain village called Aillant, in the district of Sens, which had been granted to the rulers of the monastery of St. Columba the virgin, was to be judged among them. The knights of Auxerre who had always lived there took it over from them by force; but they were preparing to make it their own again by a consummate effort. This dispute lasted many years, until one day at harvest time war broke out in the village between the two parties, in which many were killed on both sides. Eleven sons and grandsons from the afore-mentioned family were killed. In the course of time, amid increasing conflict, the quarrel remaining ever-present, the family continued to fight on, though numerically depleted, and to murder their enemies for thirty years and more.

<hr />

33

FEUDAL OBLIGATIONS

The mutual obligations between the feudal lord and his man, or vassal, were very much the same whether the contracting parties were petty knights or kings. In both cases the vassal swore first an oath of homage, promising service and obedience to the lord in return for protection and, usually, an estate or fief; then an

SOURCE Translated from *Liber Feudorum Maior, Cartularia real que se conserva en el Archivo de la Corona de Aragón,* ed. Francisco Miquel Rosell, *Textos y Estudios de la Corona de Aragón,* Vol. I (Barcelona: 1945), 3–4.

oath of fealty, promising his loyalty and fidelity and binding
the agreement by an oath taken in the presence of a priest and
possibly of holy relics. The oath of Sancho provides for the
automatic revolt of his vassals against him should he "disparage"
Ramiro by attempting to take back the towns or castle he has
granted him. The fact that kings could become one another's
vassals weakens the assumption that feudal society was strictly
hierarchical in each area, with the lordless king every man's
chief lord.

1054–1063

In the name of our Lord Jesus Christ. This is the oath which
I, Sancho, king, made with the lord King Ramiro,[1] concerning
the gift which I made of my free will along with all my chief
vassals who were with me: Señor Fortunio Lopiz, Señor Fertunio Azenariz, Señor Ennego Sanz, Señor Xemeno Azenariz.
. . . I the above-mentioned Sancho, king, out of friendship,
fidelity, aid and council as God has given them to me, give you
the castle which is called Sangossa, with all its boundaries, and
the town which is called Lerda, and Ondues. And I give and
confirm my pledge that throughout my life I will not vex you
concerning these towns, nor will I require them of you, nor the
castle. . . . And if I should basely do this—may it never be!—
I give permission to all my chief vassals who are with me, with
all their honors and lands which they have and hold of me,
to come to your aid and place themselves in your power. And
we lords whose names appear above, vow that, as is written in
this charter, we are held to this agreement in good faith, without deception, through God and his saints, and we shall not
quit you nor your service for the sake of any possession or earthly
honor.

[1] The contracting parties are Sancho IV of Navarre and Ramiro I
of Aragón.

These are the lords which are not present: Señor Garcia Xemenones, Señor Fertunio Sanz, Señor Amavita Azenariz, Señor Fertunio Azenariz, Señor Fertunio Sanz of Buradone, Señor Agauri Garzez.

Before 1086

I Fichapal swear to you Count Artallo that from this time forward I will be faithful to you in your body and in the possessions you hold today and may acquire in the future; and may I so hold to this pledge which is made between us and may I so serve you, as a man ought to do to his liege lord, in faith, without any evil design. Through God and his saints.

SOURCE Translated from *Liber Feudorum Maior,* 104.

GILBERT OF BRUGES, *CHRONICLE OF HAINAUT*

1071

The relationship between lord and vassal was intended to benefit both parties. When they were relatively unimportant men, a ceremonial and verbal exchange of oaths was usually adequate to ensure to each his just rights. But when each of the contracting parties was a powerful lord in his own right, the details of the agreement became complex and were often put into written form. This passage from the Chronicle of Gilbert of Bruges, *chancellor of the Count of Hainaut, lists the mutual obligations of the Count and his episcopal overlord.*

SOURCE Translated from *Gisleberti Balduini Hanoniae Comitis Cancelarii Chronica Hanoniae,* ed. le Marquis de Godefroy Ménilglaise (Tournai: Imprimerie de Malô et Levasseur, 1874), 20, 22, 24.

In the gift to the church of Liége of so many and such important allods and fiefs, in liege homage from such an important man as the Count of Hainaut, it was agreed that the Count of Hainaut owes the Bishop his Lord service and aid in all things and against all men with all his forces, on foot and on horseback; and this retinue is to be maintained at the Bishop's expense when the Count goes outside the County of Hainaut. If the Lord Count comes to the Lord Bishop to be invested with his lands, the Lord Bishop owes him whatever expenses he incurs after leaving the County of Hainaut. If the Lord Bishop should invite the Count of Hainaut to the court, or to any colloquy, he owes him his expenses similarly. If the Lord Roman Emperor should invite the Count of Hainaut to his court for any reason, the Bishop of Liége will defray his costs, conduct him there and bring him back in safety, and will stand for him and answer for him at the court.

Furthermore, if anyone should attack the lands of Hainaut with evil intent, the Bishop of Liége owes the Count an equal force, man for man, paid for with his own funds. If the Count besieges or is besieged at a castle belonging to his fief, the Bishop must assist him, at his own expense, with five hundred knights, and the Count must provide such food as he can buy at a just price. If the fields bear grasses and other fodder necessary for the nourishment of the horses, the Bishop and his men may make use of it at will. This aid is due the Count from the Bishop three times a year, and each time for forty days. The three castellans of Hainaut, that is, of Mons, Beaumont and Valenciennes, will do homage to the Bishop, along with the Count. On Christmas day the Bishop owes them the following: to the Count, three suits of robes, each worth six marks of silver in the weight of Liége, and to each castellan a single suit of equal value. If the Count receives an allod to be held of him in fee, if he himself acquires an allod within the boundaries of his county, with serfs of one sex or the other, he automatically holds them of the Bishop as he holds the rest of his fief.

THE MONASTERY

34

THE LETTERS OF LUPUS OF FERRIÈRES

The first letter to the monk Altwin written by Lupus, abbot of the monastery of Ferrières, near Paris, tells much about the state of learning in ninth-century France; Lupus is providing Altwin with the sort of information that would now be readily available in a few good reference works. It was the curiosity and erudition of Lupus and many lesser-known Benedictine scholars that helped preserve classical literature in the early Middle Ages. Lupus' letter to Charles the Bald, part of a widespread contemporary controversy over predestination, argued that man's sin was not God's fault, and so justified God's assigning some men to eternal punishment.

May 837

To Altwin[1]

Lupus sends warmest greeting to his dearest brother Altwin. Your holiness' letter of April 27 reached me, and professed your

SOURCE Translated from *Loup de Ferrières, Correspondance*, ed. by Léon Levillain, *Les Classiques de l'histoire de France au moyen-âge*, 10 (Paris: 1927), Vol. I, 60, 62, 64, 66, 72; II, 22, 24, 26, 28, 30.

[1] A monk of St. Alban near Mainz; he was probably head of the monastic school.

affection for me—an affection I already perceived in my soul, and had kept most strongly in memory. After all, we have lived abroad pleasantly, harmoniously, and—it may be said—profitably for a long time; how then could our strong and long-standing affection be weakened? You are aware that infirmity has recently sprung up all around me—you doubtless heard the news when it happened—but, as always and in all things, divine grace bore it away, without loss, but with the greatest profit; without disquietude, even, save that caused by fear. An infected blister on the right side of my groin threatened me with death; but my affliction occasioned so many prayers, wherever rumor spread knowledge of it, that I dare to claim that *they* procured the divine favor for me.

Returning then into France, when I discovered the state of our convent, I decided to obey those to whom I owed obedience; and, through God's favor, I now enjoy the most complete tranquillity, and—what is delightful to me—I have time for study. . . .

In the meantime, as to those things you asked of me, I discharge them here, as briefly as I can, and insofar as my knowledge allows. I feel certain that one ought to make a single syllable out of a mute and a liquid only when they are short by nature. First, because nature almost always has had an influence on art, and also because, as I perceive, pronunciation urges this practice: *peccator* thus yields the feminine form *peccatrix; amator, amatrix; venator, venatrix* and many more similarly, in which, as no one would doubt, the penultimate syllable receives the accent. For if we rule according to position, we would have to accept the antepenult in the feminine gender; but who wouldn't see how absurd, how barbarous, even, that would be? . . . In those moral verses said to be by Alcuin, the word "stătĕra" is placed thus: "Non tibi sit modius duplex, nec státĕra duplex". Only a person who overlooked the fact that *blasphemus* is written with a "ph" would hesitate before judging it to be a Greek word. A certain Greek has assured me many times that the Greeks say *blasphemus*, with the penultimate syl-

166

lable short, and our own Einhard asserted the same thing. However, Aurelius Prudentius[2], who is held by many in the highest esteem, used the noun this way: *Divisor blaspheme Dei*. Here he handled it as long, so that in *blasphemus* and *blasphemo* the accent falls on the penultimate syllable. . . . The *sistrum* is a musical instrument, which Isis, as you indicated, is portrayed carrying in her hand, and with which she announces the flooding and receding of the river Nile; from this image Vergil, with his customary penetration, described her as assuming to herself its imaginary power—"With her sistrum", he said, "she calls the troops".

Farewell, dearest friend, and continue in the friendship you feel for us. Give greeting from my insignificance to your prior and to your congregation, and beg them to pray to the Lord for me and for my father and mother.

850

To the Lord King

To the glorious lord King Charles from his faithful vassal Lupus. Recently, in the city of Bourges, you asked what my opinion was on the issues of predestination, free will, and redemption by the blood of Christ; and I disclosed to your majesty in few words that which I learned from Scripture, and had found in the works of the greatest authors. And since another opinion prevailed among certain men, who believe that I do not understand the things of God piously or faithfully, God himself, in whom I have wholly trusted ever since I attained the age of reason, will guide my mind and pen so that I may disentangle the aforementioned questions—on which many boldly air their opinions, but which few understand—briefly, truly and perceptively. Nor ought I to detain you with a long disputation, either to deceive you in anything, or to slow you down by obscurities,

[2] The fourth-century Christian Latin poet.

for I am not ignorant of your tasks in governing the republic, and, after God, I owe you singular fidelity.

God created Adam without sin, as the Holy Scripture teaches, and, through Adam, created us all without sin. Then this father of the human race, departing from his natural sinlessness, without coercion, sinned with such enormity that he condemned himself and, in so doing, condemned all men born, of both sexes. God, therefore, wisely made man's nature good but man vitiated it miserably through his voluntary sin. Then Adam was, as blessed Ambrose says, and in him we all were; Adam perished, and in him we all perished. Let us therefore praise the work of God, and we recognize that our sins merit nothing else [but death]. But God, who stands in the midst of past, present and future (for he is who he is, nor can anyone accede to his knowledge or hide from it), since he knew that the mass of the human race was corrupted through Adam, did not withhold from it the good of his creation (for he can work through evil as well as good), and before the making of the world he chose to liberate some from punishment, through grace, as the Apostle says: "According as he hath chosen us in him before the foundation of the world".[3] The rest, moreover, to whom his mercy did not extend this grace, he abandoned, by a just judgment, to that damnation their sins merited; and in this way, as the Apostle teaches, "Therefore hath he mercy on whom he will have mercy, and whom he will he hardeneth"[4]. . . .

The first man, by sinning, lost that free will to do good which he despised, however he retained free will in doing evil, which he chose. It is as if a man should wish to destroy himself by withholding food from his body; even so, once dead, he could not revive himself. In the same way, man was able to lose the use of his free will for good voluntarily, but he cannot, even if he wishes, restore it again by his own power. Therefore, he can have no free will where good is concerned, unless he be freed by divine grace. Lord Jesus "knew", as it is written, "what was

[3] Ephesians 1, 4.   [4] Romans 9, 18.

in man", making this clear, to man's profit: "Without me", he
said, "ye can do nothing",[5] meaning nothing that is good. . . .
Saint Cyprian, the most glorious martyr, and most agreeable
doctor, explicating well the words of the Apostle: "What hast
thou that thou didst not receive? Now if thou didst receive it,
why dost thou glory, as if thou hadst not received it?"[6], determined that we ought not to glory in any thing, for nothing is
ours. . . .[7]

35

EADMER, *THE LIFE OF SAINT ANSELM*

c. 1109

*The monk Eadmer was a devoted pupil of Anselm during An-
selm's tenure as Archbishop of Canterbury. Written shortly after
the saint's death in 1109, this biography is based on observations which Eadmer recorded throughout their companionship.
The first two passages, concerning Anselm's early life on the
Continent, were most probably reconstructed from the saint's
copious conversation. The following ones, taken from the second
part of the book, involve events after Anselm had gone to
England and was made archbishop, and were based on Eadmer's
more direct observation of Anselm's personal anguish over the
strife between king and church, as the English Church began
to struggle for greater freedom from state control. The work itself represents a sharp departure from the conventional saint's*

[5] John 15, 5.   [6] I Cor. 4, 7.
[7] Saint Cyprian, *Ad Quirin.* i, III, 4, in *Oeuvres*, ed. Hartel, I,
116.

life; Eadmer did not hesitate to show Anselm in moments of weakness and fear, and was convinced that his sanctity lay in qualities of mind and personality rather than in an ability to work miracles.

Being now about to commit to writing an account of the life and conversation of Anselm, Archbishop of Canterbury, I first invoke the help of God's great mercy and majesty. I shall then say something briefly about the place of Anselm's birth and the character of his parents, so that the reader may know from what root came the qualities which later shone forth in the child. His father, then, was called Gundulf; his mother Ermenberga; both of them of noble birth, so far as worldly dignity goes, and living spaciously in the city of Aosta. This city is on the border of Burgundy and Lombardy, and Ermenberga was born there. . . .

After passing almost three years from this time, partly in Burgundy and partly in France, he went to Normandy to see, to talk to, and stay with a certain master by the name of Lanfranc, a truly good man and one of real nobility in the excellence of his religious life and wisdom. His lofty fame had resounded everywhere and had drawn to him the best clerks from all parts of the world. Anselm therefore came to him and recognised the outstanding wisdom, which shone forth in him. He placed himself under his guidance and in a short time became the most intimate of his disciples. He gave himself up day and night to literary studies, not only reading with Lanfranc those things which he wished, but teaching carefully to others the things which they required.

While he was thus wearying his body with late nights, with cold and with hunger because of his studies, he began to think

source From Eadmer, *The Life of Saint Anselm, Archbishop of Canterbury*, ed. and trans. by R. W. Southern (London: Thomas Nelson and Sons, Ltd., n.d.), 3, 8, 12–13, 69–70, 81–82, 127.

that if he had become a monk somewhere, as he formerly intended, he would not have had to put up with anything more severe than what he was now suffering, nor would he lose the reward of his labour, which he was quite uncertain of retaining in his present state. . . . And so it came about that, being continually given up to God and to spiritual exercises, he attained such a height of divine speculation, that he was able by God's help to see into and unravel many most obscure and previously insoluble questions about the divinity of God and about our faith, and to prove by plain arguments that what he said was firm and catholic truth. For he had so much faith in the Holy Scriptures, that he firmly and inviolably believed that there was nothing in them which deviated in any way from the path of solid truth. Hence he applied his whole mind to this end, that according to his faith he might be found worthy to see with the eye of reason those things in the Holy Scriptures which, as he felt, lay hidden in a deep obscurity. Thus one night it happened that he was lying awake on his bed before matins exercised in mind about these matters; and as he meditated he tried to puzzle out how the prophets of old could see both past and future as if they were present and set them forth beyond doubt in speech or writing. And, behold, while he was thus absorbed and striving with all his might to understand this problem, he fixed his eyes on the wall and—right through the masonry of the church and dormitory—he saw the monks whose office it was to prepare for matins going about the altar and other parts of the church lighting the candles; and finally he saw one of them take in his hands the bell-rope and sound the bell to awaken the brethren. At this sound the whole community rose from their beds, and Anselm was astonished at the thing which had happened. From this he saw that it was a very small thing for God to show to the prophets in the spirit the things which would come to pass, since God had allowed him to see with his bodily eyes through so many obstacles the things which then were happening. . . .

When Anselm began now to think of all the peace he had

lost and all the labor he had found, his spirit was torn and tormented with bitter anguish. For he saw in his mind's eye the life which he had been accustomed to lead as prior and as abbot,— how joyfully he had reposed and delighted in the love of God and of his neighbor, how devoutly he had been heard by all to whom he ministered the words of life, how still more devoutly his hearers had hastened to put into practice what he taught, and thereby (as he hoped) added to the sum of his reward. And now how different it was! As a bishop he ought to have gone on to better things; but he saw his days and nights taken up with secular business; he saw himself unable to devote his attention either to God or to his neighbour in God's name as he had formerly done; and he saw no-one willing to listen to the Word of Life from his lips or to carry it out; and thereby he lost (as he thought) his reward. To add to these evils of his own, the cruel oppression of his men daily afflicted his ears; and he was deafened by the threats of worse to follow, made by malicious men on all sides. For it was well-known that the king's mind was worked up into a fury against him, and as a result every wicked man thought himself happy if he could hit on any device to exasperate him further. Thus he was tossed by the storms of injuries of many kinds, without having the consolation of any flattering caresses of worldly honour or prosperity. Nevertheless, he preserved a pure conscience in all things and towards all men; and he even had some relief from these trials, finding his chief consolation in burying himself in the cloister with the monks and talking to them of things pertaining to their rule of life. . . .

Nevertheless various troubles and anxieties interrupted his quiet and forced him to think of other things. There was trouble about the lands of the church which wicked men unjustly occupied with the king's complaisance; also about the monetary exactions which very greatly impoverished the whole kingdom, and especially his tenants; also about the oppressions of the monasteries which he was powerless to check and which were daily brought to his notice; and about many similar things which frequently added to his sufferings. Moreover the men who had loved him most devotedly before he became a bishop, who had made much of him and had cheerfully given to him the best they had, now began to ask for church lands, and to beg for horses, money or whatever happened to take their fancy. Then you should have seen those who had got what they wanted putting on an expression of false satisfaction and pleasure in his presence, and promising repayment and service; and the others who had not got what they wanted besmirching his good name, abusing his men with all their might, and breathing out wild threats. Meanwhile he knew how to possess his soul in patience; he was a peacemaker among those who hated peace; to those who attacked him he spoke words of gentleness and peace, desiring to overcome their evil with good. . . .

But when he came to the king at Salisbury and told him plainly what he had heard in the Council at Rome about investitures of churches, the king was disturbed and troubled beyond measure, and he showed no desire to defer to Anselm's wishes in anything, as the messengers had said. Whoever wants to know about the negotiations which took place between them on this subject during the next two and a half years, and the many great injuries and tribulations which Anselm suffered, not to mention the two occasions on which messengers were sent to Rome to obtain a change in these decrees and what they achieved, should read the work which is mentioned in the prologue of this little book; and there he will find, I think, everything plainly set forth.

36

DEFENSE OF THE CLUNIAC IDEAL: *THE LETTERS OF PETER THE VENERABLE*

after 1126

In 1098 a small band of monks broke away from the huge and elaborate monastery of Cluny to found an order more in keeping with the primitive spirit of St. Benedict's Rule. The most dynamic spokesman for this group of Cistercians was Bernard, Abbot of Clairvaux, who engaged in a lengthy polemic with the learned Abbot of Cluny, Peter the Venerable. Here Peter outlines the charges which Bernard has leveled against the Cluniacs.

To Lord Bernard, Abbot of Clairvaux

To the venerable and most beloved Bernard, Abbot of Clairvaux—venerable because of his merits, most beloved because of his heartfelt feelings towards us—brother Peter, humble abbot of the Cluniacs, present and eternal greeting.

For a long time, most beloved brother, I have been drinking in to my innermost heart the sweet-smelling fragrance of your good conversation, aromatic through spiritual sweetness, and, beginning to love before I knew you, to venerate even before I looked upon you, I desired to see you, to embrace you, and speak with you about the journeying of the soul. . . .

. . . Let us see whether the practice [of the Cluniacs] is

SOURCE Translated from *The Letters of Peter the Venerable*, ed. Giles Constable (Cambridge, Mass.: 1967) I, 53–56.

174

as you say. And so that all the charges be ranged in order, with respect to how you observe the Rule in receiving novices, it is ordained that they are not to be received before they have completed a year of spiritual probation, to test "whether they are of God." You, however, accept those who come, so to speak, on impulse, serving no purpose. The result is that, since they are received carelessly, once received, they behave still more carelessly, and since they didn't understand what they were taking upon themselves, they don't know what they ought to do now that they are bound to others. . . . Concerning brothers who transgress and those who prevaricate their vow, those indeed who stealthily withdraw from their neck the yoke of the Rule, and, fleeing from the monasteries, return to the world, the Rule orders that, if they return again and wish to repent, they may be received again, up to three times, and that if afterwards they do it again, "all entry is to be denied to those returning." But you hold this order, like the others, in contempt, and you accept these runaways back against the precept of the Rule as often as it pleases you. . . .

Of the secular possessions you hold, after the manner of laymen, what can you reply, since you seem in no way different from them? For you have accepted towns, villages, peasants, serfs and maidservants, and, what is more damning, the profits from tolls, and nearly all this sort of emolument indiscriminately, and you do not hold it rightly. . . .

37

THE SCHISM BETWEEN EAST AND WEST: *THE LETTER OF LEO, ARCHBISHOP OF BULGARIA, SENT TO A CERTAIN ROMAN BISHOP*

1053

In 1052 the Greek patriarch Michael Cerularius launched a campaign to alienate Latin Christians, still nominally bound with the Greeks in a single church. This letter, sent the following year by the Archbishop of Bulgaria to the Bishop of Trani in southern Italy, was in fact a challenge from the court of Cerularius to the Roman See. Ostensibly a listing of the dissimilarities between the Greek and Latin ritual usages, the letter was in fact an insulting condemnation of "unwholesome" Latin practices; as such it greatly exacerbated the East-West conflict which culminated in the schism of 1054.

Our great love of God and the agreeable bowels of our compassion have directed us to write to your holiness, and, through you, to all chief priests, and to the priests and monks of the

SOURCE   Translated from *Leonis Bulgariae Archiepiscopi Epistola Missa Ad Quemdam Episcopum Romanum. Patrologiae Cursus Completus. Series Graeca Posterior*, ed. J.-P. Migne, Vol. CXX (Paris: 1880), 835, 838, 839, 842–43.

Franks, and to the people, and to the same most reverend pope, to speak concerning the unleavened host and the Sabbath. The former you keep, mystically, in an inappropriate manner, and the latter you observe in the Jewish fashion.

For the unleavened host and the Sabbath were, by Moses' law, given to them to observe; but Christ is our true passover.[1] For, so that he would not be found to be in opposition to the law, he was circumcised, and celebrated the first true holy passover. Thus from his beginning he imposed upon us a new practice. And this is clear in the gospel of Matthew. Speaking of the mystical mass the evangelist also spoke thus, saying: "Now on the first day of the feast of unleavened bread the disciples came to Jesus, saying unto him, Where wilt thou that we prepare for thee to eat the passover? And he said, Go into the city to such a man, and say unto him, The Master saith, My time is at hand; I will keep the passover at thy house with my disciples."[2] And a little further on: "Now when the even was come, he sat down with the twelve. And as they did eat, he said, Verily I say unto you, that one of you shall betray me"[3]. . . .

That which you call *panem* [bread] we call *artos*. *Artos* means "raised up," and "carried on high," heated and having risen because of the leaven and salt; unleavened bread, however, is little different from lifeless stone besmeared all over with wasted earth, and is like dried mud which Moses bitterly ordered the Jews to eat once a year in their misery, saying it was the symbol of the evil suffering and tribulation. But our passover is joyful and full of gladness, and raises us up from earth to heaven for joy, like bread, fermented through its own heat, which is full of sweetness. Unleavened bread, though, containing neither malt nor leaven, is as dry as mud. Have you not heard Jesus saying to his disciples: "Ye are the salt of the earth,"[4] and "The kingdom of heaven is like unto leaven, which

[1] I Cor. 5, 7.   [2] Matthew 26, 17–18.   [3] Matthew 26, 20–21.
[4] Matthew 5, 13.

a woman took, and hid in three measures of meal, till the whole was leavened?"[5] He calls the holy church a woman; the leaven is of three kinds—Father, Son and Holy Spirit—none of whom are associated with dirty unleavened bread. . . .

And indeed how do you observe the Sabbath during Lent in the Jewish fashion? Either you do not heed the gospel saying, "Jesus went on the sabbath day through the corn; and his disciples were a hungered, and began to pluck the ears of corn, and to eat. But when the Pharisees saw it, they said unto him, Behold thy disciples do that which is not lawful to do upon the sabbath day. But he said unto them, Have ye not read what David did, when he was a hungered, and they that were with him; how he entered into the house of God, and did eat the shewbread," etc.?[6] "The sabbath was made for man, and not man for the sabbath."[7] And they would say to themselves, "This man is not of God, because he keepeth not the sabbath day"[8]. . . .

And also, you do not chant during Lent, but often in the passion season, the Alleluia which in Latin is interpreted *"Dominus venit, laudate, hymnum dicite, et benedicite eum."*[9] Nor, following this, do you chant "Lord of Lords", nor "blessed is he that cometh."[10] But this Alleluia is in truth said in Hebrew.

Why do you neither see nor understand the degree of deception in these things; why do you not correct the people, and yourselves, as those who ought to be judged accountable for these things before God? Are you not forsaking that which Peter, Benedict and Paul and others taught? You deceive yourselves, and the people too, in these matters. . . . Put off the unleavened bread, and the keeping of the wretched Jews' sabbath; . . . so that we may be pure in the true and immaculate faith, and be one flock of the one shepherd, Christ.

[5] Matthew 13, 33.   [6] Matthew 12, 1–4.   [7] Mark 2, 27.
[8] John 9, 16.   [9] Psalms 127, 27 [Douai].   [10] Matthew 21, 9.

38

WIDO OF OSNABRÜCK,
BOOK OF THE CONTROVERSY
BETWEEN HILDEBRAND AND HENRY

1118

*In 1075 Gregory VII had banned lay investiture of bishops
and abbots. This act represented a severe threat to the administrative power of Henry IV, Emperor of the Holy Roman Empire. Henry defied the pope's decision, and was answered with
prompt excommunication. Although he went to Italy in the
winter of 1077 to seek the pope's absolution (DOCUMENT 29),
the real issue remained unresolved for some time. Here Wido
advances a unique argument for the royal side in the quarrel
over lay investiture.*

To T., venerable leader of the confraternity, and brother H.:
T., humble preceptor of students of the church of Osnabrück,
their servant, professes sincere devotion in the Lord.

In the midst of the present controversy between the priestly
power and the kingdom, which is pernicious to the unanimity
of the church, desiring to find a way to bring both parties into
harmony, in an effort to gather together whatever material there

SOURCE Translated from *Excerpta Ex Widonis Osnabrugensis Li-
bro de Controversia Inter Hildebrandum et Heinricum Imperatorem*,
ed. L. Heinemann, *Monumenta Germaniae Historica, Libelli de Lite*,
I, 462, 467–68.

is among our records, I began frequently to search it out. . . .
With this as my intention, I came across, in the bookcase of our
venerable confraternity of monks, a little quarto in which I
found an anonymous treatise on the controversy between Hildebrand and Emperor Henry. The prior of the abbey informed
me, moreover, that it was written by Wido, who afterwards
was made bishop of Osnabrück, on the advice of Liemar, bishop
of Bremen, and Benno, bishop of Osnabrück. It concerned three
things principally: 1) the election and consecration of the
Roman pontiff; 2) the excommunication of the emperor; and
3) the absolution of the king's followers from their oaths. Ex-
cerpting certain passages from the treatise, which seemed to me
in some measure to touch on the present perturbation in the
church, I send them for your discretionary judgment. Whether
they please you or not, may my pure devotion toward you ever
avail me. Farewell!

*That Wipert, called Clement, was legitimately enthroned
in the apostolic see, and Hildebrand,
called Gregory VII, was justly rejected.*

"Since many, either deceived by a cloud of ignorance or inflamed by the firebrand of long, old anger, strive to reject venerable Clement's elevation to the papal office, and they do not
blush in every particular to defame him, so that they bring
confusion everywhere between the priestly rule and the kingdom, and prevent harmony and peace by their strife, we, who
are not ignorant of the truth in this matter, and who love and
desire peace among Christ's sheep, who desire and seek a kingdom and priesthood bound by the chains of peace and concord,
consider this not a useless ideal, but an utmost necessity—so
much so that we hasten on, in the hearing of all, to show by
reasoning that the above-named pope who pursues peace and
justice, through the aid of omnipotent God, came to the holy
and apostolic see justly and properly. . . . It is then agreed, as
has been said now quite often, that he ascends to the height of

the Roman see neither justly nor properly, according to the custom and decree of antiquity, who neglects the consent of the prince in so doing, both for the sake of the peace and concord of the holy church, and for the sake of the kingdom's due honor."

Here is what was said in the aforesaid bishop's treatise about the election and consecration of the Roman pope according to canonical authority and the custom of antiquity. Now, we shall see what is written concerning the excommunication of the prince.

"That honor, as Leo the Great avers, is not legitimate, which has been gained contrary to the precepts of divine law and the decrees of the holy fathers. For that reason, whoever was ordained against canon law and its procedure is neither validly elected, nor shall he have any power at all, nor is he, as a pseudo-pope, at all authorized to bind or free anyone by pontifical law."

Again in the same treatise:

"For, from the time that royal necks submitted themselves to the yoke of Christ, many Roman pontiffs have preceded Hildebrand, popes who were outstanding in true faith and constancy of religion, in whose reigns many Roman princes committed more serious crimes against the church; nevertheless no pope presumed to worsen the pontifical censure by a sentence of excommunication. Nor did they fail to do this to the extent that, in fear of losing favor among men, they feared even more to speak what is right freely, bringing on themselves the old prophecy: "the dogs will be mute, unable to bark," but rather, having before their eyes the old saying of the apostle "Let all things be done unto edifying."[1] Whence they wisely perceive that, if they corrected the sinners with a rod, still worse results might ensue, just as if they had supposed that they might more easily carry an extra burden imposed on them. Many emperors, even, with no little cleverness, have lashed out against the Roman

[1] I Corinthians 14, 26.

popes in the fire of their anger, but the popes were careful to extinguish it by bearing it with patience, rather than avenging themselves. . . . But notwithstanding the heap of agonies and injuries that have afflicted the pope's mind with no small anxiety, Nicholas I preferred to mitigate the present danger by the humility of patience rather than stir up the anger of the prince even more by the severity of vengeance. What has happened now is surely clear; for ecclesiastical and royal lands, like booty, are everywhere occupied and the surrounding areas are pillaged by all. The sheep of Christ are lost on every hand. Wars worse than civil war arise and worsen daily. Pastoral duties are neglected and the standing and procedure of the church are disrupted. And, through an impious and sacrilegious presumption, the cathedrals dedicated to God are despoiled of their gold, silver, jewels, vestments and other furnishings, placed there to represent the worthy devotion of the pope or king and the piety of the faithful toward them, and are lavished on creating battle, promoting warfare and committing murder. The goods and tithes of the holy congregation, the legacies and provisions of wards and orphans are divided and wasted. . . . It follows from all this that Hildebrand acted wickedly and impiously when, moved by his anger and enmity, he presumed to alienate the Roman prince, though he had no example from his wiser predecessors, by his unjust excommunication.

Moreover, Hildebrand, in a certain letter, introduced Ambrose of Milan's excommunication of the Emperor Theodosius (since he could not choose an example of this sort from the lives of the Roman popes), to prove by this (since Ambrose was a metropolitan bishop) that it was all the more legal for him to do, as a greater churchman and as Roman pope. But because he impaired his example by incorporating a falsehood into his argumentation, none of this evidence of probability confirmed the intention of his effort. For Theodosius, inflamed by the madness of his anger, with no precedent, ordered the deaths of seven thousand men at Thessalonica. Ambrose, hearing of this unutterable disaster, acted thus. When the prince came to Milan and desired solemnly to enter the holy church, Ambrose, meeting him outside at the door, in a gentle and sweet warning refused him entrance to the holy threshold with pious and salubrious arguments, lest he magnify his first sin by adding a second; and, without arrogantly attributing to himself any power of binding, he said humbly: "Accept, O Emperor, the chain by which the Lord bound you to all men; for it is the most healthful medicine." Therefore unfittingly and fallaciously did Hildebrand take his example from Ambrose when he excommunicated the Roman prince and suspended his vassals from communion with their lord and from their oaths of allegiance. For even Ambrose did not, by an angry judgment or out of prideful tyranny, presume to excommunicate Theodosius, even though he was guilty of so many thousand murders, nor did he suspend any of the emperor's vassals from his service or company, nor absolve them from the oath they had made to him, nor was he moved to deprive him of his imperial authority or of his life."

39

THE CRUSADING IDEAL:
BERNARD OF CLAIRVAUX,
IN PRAISE OF THE NEW MILITIA
OF THE TEMPLE

between January 1128 and May 1136

*The Knights Templars were founded in 1118, as defenders of
the Christian holy places in the East. The Cistercian abbot
Bernard, one of the most powerful promoters of the Second
Crusade, praises the order as a synthesis of the monastic and
military lives. His extreme exaltation of death in battle and his
characterization of the killing of pagans as "malicide" marks this
as one of the most fanatical pieces of crusade propaganda written in the Middle Ages.*

A new kind of knighthood is now heard of in the land; it
has arisen in that region once visited by the Rising Star from
on high, and from whence he drove out the princes of darkness with the strength of his hand—where even now with the
hands of his worthies he is crushing their minions, sons of dis-
loyalty, and driving them out, and is accomplishing the redemption of his people, raising again the trumpet of our salvation in
the house of his son David. . . .

SOURCE Translated from Bernard of Clairvaux, *Liber ad Milites
Templi De Laude Novae Militiae, Sancti Bernardi Opera,* ed. J.
Leclercq, III, 214, 216–17.

He is a fearless knight, in truth, and secure on all sides, who, as he has girded his body with iron, so has girded his soul with the shield of faith. Surely, fortified with both these weapons, he fears neither demon nor man. Nor does he who desires to die fear death. For what should he fear in living or in dying, for whom to live is Christ, to die is gain?[1] To be sure, he stands faithfully and willingly for Christ; but he desires even more to be dissolved and be with Christ, for this is better. . . .

of worldly knighthood

What end and reward therefore does it have, this worldly—I do not say knighthood [*militia*] but roguery [*malitia*]—if as a murderer a man sins mortally and when killed, perishes eternally? . . . You [worldly knights] cover your horses with silks; you have I know not what little cloths hanging from your cuirasses; you paint your lances, shields and saddles; you encrust your reins and spurs with gold, silver and gems; and in this splendor, with shameful fury, impudently oblivious, you race on to your death. Are these the trappings of a military man, or are they rather womanly ornaments? . . .

Of the new knighthood

The knight of Christ, I say, is safe in slaying, safer if he is slain. He is accountable to himself when he is slain, to Christ when he slays. "For he beareth not the sword in vain: for he is the minister of God, a revenger to execute wrath upon him that doeth evil, to praise him that doeth good."[2] For when he kills a malefactor, he does not commit homicide but, I might say, malicide, and is clearly reputed to be the vindicator of Christ, bringing punishment to evildoers, and praise in truth to good men. Moreover, when he is himself killed, it is known

[1] Philippians 1, 21.
[2] Romans 13, 4.

that he does not perish, but triumphs. The death he inflicts is Christ's gain; the death he dies, his own. The Christian is glorified in the death of a pagan, because thereby Christ is glorified; in the death of a Christian, the liberality of the King is shown, when the knight is led to his reward. . . . .

LITERATURE

40

DICUIL,
BOOK OF THE MEASUREMENT OF THE EARTH
fl. before 787 – c. 816

Dicuil, one of many scholarly Irish monks to come to the Continent in the latter part of the eighth century, was probably a teacher in the palace school of Louis the Pious. His treatise, although heavily dependent on ancient sources, represents some of the most accurate geographical knowledge in the West in the early ninth century.

1. Having composed my letter on ten questions of the art of grammar, I considered that a book might follow on the measurement of the provinces of the earth, according to the authority of the men whom the holy Emperor Theodosius had sent to

SOURCE From *Dicuili Liber de Mensura Orbis Terrae*, ed. and trans. by J. J. Tierney, *Scriptores Latini Hiberniae*, VI (Dublin: The Dublin Institute for Advanced Study, 1967), 45, 57, 59, 63.

measure the said provinces; and I desire to indicate their dimensions, supplementing this information on the high authority of Plinius Secundus.

2. But I have two reasons for prefixing the account of the envoys of Theodosius to the words of Plinius Secundus in the order of my writing, as against the chronological order, one that the former, in their last twelve lines, assert that their work has been done more carefully than that of the ancients, and the other, that I saw before hand that the volumes of the Natural History of Plinius Secundus which I had examined, were very much jumbled up by the scribes of recent times.

3. I shall, indeed, devote my attention to correcting, in so far as I can, the reports of the above-mentioned envoys, as they have been composed with fewer mistakes.

4. But where in the books of Plinius Secundus I find figures which I realize to be undoubtedly corrupt, I shall leave their places vacant for the moment, so that if I do not find trusty copies whoever does find them may emend them. Where I am in doubt as to whether the figures are correct or not, I shall write them down as correct, so that, as I have said, whoever finds the true figures may make the appropriate correction.

5. Discrepancies in the number of miles between Plinius Secundus and the emperor's envoys should occasion no surprise to anyone, since the latter truly testify, as I have said, that they accomplished their work with more care than did the ancients. . . .

The latitude of the earth from south to north makes up less by nearly a half, being three thousand three hundred and forty-eight miles. This shows how much the heat has removed on the one hand, and the sea on the other. For I do not think that the earth ceases to be spherical (i.e., at the extreme north and south), or is not spherical at all, but that it is uninhabitable at both extremes and is therefore unknown.

If we measure the longitude given above from the eastern part of India as far as the islands of Cádiz by means of the mile-signs, for example by means of the milestones, each marking the end of a mile, the extent will be six thousand six hundred and thirty miles, and the latitude from north to south will be three thousand three hundred and forty-eight, omitting the aforesaid areas where the cold or the heat is unbearable. Here ends the survey of the earth. . . .

Plinius Secundus makes these statements about the Nile in his fifth book: Egypt is situated next to Africa, extending inwards towards the south to where Ethiopia stretches out behind it. The Nile, dividing into a right-hand and a left-hand channel, embraces and forms the bounds of its more low-lying part, the Canopic mouth lying towards Africa, the Pelusiac towards Asia, at an interval of two hundred and seventy miles. Hence some authors have regarded Egypt as an island, this division of the Nile giving the country the shape of a triangle; and therefore many people have called Egypt Delta by the name of the Greek letter. . . .

The Nile begins to rise from the time of the new moon which follows the summer solstice. The rise is gradual and moderate while the sun is moving through the Crab, and strongest as it passes through the Lion, and while in the Virgin it subsides at the same rate as that at which it rose. It withdraws, however, entirely within its banks, as Herodotus states, on the hundredth day, when the sun is in the Scales.

It is regarded as a religious offense for kings or for those in authority to sail on the Nile while it is rising. The rising is observed by means of walls which have measuring-marks. The regular rise is one of sixteen cubits. A less amount of water does not irrigate the whole area, while a larger amount recedes more slowly and so delays operations; the latter takes up the time for sowing because the soil remains wet, the former does not allow sufficient time since the soil is parched; both of these things are carefully reckoned by the province. . . .

Although we read in no authority that a branch of the Nile flows into the Red Sea, yet brother Fidelis asserted this and related it, in my presence, to my teacher Suibne (to whom, under God, I owe any progress that I have made), saying that, for purposes of worship, in the city of Jerusalem, both clerics and laymen . . . sailed in a . . .[1] as far as the Nile.

Then, after a long sail on the Nile, they saw, like mountains, and admired from a distance, the seven barns built by holy Joseph, according to the number of the years of abundance, four in one place, and three in another.

From here they went to the three barns to admire them and found beside them a lion and eight people, men and women, lying dead. The lion had killed them in his strength, and they had killed him with spears and swords; both places in which the seven barns are built are desert.

After this he carefully examined the three barns and again was filled with amazement that they were entirely made of stone from their very base to the summit. The barns were square at the base, but rounded at the top; at the very apex they have, as it were, a slender point.

Then the brother whom I have mentioned measured one side of one barn, from corner to corner, as four hundred feet.

Next, embarking on their boats, they sailed along the Nile as far as the entrance of the Red Sea. From this harbour it is a small distance eastwards to the passage of Moses across the Red Sea. He who measured the side of the barn wished to go as far as the harbour where Moses with his people entered the sea, not only to enter the harbour, but in order to see in it the tracks of the chariots and the ruts of Pharaoh's wheels; but the sailors would not oblige. The width of the sea at that place seemed to him to be about six miles.

From thence they made a fast voyage in the western part of the Red Sea, that is, in the gulf which extends far towards the north. That is the sea which prevented the people of Israel, when murmuring in the desert, from being able to return to the land of Egypt.

[1] The text is corrupt here.

_____

BISHOP PATRICK,
ON THE HONOR OF THE HUMAN CONDITION

c. 1074–84

Another Irish scholar, Patrick, was bishop of the small Norse-Irish city of Dublin from 1074 to 1084, and may have been the founder of the first Benedictine community in that city. Although his analysis of the human mind is wholly Augustinian, his emphasis on the power of discernment and on the unique ability of man to control his will exalt man in a way reminiscent of classical Roman writers and prefiguring the fifteenth-century humanists.

He who wishes to know how high the honour stands of man's
    nature,
Let him see it from the sequence of my reasoning.

When God was about to make man He did not form him solely
By word, as He made all other things.
For He said 'Let them be made', and straightway they were
    made
As He ordered them to come forth within the space of six days.
But when about to make man He said: 'Let us make such a form
To which we may grant the sense of discernment:

SOURCE From *The Writings of Bishop Patrick,* trans. by Aubrey Gwynn, *Scriptores Latini Hiberniae,* I (Dublin: The Dublin Institute for Advanced Study, 1955), 73, 75.

Let him be master of himself, let him be lord of the earth,
And let him serve his Creator in subjection'.
Mortal man, made of such compound nature,
God endowed with both sense and reason.
For all other animal beasts, though they breathe and live,
Are (save only man) lacking in reason.
He alone is made like to angelic spirits,
For [in his being] he certainly is [made] master of his own
    free will.

Great is his honour: for God gave him life in council,
Whereas it is known that He created all others by word alone.
Let him therefore take thought how much his Maker is worthy
    of love,
Who has formed a creature of such honour.

After such a preface it is fitting that we come now to our theme,
To teach those made in God's image what that image is:
So that mortal man, made of slime and brought back to slime,
May be able to see Him by whom time and eternity have being.
The immortal King, we are taught, is not confined to space.
For God is perfect and whole everywhere,
Giving life and movement to all, and ruling all by movement.
In all things he abides, whole in all and whole in each:
Not greater in a greater part nor less in less.
But all parts hold Him wholly and each wholly.

Man's spirit, thus made by its Creator,
Is sent, undivided, to be in mortal body:
Giving life and movement, and ruling the limbs in movement.
It lives equal in all, and in each separate limb:
It is equally present in the greater and lesser limbs,
Whole and entire, penetrating alone the innermost parts:
And it so orders the functions of the limbs
As to be life, health, power, harmony of all.
Our mind is also most like to the threefold Lord,

As I shall show to you in verse according to my small measure.
For God, unchanging, is, lives, and knows—ever the same:
So man's spirit is, lives, and knows—ever the same.
There is another gift possessed by this same spirit
Rather than by any irrational animal:
Namely this, that man wills, understands, and contemplates,
Feels and desires, and later recalls in memory:
All this is stored in the mind's memory, not in vain.
For these three faculties seem to show forth the three Persons:
Our understanding shows forth God the Father, our will God
    the Son,
So our memory, the third faculty, comes forth and is born of
    both.
But intellect comes forth, and to it the will
Is added: from these memory, the third, proceeds.
Without these three man's mind seems imperfect,
And any of the three is useless without the two others.
As the Father and Son and kindly Spirit are God,
One God, not three: so in no body are there three souls,
Nor a threefold soul, but to each is given his single soul.
Frequently we call this same soul 'breath',
Bound by strict metre: but it is also our spirit.
So indeed does one substance signify many things:
Our intellect is mind, our memory is mind, our will is mind.
Our intellect does not thus become memory or will,
Nor does memory or will become the same as the others:
And these three are one substance, which is called mind:
Nor are there three minds, but one simple mind is found in all.
Nor are they less strong apart than all three joined together,
Nor, joined together, are they stronger than each alone.
These three belong to the soul, which is called life of the body:
Of which God is the life, by whom the soul is made and is
    given life.

Thus is the simple soul adorned with threefold honour,
And is believed to bear the likeness of its Maker. . . .

42

THE MATTER OF BRITAIN:
GEOFFREY OF MONMOUTH,
HISTORY OF THE KINGS OF BRITAIN

1139

Geoffrey's History, based on legends of Arthur, the Celtic chief-tain of the fifth century, surrounded his hero with the ac-couterments of contemporary monarchs and made a new code of noble behavior—chivalry—flourish at his imaginary court. The fame of Roland, celebrated in the late eleventh-century French epic The Song of Roland, *may have motivated Geoffrey to elaborate the Arthurian legends in order to create an English heroic figure of equal stature.*

In the meantime it so fell out, as may be found in the Roman histories, that after he had conquered Gaul, Julius Caesar came to the coast of Flanders. And when he had espied from thence the island of Britain, he asked of them that stood around what land it might be and who were they that dwelt therein? Whilst that he was still looking out to seaward after he had learnt the name of the kingdom and of the people, "By Hercules," saith he, "we Romans and these Britons be of one ancestry, for we also do come of Trojan stock. For after the destruction of Troy,

SOURCE From *History of the Kings of Britain* by Geoffrey of Monmouth, trans. by Sebastian Evans, pp. 66, 83, 188–89, 193–95, 198–202. Copyright, ©, 1958, by E. P. Dutton & Co., Inc. Re-printed with permission of the publishers.

Aeneas was first father unto us, as unto them was Brute, whom Silvius, son of Ascanius, son of Aeneas, did beget. But, and if I mistake not, they be sore degenerate from us, and know not what warfare meaneth, seeing that they lie thus sundered from the world in the outer ocean. Lightly may they be compelled to give us tribute, and to offer perpetual obedience unto the dignity of Rome. Natheless,[1] first of all let us send them word, bidding them pay us toll and tallage unvisited and untouched of the Roman people, and, like the rest of the nations, do homage to the Senate, lest haply, by shedding the blood of these our kinsmen, we should offend the ancient nobility of Priam, father of us all". . . . .

After the death of Uther Pendragon, the barons of Britain did come together from the divers provinces unto the city of Silchester, and did bear on hand Dubric, Archbishop of Caerleon, that he should crown as king Arthur, the late King's son. For sore was need upon them; seeing that when the Saxons heard of Uther's death they had invited their fellow-countrymen from Germany, and under their Duke Colgrin were bent upon exterminating the Britons. . . . Arthur himself doing upon him a habergeon worthy of a king so noble, did set upon his head a helm of gold graven with the semblance of a dragon. Upon his shoulders, moreover, did he bear the shield that was named Pridwen, wherein, upon the inner side, was painted the image of holy Mary, Mother of God, that many a time and oft did call her back unto his memory. Girt was he also with Caliburn, best of swords, that was forged within the Isle of Avallon; and the lance that did grace his right hand was called by the name Ron, a tall lance and a stout, full meet to do slaughter withal. Then, stationing his companies, he made hardy assault upon the Saxons that after their wont were ranked wedge-wise in battalions. Natheless, all day long did they stand their ground manfully maugre[2] the Britons that did deliver assault upon as-

[1] nonetheless.
[2] despite.

sault against them. . . . Whomsoever he [Arthur] touched, calling upon God, he slew at a single blow, nor did he once slacken in his onslaught until that he had slain four hundred and seventy men single-handed with his sword Caliburn. This when the Britons beheld, they followed him up in close rank dealing slaughter on every side. Colgrin and Badulf his brother fell amongst the first, and many thousands fell besides. . . .

When the next summer came on he fitted out his fleet and sailed unto the island of Ireland, that he desired to subdue unto himself. No sooner had he landed than Gillamaur, before-mentioned, came to meet him with a host past numbering, purposing to do battle with him. But as soon as the fight began, his folk, naked and utterly unarmed, fled withersoever they might find a place of refuge. Gillamaur was forthwith taken prisoner and compelled to surrender, and the rest of the princes of the country, smitten with dismay, likewise surrendered them after their King's ensample. All parts of Ireland thus subdued, he made with his fleet for Iceland, and there also defeated the people and subjugated the island. Next, for far and wide amongst the other islands it was rumoured that no country could stand against him, Doldavius, King of Gothland, and Gunvasius, King of the Orkneys, came of their own accord, and promising a tribute, did homage unto him. At the end of winter he returned into Britain, and re-establishing his peace firmly throughout the realm, did abide therein for the next twelve years.

At the end of this time he invited unto him all soever of most prowess from far-off kingdoms and began to multiply his household retinue, and to hold such courtly fashion in his household as begat rivalry amongst peoples at a distance, insomuch as the noblest in the land, fain to vie with him, would hold himself as nought, save in the cut of his clothes and the manner of his arms he followed the pattern of Arthur's knights. At last the fame of his country and his prowess was upon every man's tongue, even unto the uttermost ends of the earth, and a fear fell upon the Kings of realms oversea lest he might fall upon them in arms and they might lose the nations under their dominion. . . . And when this was notified unto Arthur, his heart was uplifted for that he was a terror unto them all, and he set his desire upon subduing the whole of Europe unto himself. . . .

When the high festival of Whitsuntide began to draw nigh, Arthur, filled with exceeding great joy at having achieved so great success, was fain to hold high court, and to set the crown of the kingdom upon his head, to convene the Kings and Dukes that were his vassals to the festival so that he might the more worshipfully celebrate the same, and renew his peace more firmly amongst his barons. Howbeit, when he made known his desire unto his familiars, he, by their counsel, made choice of Caerleon wherein to fulfil his design. . . . It had, moreover, a school of two hundred philosophers learned in astronomy and in the other arts, that did diligently observe the courses of the stars, and did by true inferences foretell the prodigies which at that time were about to befall unto King Arthur. . . .

When all at last were assembled in the city on the high day of the festival, the archbishops were conducted unto the palace to crown the King with the royal diadem. Dubric, therefore, upon whom the charge fell, for that the court was held within his diocese, was ready to celebrate the service. As soon as the King had been invested with the ensigns of kingship, he was led in right comely wise to the church of the Metropolitan See, two archbishops supporting him, the one upon his right hand side the other upon his left. Four Kings, moreover, to wit, those of Scotland, Cornwall, and North and South Wales, went before him, bearing before him, as was their right, four golden swords. A company of clerics in holy orders of every degree went chanting music marvellous sweet in front. . . . At last, when the procession was over, so manifold was the music of the organs and so many were the hymns that were chanted in both churches, that the knights who were there scarce knew which church they should enter first for the exceeding sweetness of the harmonies in both. First into the one and then into the other they flocked in crowds, nor, had the whole day been given up to the celebration, would any have felt a moment's weariness thereof. . . . For at that time was Britain exalted unto so high a pitch of dignity as that it did surpass all other kingdoms in plenty of riches, in luxury of adornment, and in the courteous wit of them that dwelt therein. Whatsoever knight in the land was of renown for his prowess did wear his clothes and his arms all of one same colour. And the dames, no less witty, would apparel them in like manner in a single colour, nor would they deign have the love of none save he had thrice approved him in the wars. Wherefore at that time did dames wax chaste and knights the nobler for their love.

THE UNIVERSITIES

43

ABELARD, *ETHICS,* OR *KNOW THYSELF*

probably 1136 – 39

Abelard's (1079–1142) controversial career as a brilliant teacher of logic in the schools of Paris was abruptly ended by the scandal surrounding his marriage to Heloise and his subsequent castration by her vengeful relatives; humiliated, he embraced the monastic life and produced works on theology and philosophy which continued to gain him enemies. Abelard's firm faith in reason led him to examine accepted ideas critically; in the Ethics *he gives a new definition of sin and changes its*

SOURCE From *Abailard's Ethics,* trans. by J. R. McCallum (Oxford: Basil Blackwell, 1935), 15, 17–18, 22–23.

psychological basis. The final passage opens the way for the elimination of priestly confession and suggests that the emotional transformation of the sinner from within is much more important than the ritual accompanying it.

In the study of morals we deal with the defects or qualities of the mind which dispose us to bad or good actions. Defects and qualities are not only mental, but also physical. There is bodily weakness; there is also the endurance which we call strength. There is sluggishness or speed; blindness or sight. When we now speak of defects, therefore, we presuppose defects of the mind, so as to distinguish them from the physical ones. The defects of the mind are opposed to the qualities; injustice to justice; cowardice to constancy; intemperance to temperance.

CHAPTER I *The Defect of Mind bearing upon Conduct*

Certain defects or merits of mind have no connection with morals. They do not make human life a matter of praise or blame. Such are dull wits or quick insight; a good or a bad memory; ignorance or knowledge. Each of these features is found in good and bad alike. They have nothing to do with the system of morals, nor with making life base or honorable. To exclude these we safeguarded above the phrase 'defects of mind' by adding 'which dispose to bad actions,' that is, those defects which incline the will to what least of all either should be done or should be left undone.

CHAPTER II *How does sin differ from a disposition to evil?*

Defect of this mental kind is not the same thing as sin. Sin, too, is not the same as a bad action. For example, to be irascible, that is, prone or easily roused to the agitation of anger is a defect and moves the mind to unpleasantly impetuous and irrational action. This defect, however, is in the mind so that the mind is liable to wrath, even when it is not actually roused to it. Similarly, lameness, by reason of which a man is said to be lame, is in the man himself even when he does not walk and reveal his lameness. For the defect is there though action be lacking. So, also, nature or constitution renders many liable to luxury. Yet they do not sin because they are like this, but from this very fact they have the material of a struggle whereby they may, in the virtue of temperance, triumph over themselves and win the crown. As Solomon says: 'Better a patient than a strong man; and the Lord of his soul than he that taketh a city.' (Prov. xvi, 32.) For religion does not think it degrading to be beaten by man; but it is degrading to be beaten by one's lower self. . . .

Sin, therefore, is sometimes committed without an evil will. Thus sin cannot be defined as 'will'. True, you will say, when we sin under constraint, but not when we sin willingly, for instance, when we will to do something which we know ought not to be done by us. There the evil will and sin seem to be the same thing. For example a man sees a woman; his concupiscence is aroused; his mind is enticed by fleshly lust and stirred to base desire. This wish, this lascivious longing, what else can it be, you say, than sin?

I reply: What if that wish may be bridled by the power of temperance? What if its nature is never to be entirely extinguished but to persist in struggle and not fully fail even in defeat? For where is the battle if the antagonist is away? Whence the great reward without grave endurance? When the fight is over nothing remains but to reap the reward. Here we strive in contest in order elsewhere to obtain as victors a crown. Now, for a contest, an opponent is needed who will resist, not one who simply submits. This opponent is our evil will over which we triumph when we subjugate it to the divine will. But we do not entirely destroy it. For we needs must ever expect to encounter our enemy. What achievement before God is it if we undergo nothing contrary to our own will, but merely practice what we please? Who will be grateful to us if in what we say we do for him we merely satisfy our own fancy? . . .

The sin, then, consists not in desiring a woman, but in consent to the desire, and not the wish for whoredom, but the consent to the wish is damnation.

Let us see how our conclusions about sexual intemperance apply to theft. A man crosses another's garden. At the sight of the delectable fruit his desire is aroused. He does not, however, give way to desire so as to take anything by theft or rapine, although his mind was moved to strong inclination by the thought of the delight of eating. Where there is desire, there, without doubt, will exists. The man desires the eating of that fruit wherein he doubts not that there will be delight. The weakness of nature in this man is compelled to desire the fruit which, without the master's permission, he has no right to take. He conquers the desire, but does not extinguish it. Since, however, he is not enticed into consent, he does not descend to sin. . . . It should be clear from such instances, that the wish or desire itself of doing what is not seemly is never to be called sin, but rather, as we said, the consent is sin. . . .

Some are intensely indignant when they hear us assert that the act of sinning adds nothing to guilt or damnation before God. Their contention is that in this act of sinning a certain delight supervenes, which increases the sin, as in sexual intercourse or indulgence in food which we referred to above. Their statement is absurd unless they can prove that physical delight of this kind is itself sin, and that such pleasure cannot be taken without a sin being thereby committed. If it be as they suppose, then no one is permitted to enjoy physical pleasure. The married do not escape sin when they employ their physical privilege; nor yet the man who eats with relish his own fruits. . . .

God considers not the action, but the spirit of the action. It is the intention, not the deed wherein the merit or praise of the doer consists. Often, indeed, the same action is done from different motives: for justice sake by one man, for an evil reason by another. Two men, for instance, hang a guilty person. The one does it out of zeal for justice, the other in resentment for an earlier enmity. The action of hanging is the same. Both men do what is good and what justice demands. Yet the diversity of their intentions causes the same deed to be done from different motives, in the one case good, in the other bad. . . .

Briefly to summarize the above argument: Four things were postulated which must be carefully distinguished from one another.

1. Imperfection of soul, making us liable to sin.
2. Sin itself, which we decided is consent to evil or contempt of God.
3. The will or desire of evil.
4. The evil deed.

To wish is not the same thing as to fulfil a wish. Equally, to sin is not the same as to carry out a sin. In the first case, we sin by consent of the soul: the second is a matter of the external effect of an action, namely, when we fulfil in deed that whereunto we have previously consented. When, therefore, temptation is said to proceed through three stages, suggestion, delight, consent, it must be understood that, like our first parents, we are frequently led along these three paths to the commission of sin. The devil's persuasion comes *first* promising from the taste of the forbidden fruit immortality. Delight follows. When the woman sees the beautiful tree, and perceives that the fruit is good, her appetite is whetted by the anticipated pleasure of tasting. This desire she ought to have repressed, so as to obey God's command. But in consenting to it, she was drawn *secondly* into sin. By penitence she should have put right this fault, and obtained pardon. Instead, she *thirdly* consummated the sin by the deed. Eve thus passed through the three stages to the commission of sin. . . .

CHAPTER XXIV *Confession*

We must now treat of the confession of sins. The Apostle James exhorts us in these words: 'Confess your sins to one another, and pray for each other that you may be saved. The earnest prayer of a just man availeth much.' (James v, 16.) It is maintained by some that confession should be made to God alone, a practice which the Greeks are said to follow.

But what is the good of confession to God who knows all? I cannot see what indulgence the tongue can implore for us albeit the Psalmist cries: 'I have made known to Thee my sin, and my iniquity have I not hid.' (Ps. xxxii, 5.) For many reasons the faithful confess their sins in the manner referred to by the Apostle. There is the notion that the prayers of those to whom we confess aid us all the more. Again, in the humility of confession a great part of the penance is enacted. In the easing of the mind in penitence we meet with an increase of indulgence. When David was accused by Nathan the prophet, he replied: 'I have sinned.' (2 Kings xii, 13.) Straightway the prophet said: 'The Lord hath taken away thy sin. (ibid.) God accepted immediately this act of pious abasement by so exalted a monarch. Priests who have the souls of the faithful entrusted to them are able to impose penance upon them. People who have used their will proudly and ill, by contempt of God, can be corrected by the will of another authority. Their penitence is the more sure because they follow the will of their priests, in obedience to them, and not their own will. If the priest counsels wrongly, and the penitent has obeyed, the blame lies rather upon the penitent than upon the priest. 'We must not leave out of account,' says the Apostle, 'the wiles of Satan.' (2 Cor. ii, 11.) Nor must we overlook how the devil manoeuvres to incite us to sin and deter us from confession. He stimulates us by removing fear and shame so that nothing is left to prevent us from offence. . . .

CHAPTER XXV *Confession not always needed*

Let us notice that a healthy attitude of regret may render confession unnecessary. We feel that this was the case with Peter. His tears testify to us of his denial of the Lord. But we read of no other confession or penance. In his comment on this passage about Peter's denial, in Luke, Ambrose remarks: 'I do not discover any word spoken, but simply that the disciple wept; tears, I read of, not penance uttered. These tears remove the sin which the voice is ashamed to acknowledge. They suggest remission and shame. Tears without any shrinking tell the fault, and confess the guilt without offence. Tears do not demand forgiveness: they deserve it'. . . .

44

GRATIAN, *THE CONCORD OF DISCORDANT CANONS*

1139 – c. 50

Gratian (d. 1197), a Camaldolese monk of Bologna, completed The Concord of Discordant Canons *or "Decretum" between 1139 and about 1150. Gratian's work was intended to unify the diverse customs and rules relating to church discipline; as such it was the beginning of the study of church, or canon, law. After summarizing the divisions of the law following Roman categories, Gratian lists specific cases or examples of legal tangles and offers the often contradictory rulings of theologians, popes, and councils that pertain to them. In each case he adds his own often original and ingenious solution.*

SOURCE Translated from Gratian, *Concordia Discordantium Canonum*, in *Patrologia Latina*, ed. by J.-P. Migne, 187 (Paris: 1891), 30–32, 1661–62, 1666–68. The editor is grateful to John T. Noonan for permission to quote Cause XXIX from his translation of the marriage sections of the *Decretum*, copyright, © 1967.

GRATIAN: Mankind is ruled by two things—that is, natural law and customs. Natural law is that which is contained in the law and the Gospel, by which anyone is ordered to do to another that which he desires to have done to himself, and is prohibited from doing to others what he does not want done to himself. Whence Christ says in the Gospel: "Therefore all things whatsoever ye would that men should do to you, do ye even to them: for this is the law and the prophets."[1]

> Isidore in the *Etymologies,* Book V, Chapter 2, says: Divine laws are established in the laws of nature; human laws, in custom.
>
> All laws are either divine or human. Those of nature make up the divine; those of custom, the human: these latter differ among themselves, because each set seems good to a certain people.
>
> Divine law is called *fas* [literally, "what is permitted"]: human law *jus* [literally, "what is right"]. To cross another's field is acceptable to divine law, but not to human.

GRATIAN: From the words of this author, we are evidently given to understand how divine and human law differ, since everything which is *fas* goes by the name of divine or natural law; by "human law", customs, written law and tradition are understood.

> *Jus* is a general name containing many divisions within it. . . .
>
> What law is.
>
> Law is the written constitution.
>
> What custom is.
>
> Custom is long use; we must now deal with custom.

[1] Matthew 7, 12.

What use is.

Custom is a certain practice which becomes usual, which is accepted as law, when there is no written law. It makes no difference whether it depends on writing or reason, for reason commends the written law. . . . That which is in common use is called custom.

GRATIAN: Therefore we read: "they do not differ, whether custom depends on writing or depends on reason." It appears that custom is partly put into written form, partly remaining in the form of the usual practice. That which has not been put in written form is called by the general term custom [*consuetudo*].

There is, moreover, another division of the law, as Isidore says in Book V, Chapter 4:

What the kinds of law are.

Law, then, is either natural, or civil, or the law of peoples.

What natural law is.

GRATIAN: Natural law is common to all nations, that which prevails everywhere by natural instinct, not by formal legislation, as in the case of the union of man and woman, the inheritance and education of children, possession of all goods in common and the existence of one freedom for all, the taking of goods from the heavens, earth and sea; also the restitution of property that has been deposited or of money commended to another's care, the repulsing of violence by force.

For in these, or any similar cases, there is no injustice— it is merely that natural equity prevails.

What civil law is.

Civil law is that which a certain people or city made to govern itself, at the instigation of God and man.

What the law of nations [*jus gentium*] is.

The law of nations concerns the seizing of dwellings, building, arming, making war, captives, slaves, the restoration of civil privileges, pacts, peace treaties, armistices, the non-violation of the rights of ambassadors, prohibition of marriage between persons of different races.

These things are called the law of nations; almost every race keeps them. . . .

CAUSE XXIX

GRATIAN: A certain noblewoman was informed that she was sought in marriage by the son of a certain noble. She gave her consent. But one who was not a noble and who was of slave condition offered himself in the name of the first man and took her as a wife. The one who had first pleased her finally came and sought her in marriage. She complained that she was deceived and wanted to be joined to the first man. It is first asked here: was there marriage between them? Secondly, if she first thought that he was a free man and afterwards learned that he was a slave, is it lawful for her to withdraw at once from him?

Question 1

GRATIAN: That there is marriage between them is proved in this way. Marriage or matrimony is a union of man and woman keeping an undivided way of life. The consent of both makes the marriage. Those, therefore, who are joined in order to keep an undivided way of life, each consenting to the other, are called married.

To the foregoing, it will be responded as follows: Consent is the perception of two or more as to the same thing. He who is in error, however, does not perceive: so he does not consent—that is, sense the same thing with others. He has made an error, and so does not consent. Thus she is not to be called married, because there was not the consent of each one, without which there can be no marriage. Just as one errs who is ordained by a man he thinks to be a bishop and who is still a layman; and just as such one is not called ordained, but is still to be ordained by a bishop; so she erred and is not coupled in marriage, but is still to be coupled.

Against this: Not every error eliminates consent. One who takes as a wife her whom he thinks to be a virgin, or one who takes a prostitute whom he thinks to be chaste, errs because he thinks she who has been corrupted is a virgin, or he accounts a prostitute to be chaste. Are they then to be said not to consent to these women? Or is either man to be given the option of sending away the woman and taking another? True it is that not every error excludes consent. But an error as to person is one thing; error as to fortune is another; error as to condition is another; error as to quality is another. An error as to person is when one is thought to be Virgil and he is Plato. An error as to fortune is when one is thought to be rich when he is poor, or conversely. An error as to condition is when one is thought to be free who is a slave. An error as to quality is when one is thought to be good who is bad. An error as to fortune and as to quality does not exclude consent to marriage. But an error as to person and as to condition does not allow consent to marriage. If one agrees that he will sell a field to Marcellus and later Paul comes saying that he is Marcellus and buys the field from him, did he agree with Paul about the price or is it to be said that he sold the field to him? Again, if one promises that he will sell me gold and in place of gold offers me yellow ore and so deceives me, am I to be said to consent to the yellow ore? I never wished to buy yellow ore, and I did not at some time consent to it, because there is no consent unless it is of the will. Just as error as to the matter here excludes consent, so does error of person in marriage. He does not consent to this one but to that one whom he thinks to be this one. . . .

An error as to fortune and quality does not exclude consent. When one consents to be the prelate of some church which he thinks is rich and it is less well off, although deceived by the error as to fortune, he still cannot renounce the prelacy accepted. Similarly, one who marries a poor man thinking he is rich cannot renounce this condition although she erred. Similarly an error as to quality does not exclude consent. When one buys a field or a vineyard which he thinks is very fruitful and errs as to the quality of the property and buys one less fertile, he still cannot rescind the sale. Similarly, one who takes as a wife a prostitute or one who has been corrupted whom he thinks to be chaste or a virgin cannot send her away and take another. . . .

CHAPTER I

It is lawful for slaves to contract marriages.

Again, Pope Julius:

> There is one Father in heaven for all of us; and each one of us, rich and poor, free and slave, will equally render an account for himself and his soul. Therefore we do not doubt that all, whatever their condition, have one law as to the Lord. If, however, all have one law, then a free man cannot be sent away nor can a slave once coupled in marriage be sent away. . . .

GRATIAN: To the foregoing it will be answered in this way: It is not denied that a free woman can marry a slave, but it is said that if his slave condition is not known he can be freely sent away when his slavery is discovered. What is said by the Apostle and Pope Julius is to be understood about those whose condition was known to both, but the condition of this man was unknown to the woman. Therefore, she is not compelled by the said authorities to stay with him; but she is shown to be free to stay with him or to withdraw. . . .

CAUSE XXXV

GRATIAN: A certain man, after the death of his wife, married a woman related to his deceased wife in the fourth degree, and to himself in the sixth. After three years, when she had presented him with children, he was accused before the church; he pleaded ignorance. (Question 1) First this must be resolved, whether a man may marry a woman who is his blood relation? (Question 2) Secondly, whether a man may marry a woman who is his wife's blood relation? (Question 3) Thirdly, up to what degree of consanguinity ought anyone to refrain from taking a wife from among his own or his wife's relatives? (Question 4) Why is consanguinity calculated up to the seventh degree only—neither continued beyond it nor stopped before it? (Question 5) Fifthly, how are the degrees of consanguinity computed? (Question 6) Who ought to affirm the relationship by oath? (Question 7) Are the sons born of incestuous parents considered legitimate? (Question 8) If she is ignorant of the consanguinity or affinity to the man she marries, may she remain his wife by a dispensation? (Question 9) If the church should have mistakenly separated a woman from her husband because of supposed consanguinity, and after forty days she marries again, if it is subsequently discovered that she was not related to her first husband, ought the second marriage to be declared null, and the first reinstated? (Question 10) If a widow marries for a second time outside her affinity, can the children born of the second marriage attempt to marry anyone who has affinity to the mother's former husband? . . .

Questions 2 and 3

GRATIAN: Since, therefore, it has been shown that one ought to abstain from marrying blood relatives, it is now to be seen to what degree of consanguinity one ought to abstain, and whether or not a man may take in marriage a woman related to one's own wife.

Concerning this, Pope Gregory[1] wrote at the Council of Meaux:

No one may marry a woman related to him within seven generations. It is decreed that one ought to observe [the laws concerning] the blood-relationship by degrees of lineage up to the seventh generation. Inheritance, hallowed by the legal limits of testaments, extends hereditary succession to the seventh degree. For none succeed to their inheritances unless they ought to by virtue of descent.

Let those who marry women related to them by blood be marked with infamy.

[1] This dictum is traceable neither to Gregory nor to the Council of Meaux.

Also Pope Calixtus[2] in his second letter to the bishops of Gaul:

Prohibit related persons to marry, because both divine and secular laws prohibit them. By divine law, those who do this, and their children, are not only to be cursed, but called evildoers. Secular law calls them infamous, and denies them their inheritance. We, also, following our fathers and cleaving to their footsteps, mark them with infamy, and judge them to be infamous because they are spotted with blotches of infamy, and we ought not to harbor them nor accept the accusations of those whom secular law rejects. . . . We call those blood relatives who are related within the bounds of consanguinity, whom divine law, and imperial and Roman law, and even Greek law recognize as such, and whom those laws accept as heirs, and cannot reject.

In-laws may unite in the fifth generation; in the fourth, if they have already done so, they are not to be separated.

Also, Pope Fabian:[3]

As to near relatives, related through their wife or husband, if the wife or husband dies, they may unite if related in the fifth generation; if related in the fourth, if they are discovered to be already united, they are not to be separated. If in the third degree, he cannot take another wife after his wife's death. It is the same when a man marries a woman who is related to him, and if, after his wife's death, he marries a female relative of hers. . . .

The same:[4]

Those who marry women related to them by blood, and then put them away, may not, as long as both still live,

[2] Actually from the pseudo-Isadorian decretals.

[3] Actually from a penitential of Theodore.

[4] The reference to "Pope Fabian" is again a fiction, but the actual source of this dictum is unknown.

marry other women [here Gratian adds: "unless they are excused through a plea of ignorance"].

Whence in the council at Verberie:

A man who has consciously committed incest is not prohibited from marrying.

The same again:

If a man shall have fornicated with a woman, and his brother, unwittingly, marries her, the brother ought to do penance for seven years because he concealed the crime from his brother, and after his penance he may marry. The woman, however, ought to do penance until her death, and remain without hope of ever having a husband.

GRATIAN: Concerning those who marry unwittingly, other authorities are to be consulted.

Pope Julius:[5]

No one may marry a woman related within seven degrees to him or to his wife.

We do not permit anyone of either sex to marry someone related to him by blood or to his spouse up to the seventh degree of lineage, or to be united under the stigma of incest. . . .

No couple, incestuously united, is worthy of the name of married persons.

Also, from the Council of St. Agatha, Chapter 61:

As to spouses incestuously united, we reserve no indulgence for them at all, unless their adultery be healed through separation. Incestuous spouses ought not to be called by the name of spouse, since even to designate them as such is horrible.

For we judge it to be incestuous if the man shall have defiled a woman, the widow of his brother (who heretofore was almost a sister to him), through a carnal union; or if the man should take his half brother's wife; or if a man shall have married his stepmother. . . .

[5] Actually from the Council of Orléans, 538.

45

THE DISPUTE OF THE CHURCH AND THE SYNAGOGUE

c. 938–966

Jews formed a special group in the midst of medieval Europe's overwhelming unity of religion. Mistrust and prejudice sought their justification in the popular belief that with the incarnation of Christ, Judaism had lost all favor with God. This dialogue, written between 938 and 966, used the word synagogue to symbolize Jews in general, and church to refer to Christians in general. Its place of origin was probably England, which had a small Jewish community by the tenth century. The work treats the Jewish viewpoint with remarkable insight and respect, and gives no hint of the violent waves of anti-Semitism that were to roll across Europe from the time of the First Crusade.

The Voice of the Church: You, O Synagogue, who once were the chosen and beloved of the great king, but afterwards you were repudiated and cast out—deservedly, because of your sins—I address you. Your arrogance, which prompts you not to blush, compels me to assert you just, even though you are full

SOURCE Translated from "'Altercatio Aecclesie contra Sinagogam,' Texte inédit du Xᵉ siècle," *Revue du moyen-âge Latin*, X, 1–2 (January–June, 1954), 53–56, 110, 112.

of all manner of crimes; and the abominable blasphemies and detractions with which you provoked my Lord and myself, now his servant, compel me to refute your fatuities and calumnies with an account of the truth. . . .

The Synagogue: Since you say I am repudiated and cast out and you delight in being taken into my place, and since you bear witness to my degeneration from the faith and nobility of my fathers, you compel me to answer your objections and assertions. Tell me first, then, how you claim that I have degenerated from the birthright of my fathers. For I have taken pains always to preserve uncontaminated that birthright which I accepted from them, nor have I mixed my people with ignoble or alien peoples in marriage, except with those who have passed over to embrace my race and my law. . . . I hold the glory of the faith which you know was so eminent in my fathers and from which you, boldly and wickedly, recently declared me relapsed; I hold the glory which I knew the reverend fathers had from God; and I believe in and worship one God, creator of all and, because I trust that he can never fail, I look for [the fulfillment of] those promises which he foretold by means of his prophets of our race. . . .

The Church: When I carefully search into and diligently study the things foretold about the coming of Christ by the holy prophets—both the hidden and the visible signs, the weak and the strong, the gentle and the terrible—I see that he, who was foretold, was to have come, a man hidden and in the open, weak and strong, gentle and terrible, to be judged and to judge. You, indeed, who reflect upon those signs which witness to his visible work and power; why do you not recall those which witness to his hidden works and weakness? . . . Thus Isaiah says: we saw him and there was no beauty in him nor comeliness and his face was as if hidden away and contemptible. So we did not recognize him. . . .

The Synagogue: It seems inconsistent that one and the same [man] should undergo agony and slanderous affronts, and yet be lifted up amid glory, as is written of him; for the same man to be condemned to death and yet to be given dominion over the whole world: rather, if it all was necessary, one man should be understood to have sustained the affronts, and another one altogether deserves to reign eternally. If, indeed, as you try to assert, he must be understood to be God's own son, it should seem much more of an indignity, when they say that he could endure so much.

46

———————

A TRAVELER'S GUIDE TO ROME:
WILLIAM OF MALMESBURY,
CHRONICLE OF THE KINGS OF ENGLAND

c. 1135

William (d. 1142), librarian of the English monastery of Malmesbury, was among the important representatives of twelfth-century Benedictine culture who enjoyed the respect of his contemporaries as a scholar and a great lover of books. His Chronicle, written in about 1135, gives ample evidence of his mastery of classical Latin and attests to the nostalgic reverence for Rome that he shared with other belletristic writers. The sections describing the plan of the city were doubtless intended to orient the increasing number of pilgrims drawn to Rome, the symbolic center of secular and ecclesiastical splendor, each year.

Of Rome, formerly the mistress of the globe, but which now, in comparison of its ancient state, appears a small town; and of

SOURCE From William of Malmesbury, *Chronicle of the Kings of England*, trans. by J. A. Giles (London: Henry G. Bohn, 1847), 367–71.

the Romans, once "Sovereigns over all and the gowned nation,"[1] who are now the most fickle of men, bartering justice for gold, and dispensing with the canons for money; of this city and its inhabitants, I say, whatever I might attempt to write, has been anticipated by the verses of Hildebert, first, bishop of Mans, and afterwards archbishop of Tours. Which I insert, not to assume the honour acquired by another man's labour, but rather as a proof of a liberal mind, while not envying his fame, I give testimony to his charming poetry.

> Rome, still thy ruins grand beyond compare,
> Thy former greatness mournfully declare,
> Though time thy stately palaces around
> Hath strewed, and cast thy temples to the ground.
> Fall'n is the power, the power Araxes dire
> Regrets now gone, and dreaded when entire;
> Which arms and laws, and ev'n the gods on high
> Bade o'er the world assume the mastery;
> Which guilty Caesar rather had enjoyed
> Alone, than e'er a fostering hand employed.
> Which gave to foes, to vice, to friends its care,
> Subdued, restrained, or bade its kindness share
> This growing power the holy fathers reared,
> Where near the stream the fav'ring spot appeared
> From either pole, materials, artists meet,
> And rising walls their proper station greet;
> Kings gave their treasures, fav'ring too was fate,
> And arts and riches on the structure wait.
> Fall'n is that city, whose proud fame to reach,
> I merely say, "Rome was," there fails my speech.
> Still neither time's decay, nor sword, nor fire,
> Shall cause its beauty wholly to expire.
> Human exertions raised that splendid Rome,
> Which gods in vain shall strive to overcome.
> Bid wealth, bid marble, and bid fate attend,

---

[1] Virgil, *Aeneid* i. 281.

And watchful artists o'er the labour bend,
Still shall the matchless ruin art defy
The old to rival, or its loss supply.
Here gods themselves their sculptur'd forms admire,
And only to reflect those forms aspire;
Nature unable such like gods to form,
Left them to man's creative genius warm;
Life breathes within them, and the suppliant falls,
Not to the God, but statues in the walls.
City thrice blessed! were tyrants but away,
Or shame compelled them justice to obey.

Are not these sufficient to point out in such a city, both the dignity of its former advantages, and the majesty of its present ruin? But that nothing may be wanting to its honour, I will add the number of its gates, and the multitude of its sacred relics; and that no person may complain of his being deprived of any knowledge by the obscurity of the narrative, the description shall run in an easy and familiar style.

The first is the Cornelian gate, which is now called the gate of St. Peter, and the Cornelian way. Near it is situated the church of St. Peter, in which his body lies, decked with gold and silver, and precious stones: and no one knows the number of the holy martyrs who rest in that church. On the same way is another church, in which lie the holy virgins Rufina and Secunda. In a third church, are Marius and Martha, and Audifax and Abacuc, their sons.

The second is the Flaminian gate, which is now called the gate of St. Valentine, and the Flaminian way, and when it arrives at the Milvian bridge, it takes the name of the Ravennanian way, because it leads to Ravenna; and there, at the first stone without the gate, St. Valentine rests in his church. The third is called the Porcinian gate, and the way the same; but where it joins the Salarian, it loses its name, and there, nearly in the spot which is called Cucumeris, lie the martyrs, Festus, Johannes, Liberalis, Diogenes, Blastus, Lucina, and in one sepulchre, the Two Hundred and Sixty, in another, the Thirty. . . .

The eleventh is called the Appian gate and way. There lie St. Sebastian, and Quirinus, and originally the bodies of the apostles rested there. A little nearer Rome, are the martyrs, Januarius, Urbanus, Xenon, Quirinus, Agapetus, Felicissimus: and in another church, Tyburtius, Valerianus, Maximus. Not far distant is the church of the martyr Cecilia; and there are buried Stephanus, Sixtus, Zefferinus, Eusebius, Melchiades, Marcellus, Eutychianus, Dionysius Antheros, Pontianus, pope Lucius, Optacius, Julianus, Calocerus, Parthenius, Tharsicius, Politanus, martyrs: there too is the church and body of St. Cornelius: and in another church, St. Sotheris: and not far off, rest the martyrs, Hippolytus, Adrianus, Eusebius, Maria, Martha, Paulina, Valeria, Marcellus, and near, pope Marcus in his church. Between the Appian and Ostensian way, is the Ardeatine way, where are St. Marcus, and Marcellianus. And there lies pope Damasus in his church; and near him St. Petronilla, and Nereus, and Achilleus, and many more. . . .

Such are the Roman sanctuaries; such the sacred pledges upon earth; . . .

47

A WESTERN VIEW OF ISLAM:
PETER THE VENERABLE, *LETTER TO BERNARD*

1144

Western Christendom's contacts with the Moslem world were vastly accelerated by the First Crusade (1096–99). By the early twelfth century, Moslem thought had ceased to seem in-

SOURCE Translated from Giles Constable, ed., *The Letters of Peter the Venerable* (Cambridge, Mass., 1967), Vol. I, 294–95.

*triguing and was seen as a dangerous ideological threat. Peter
the Venerable (d. 1156), Abbot of Cluny, commissioned a
Spanish scholar to translate late Moslem works into Latin, hoping to fight the "heresy" by exposing its true nature.*

. . . I sent you also our new translation against the most
detestable, worthless defense of the Moslem heresy which I recently had turned into Latin from the Arabic while I was in
Spain. I had it done by a man skilled in both tongues, Master
Peter of Toledo. . . . Moreover, my intention in having the
translation made was to imitate those Fathers who did not allow
any of what I call heresy which appeared in their day, even
the most superficial sort, to pass unnoticed, without resisting
it with all the strength of their faith and, through works and
disputations, revealing it to be damnable and worthy of detesta-
tion. I wanted to do the same for this chief error of errors, for
this, the dregs of all heresies, in which the remnants of all the
diabolical sects which have arisen since the advent of the Savior
have come together, so that when its filthy curse is well known,
and has poisoned almost half the earth, its foolishness and vile-
ness will become known to those ignorant of it at present, as to
how it is to be execrated and trampled under foot. . . . And
so that nothing of the damnable sect be hid from me, I had
translated the whole of that law of theirs, which in their language they call *Alkoran* or *Alkyren*, in its entirety and in its
proper order. . . .

PART THREE

THE HIGH MIDDLE AGES

THE CHANNELS OF PUBLIC LIFE

GOVERNMENT, COMMERCE AND COMMUNICATIONS

48

GUILD PRIVILEGES:
A CHARTER OF HENRY II
TO THE TANNERS OF ROUEN

1170 – 89

In this document Henry II confirms the privileges of the tanner's guild, and extends to its members the legal protection of the royal court system. Agreements of this kind were one means of gaining royal control over towns and their commercial activities.

Henry, by the grace of God king of England, Duke of Normandy and Aquitaine and Count of Anjou, to all his counts, barons, justiciars, viscounts, ministers and all his faithful men, greeting. Know that I have conceded and, by this my charter, have confirmed to my tanners of Rouen their guild, dyeing and greasing processes, and all customs and laws of their guild freely and in peace, fully and honorably, and [I have confirmed] that no one may perform their craft in Rouen, nor within the

SOURCE Translated from *Documents relatifs à l'histoire de l'industrie et du commerce en France*, ed. Gustave Fagniez, *Collection de textes pour servir à l'étude et à l'enseignement de l'histoire*, Vol. I (Paris: Alphonse Picard et Fils, 1898), 89.

jurisdictional area of Rouen unless allowed to do so by them; and this I do in return for the service which those tanners performed for me. For this reason I desire and firmly order that no one vex or disturb them nor bring them to court concerning their craft unless it be before me. Witnessed by Giles, Bishop of Évreux and Nicholas de Stuteville; at Eu.

49

───────────

A THIRTEENTH-CENTURY LEGAL PROCEEDING

1258 – 59

Among the documents in the chartulary of the Benedictine priory of Boxgrove, near Chichester, are the records of legal proceedings affecting the priory's property, which included lands near Boxgrove received as alms. This document records a rather complicated property trial. Abraham Pinche loaned money to Bartholomew de Elnested on the security of certain land. Abraham seems to have been double-crossed, as Bartholomew had already given the land to Philip de Croft, who had in turn given it to the priory. Because Abraham Pinche was a Jew, at his death all his assets were forfeited to the king, who then claimed the amount of the loan from the prior of Boxgrove. The name of John of Gatesden enters the dispute because he owned other land in the same neighborhood, which the king mistakes as that which is rightfully his.

This series of writs and proceedings gives some indication of

SOURCE From *The Chartulary of Boxgrove Priory*, trans. and ed. by Lindsay Fleming, Publications of the Sussex Record Society, LIX (Cambridge, 1960), 41–44.

the intricacy of the royal court system, as well as of the irritating and costly delays it could necessitate.

Proceedings by John of Gatesden against the Prior of Boxgrove concerning a debt to Abraham Pinche a Jew

Be it known that in the year of our Lord 1258, the forty-first day of the reign of King Henry son of King John, on the 12th day of July, John de Gatesden brought proceedings to summon the Prior of Boxgrove to acquit him to the lord King of 50 marks of a debt in which Bartholomew de Elnested was held to Abraham Pinche, a Jew of Winchester, by bonds which are in the hand of the lord King, by this writ:

"Henry by the grace of God, etc., to the sheriff of Sussex, greeting. Instruct the prior of Boxgrove that justly and without delay he acquit John de Gatesden to us of a debt of 50 marks in which Bartholomew de Elnested was held by Abraham Pinche, which debt is in our hand on account of the death of the aforesaid Jew. . . . And if he does not and the said John assures you of the prosecution of his claim, then you should make him appear before our justices assigned for the control of Jews, at Westminster. . . ."

The prior comes and says that Bartholomew on the said Wednesday did not have seisin of the lands, rents and tenements which John de Gatesden holds. . . . And of this the prior appeals to a jury. Therefore the sheriff was ordered to summon to the presence, etc. in the octave of St. Hilary, 12 honest men as well knights as others of the neighborhood of Elnested, who had no connection etc. to testify on their oath whether Bartholomew had seisin of the lands. . . .

At which day no jury came so it was ordered that the same writ should again be issued, to come on the morrow of All Souls' Day; at which day there did not come a sufficient jury so that the truth of the matters premised could not be known. So the sheriff was ordered to summon in the octave of the Purification of the Blessed Mary 12 honest and lawful men as well knights as others of the Hundred of Elnested, together with the aforesaid Thomas, Aufrid, Hugh, William, John, William, Godfrey, Robert, William, Godfrey, Adam, Robert . . . to discover the truth of the premisses.

At which day came Amfrid de Ferring', William de Worth, John de Hamton', William Beaufiz, Godfrey de Horsham, William de Budeketon', Adam de Perham, Robert le Mestre, Thomas de Wautham, William Houbanc, . . . who say on oath that Bartholomew enfeoffed Philip de Croft, three years and more past, by the charter which Bartholomew pledged to Abraham Pinch the Jew, that is to say before the said Wednesday next after Epiphany in the 18th year etc. So that Bartholomew could not pledge that charter to the Jews for the debt which he borrowed from them. Therefore it was considered that the prior withdraws from the case quit and absolved. . . .

In the 43rd year of King Henry son of King John [1258–59]. Enacted in the octave of Candlemas before Simon Passelewe, Adam de Greinuill, Thomas Esperon and Ralph de Houtoth', justices then deputed for the custody of Jews, and other lieges of the lord King, then present at the same place, that is to say, Sir Robert de Sancto Johanne, William Aguylun, then constable of the Tower of London, and many others Christians and Jews. That judgment was enrolled in four rolls of the said justices in Latin and Hebrew in rolls of the Jews by hand of Vivon the Jew who was present.

50

THE DEVELOPMENT OF THE FRENCH *PARLEMENT*

The French parlement *differs from its English analogue in that its functions were primarily judicial. These documents represent an early stage in the development of the* parlement; *they give evidence of the high degree of royal control over the institution, the kinds of cases decided by it, and the general nature of thirteenth- and early fourteenth-century government in France.*

Parlement of Pentecost
June 15, 1265
The king in the Parlement.

On the Monday after the feast of St. Barnaby the Apostle, in this same parlement, the lord king held, by the council of many prelates and other good [men] that he has in his hand at Paris and ought to have, in the domain of the bishop of Paris, the justice and fines of those of that bishop's subjects who disobey this order and prohibition of the lord king not to receive coins. . . . And the lord king ordered the same bishop not to set himself in opposition to the lord king's peaceful enjoyment of the

SOURCE Translated from *Textes relatifs à l'histoire du parlement depuis les origines jusqu'en 1314,* ed. Charles-V. Langlois, *Collection de textes pour servir à l'étude et à l'enseignement de l'histoire,* Vol. V (Paris: Alphonse Picard et Fils, 1888), 71, 181; and *Les Olim, ou registres des arrêts rendus par la cour du roi . . . ,* ed. Arthur Beugnot, 4 vols. (Paris, 1839–1848) I, 537. I am grateful to Thomas N. Bisson for the generous help he gave me in translating these passages.

aforesaid [order and prohibition] but rather to rejoice in peace with the lord king over the aforementioned matters.

Item, on the same day, the lord king took counsel with the same prelates and good men [to the effect] that the lord king has and ought to have in hand likewise at Paris the justice and fines of burghers and other subjects of the same bishop of his [the bishop's] land who fail to do guard duty at the order of the *prévôt* of Paris. . . . And the lord king acted in the way described above concerning the coining of money. The lord king afterward ordained further concerning these two matters, and then his letters patent and letters of the bishop of Paris were drawn up.

Postponement of a Parlement

October 3, 1308
Order to the *bailli*[1] of Vermandois that he shall see to the publishing of the postponement of parlement

Philip, etc., to the *bailli* of Vermandois, greeting. Since we have, for cause, postponed the coming parlement of the octave of All Saints [8 November] until the octave of the next feast of the lord's nativity [1 January] and we have caused the day of your bailiwick at the said parlement thus postponed to be assigned to the day after the octaves of the aforesaid nativity of the lord [2 January], we order you to make known solemnly on our behalf the aforesaid postponed and appointed time in your assizes and through the good villages of your bailiwick and its surrounding area, and [to do] so in time so that those who ought to may know of the aforesaid postponed and appointed time in due season; with the understanding that if, because of the lack of the said announcement, damage shall be incurred by any party, we shall cause [the same party] effectively to have recourse against you in the indemnification of the same [person] in this matter.

[1] bailiff, royal official.

And whatever you do about this, write by your patent letter on the same day of our court.

Dated at Paris, on Thursday after the feast of St. Michael, in the year of the lord 1308.

Judgments
1262

I. A certain knight, son of the lord William of Setaracio, petitioned that a certain estate which had belonged to his father be returned to him. The testimony of master Henry of Virziliaco was heard, and this decision was handed down to the knight: that he should not regain the land, because his father had alienated it.

II. The *bailli* of Vermandois, on behalf of the king, requested from the men of Duriaco a certain payment which they were accustomed to make to the king through the lord of Meyaco. They answered that, on the contrary, they were not obliged to pay, because the lord king had freed them, by his charter, from the yoke of servitude. The aforementioned charter having been heard and examined, it was decided that the men were obliged to make the said payment.

51

THE CHURCH-STATE DISPUTE:
THE CHRONICLE OF BURY ST. EDMUNDS

1282 – 1335

Founded by King Canute in honor of St. Edmund, King of East Anglia killed while doing battle with the Danes, the Abbey of Bury St. Edmunds was among the wealthiest and most important monasteries in England. Generous royal patronage over several centuries assured the abbey not only of wealth but of power; the abbot, acting as a royal vicegerent, ruled a large area called St. Edmund's Liberty and exercised full secular power within it.

Like most medieval chronicles, The Chronicle of Bury is the work of several writers. The majority of it was written at the end of the thirteenth century; the later entries included in this passage come from a fourteenth-century continuation. The Chronicle illustrates the unusually close ties between the royal house and the abbey. In addition, it illustrates some of the commonest characteristics of medieval chronicles: their tendency to be strongly reflective of local circumstances; their often amorphous and seemingly miscellaneous structure; their curious mixture of weighty matters and trivia.

Pirates from Zeeland and Holland ruled the sea as tyrants round Yarmouth and Dunwich; they raided whatever ships they

SOURCE From *The Chronicle of Bury St. Edmunds 1212–1301*, ed. and trans. by Antonia Gransden (London: Thomas Nelson, 1964), 76–77, 118–20, 138–39, 155, 164.

met, killed the crews and sailed off with not a few boats and their cargo. Florence, count of Holland, in revenge for the death of his father William, who had long before been murdered by the men of Frisia[1] and ignominiously buried in their land, won a glorious victory over them. He killed fifteen thousand Frisians; some from fear of the count fled the country and went into voluntary exile elsewhere. The count then took his father's body, so shamefully buried among the Frisians in the presence of only a few people, and carried it home in solemn procession and gave him a decent burial with full rites in his own country. Richard, archdeacon of Winchester, who had formerly been elected bishop of Winchester, surrendered to the pope his election to the see, as recorded above. The pope immediately gave the see to Master John de Pontissara, archdeacon of Exeter. The king of the Tartars joined with the Hospitallers to fight the sultan. In the war infidels were slain and the sultan himself captured and closely guarded in Cairo. Eleanor, queen of England, gave birth to a daughter at Rhuddlan, whom she named Elizabeth. Isabel, countess of Arundel, died and was buried at Marham. Master Thomas de Cantilupe, bishop of Hereford, died at the Roman court. Master Richard de Swinfield, archdeacon of London, was elected to succeed him. Hartmann, son of the king of Germany, who was to marry the king of England's daughter, walked incautiously on some ice, and as there was a thaw and the ice was broken, he was swept away by the water and drowned. On the day of St. Francis[2] a first son was born to John de Hastings; he called him William. Thomas Leneband, archdeacon of Suffolk, died on St. Lucy's eve[3] at Horham. The king kept Christmas at Rhuddlan in Wales. . . .

The king came with pious devotion to Bury St. Edmunds on the feast of St. Edward the king and martyr.[4] He stayed only one night and on the morrow entertained the convent with great magnificence and generosity. Up till now Edward, king of England, had in all his acts shown himself energetic, generous and

---

[1] William was killed in 1256.   [2] October 4th.
[3] October 4th.   [4] September 20th.

229

triumphant, like another Solomon. But he became infatuated with an unlawful love for his relative Blanche, the sister of Philip, king of France. She was related to him in the second degree.[5] Edward asked for and obtained a dispensation from the Roman court to contract a marriage with her. For the sake of this he resigned in good faith all his lands in Aquitaine and Gascony with all their appurtenances (as though he could expect to receive them back together with Blanche in free marriage) to the king of France of his own free will without the advice of his liege men. The letters of resignation were drawn up at Bury St. Edmunds, where the king was still staying, and the king summoned the chancellor in Lent to come with the seal from London. The loss of these lands was attributed by some to another cause. Now the king of England held these lands from the king of France as his lord-in-chief in exchange for certain services which he owed to (the king of France), and in order to perform the services due from those lands by ancient custom he had been summoned time and time again to attend the court of France, but (as the French asserted) had never appeared either in person or by adequate attorney. At last, therefore the whole court of France tried the case and carefully considered the matter and pronounced judgment on Edward in Paris after Easter: the king of England, for himself and his heirs, as contumacious and rebellious, forfeited by judicial sentence the lands in question. And so he was plundered and robbed and his plans frustrated. Some people, however, put forward a rash theory, that by entering into such an agreement, in view of the oath he had taken to go on the Crusade, the king was taking thought for the greater peace and security of his overseas territories. When, however, the king of England, not so much voluntarily as thoughtlessly and ill-advisedly, had thus handed over the free, full and peaceful possession and control of his lands, the woman who was the cause of the trouble wrote and informed him that she did not wish ever to marry any man,

[5] Blanche, daughter of Philip III, was Edward's first cousin once removed.

especially such an old one. And so the illegal marriage which Edward had desired was deservedly frustrated and, alas, he was deprived of the ancient inheritance of his forebears. The king of England at last came to himself and repented, although too late, his rash deed. . . . The king held his parliament, with the laity who alone had been summoned, at Salisbury on Ash Wednesday[6] to discuss the question of his military expedition against the king of France. There the king asked certain earls, that is the constable[7] and marshal[8] of England, to cross the Channel with him or at least go to Gascony. They did not consent to his request and explained firmly by way of excuse that they neither could nor would quit their own country when it was surrounded by so many enemies and leave it deserted. From that day the king bore their reply in mind without saying anything.

It must be remembered that on Ash Wednesday all the goods of the abbot and convent of Bury St. Edmunds were confiscated and all their manors together with St. Edmunds borough. The whole clergy met for the third time in London about the middle of Lent to discuss in detail the innumerable exactions, injuries and unjust losses daily inflicted on the Church and clergy. . . .

The year of the Lord 1300 was a jubilee year or year of absolution, and a leap-year. Easter day was 10 April. . . .

In this year people of both sexes and every age from all over the Christian world hastened to the Roman court. For on account of the jubilee year the pope absolved all pilgrims, who had truly confessed and were contrite, from all their sins and punishments for sins. . . . In the year of the Lord 1326 the same Edward was crowned king on the day of the Conversion of St. Paul. In the year of the Lord 1329 Peter de Corberia,[9] a member of the order of Friars Minor, had himself crowned pope in the city of Rome on the advice and with the help of

[6] February 27th.

[7] Humphrey de Bohun, 7th earl of Hereford 1275–1298, hereditary constable of England.

[8] Roger Bigod, 5th earl of Norfolk 1270–1306, hereditary marshal.

[9] Peter de Corberia declared Pope Nicholas V on 12 May 1328 (not in 1329 as the chronicle records).

Ludwig, duke of Bavaria.[10] This antipope created cardinals and other officials just like a true pope. . . .

In the year of the Lord 1335 a woman called Joneta, who had neither eaten nor drunk for thirty-one years, died in Norfolk.
[The Chronicle ends here.]

[10] Ludwig, duke of Bavaria 1294–1347, emperor of Germany 1314–1347.

52
_____

WESTERN IMPERIALISM: PIERRE DUBOIS,
ON *THE RETAKING OF THE HOLY LAND*

1304

The Norman lawyer Pierre Dubois, ambitious to become one of Philip IV's intimate advisers, supported the royal interests in a series of pamphlets and treatises in the early fourteenth century. The work On the Retaking of the Holy Land *was a scheme for the military reconquest of the holy places recently lost to the West; unlike earlier crusades undertaken by European kings, this one was to promote the glory and wealth of France alone, and Dubois dwelt at length on its commercial advantages. This passage envisions a vast educational system for French children, intended to prepare them for service in the East.*

It would be profitable for those ruling the kingdom of Jerusalem to have in their service a number of faithful and experi-

SOURCE Translated from Pierre Dubois, *De Recuperatione Terre Sancte*, ed. Ch.-V. Langlois (Paris: Alphonse Picard, 1891), *Collection d'études pour servir à l'étude et à l'enseignement de l'histoire*, Vol. IX, 47–48, 53.

enced secretaries who were knowledgeable in the tongues of the Arabs, their scriptures, and others of the world's languages. It is said that there is a certain Catholic people in the East, who do not obey the Roman church, differing from her on certain articles of faith which she holds, whose highest bishop, to whom all (as we to the Roman bishop) owe obedience, is called *pentharcos*[1] and he has 900 bishops under him, so that he is said to have more under him than the lord pope. It would be profitable to those same rulers of the kingdom of Jerusalem to unite those dissident bishops and their flocks, as well as to many others, whose observances and allegiances are other than to the Roman church, to be united and made obedient to her, and to communicate with her. This cannot occur unless the Roman church has many members who are well instructed in their language, through whom she can write to them. . . .

How then can the Roman pope—who does not know their language, who cannot understand them when they speak, nor they him—draw them into the unity and obedience of Rome? How can he remove the errors from their hearts, unless it be through prudent, faithful interpreters, who, having first learned both tongues, can express their mutual wills; whose answers to the arguments of the barbarians are filled with such outstanding logic that their erroneous opinions are destroyed; and who can, by incontrovertible reasoning, move and attract them to the truth of the Christian profession. . . .

Through provision for studies of this kind, the sending of instructors of both sexes into the East, it may happen that precious goods, so abundant there, will be carried back to us in the West, things which we now lack and which are most esteemed by us. . . .

Any whatever of this world's goods, if they be found only rarely among us, we hold precious and treasured, whereas in other places where they are common they are accounted of small worth.

If the reason behind this is sought, it can be found in the

[1] Probably the Greek patriarch.

words of the Philosopher, who, in speaking of the cause of the situating of the four elements said: Not without cause did glorious and sublime God dispose his created things in the world in this manner, who made all things which exist in the lower world for man and ordained nothing in vain.

53

A CONTRACT OF EXCHANGE

The economic expansion characteristic of the High Middle Ages was strongly in evidence in northern Italy by the late twelfth century. Because theological restrictions prohibited interest-bearing loans, moneylenders disguised these loans as contracts of exchange, in which sums were converted from one currency into another. The lender's profit was absorbed into the exchange rate.

Witnesses: Coenna of Lucca, Girardo Encina, Giovanni Corrigia. I, Alcherio, banker, have received from you, Martina Corrigia, a number of deniers for which I promise to pay, personally or through my messenger to you or to your accredited messenger, £9 s.13½ Pavese before the next feast of Saint Andrew [November 30]. Otherwise I promise you, making the stipulation, the penalty of the double, etc. Done in Genoa, in front of the house of Barucio, in the bank of Alcherio, the last day of January.

SOURCE From Robert S. Lopez and Irving W. Raymond, *Medieval Trade in the Mediterranean World*, Columbia University Records of Civilization (New York: Columbia University Press, 1955), 164.

54

FRANCISCO DI BALDUCCIO PEGOLOTTI, *THE PRACTICE OF COMMERCE*

between 1310 and 1340

This passage from the most famous medieval handbook for merchants, The Practice of Commerce, *includes practical advice for those traveling to the East for business purposes. This passage gives an itinerary; others cover details of financial transactions, foreign moneys, maps and tables for calculating interest.*

First [of all], from Tana to Astrakhan it is twenty-five days by ox wagon, and from ten to twelve days by horse wagon. Along the road you meet many Mongolians, that is, armed men.

And from Astrakhan to Sarai it is one day by water on a river, and from Sarai to Saraichuk it is eight days by water on a river. And you can travel [both] by land and by water, but people travel by water to spend less [on transportation] of wares.

And from Saraichuk to Urjench it is twenty days by camel wagon—and for those who are carrying wares it is convenient to go through Urjench, because that is a good market for wares—and from Urjench to Utrar it is from thirty-five to forty days by camel wagon. And should you leave Saraichuk and travel straight to Utrar, you would travel fifty days; and for one who

SOURCE From Robert S. Lopez and Irving W. Raymond, *Medieval Trade in the Mediterranean World*, Columbia University Records of Civilization (New York: Columbia University Press, 1955), 355, 356, 357.

has no wares it would be a better way than traveling through Urjench.

And from Utrar to Almaligh it is forty-five days by pack asses. And you meet Mongolians every day.

And from Almaligh to Kan-chow it is seventy days by asses.

And from Kan-chow to a river . . . it is forty-five days by horses.

And from the river you can travel to Wuinsay [Hang-chow] and sell there any silver sommi[1] you have, because that is a good market for wares. And from Quinsay on you travel with the money you get for the silver sommi you have sold there, that is, with paper money. And said money is called balisci, four of these are worth one silver sommo throughout the country of Cathay.

And from Quinsay to Khanbaligh [Peking], which is the master city in the country of Cathay, it is thirty days.

Things Necessary For A Merchant Wishing To Make The Said Journey To Cathay

First of all, it is advisable for him to let his beard grow long and not shave. And at Tana he should furnish himself with dragomans, and he should not try to save by hiring a poor one instead of a good one, since a good one does not cost. . . . And besides dragomans he ought to take along at least two good menservants who know the Cumanic tongue well. And if the merchant wishes to take along from Tana any woman with him, he may do so—and if he does not wish to take one, there is no obligation; yet if he takes one, he will be regarded as a man of higher condition than if he does not take one. . . .

[1] A *sommo* was both a silver ingot and the money of account of the Kipchak khanate. It corresponded to the weight of 202 *aspri* (real coins) but the mint in Tana when receiving from private parties an ingot weighing 2 *sommo* delivered only 190 *aspri*, keeping back the rest for seigniorage. A Genoese statute of 1304 reckoned the Kipchak *aspro* at ten Genoese deniers. [Lopez and Raymond's note.]

The road leading from Tana to Cathay is quite safe both by day and by night, according to what the merchants report who have used it—except that if the merchant should die along the road, when going or returning, everything would go to the lord of the country where the merchant dies, and the officers of the lord would take everything—and in like manner if he should die in Cathay.

55

GUILD REGULATIONS:

JUDGMENT AGAINST A DRAPER

THE REGULATION OF APPRENTICESHIP

With the progressive elaboration of the guild system and the vast increase in commercial wealth in the later Middle Ages, factions arose within the guilds between the various membership levels. The masters' attempts to retain control of the market for their particular product led to greater and greater restrictions on those aspiring to become masters themselves, and to the hostility of journeymen and apprentices. The dispute between masters and journeymen described in the first document, from the middle of the fourteenth century, was severe enough to require the arbitration of city officials. The judgment in the next document suggests the presence of commercial deception in all ages; again, the civil authorities, not the guilds, administer punishment to the guilty merchant.

source Translated from *Recueil de documents relatifs à l'histoire de l'industrie drapière en Flandre*, ed. Georges Espinas and Henri Pirenne, Vol. I (Brussels: 1906), 202–3.

JUDGMENT AGAINST A DRAPER

mid-fourteenth century

When Jacquemars des Mares, a draper, brought one of his cloths to the great cloth hall of Arras and sold it, the aforesaid cloth was examined by the *espincheurs* as is customary, and at the time they had it weighed, it was half a pound over the legal weight. Then, because of certain suspicions which arose, they had the cloth dried, and when it was dry, it weighed a half pound less than the legal weight. The *espincheur* brought the misdeed to the attention of the Twenty; Jacquemars was fined 100 shillings.

THE REGULATION OF APPRENTICESHIP

1345

A point of discussion was mooted between the apprentice fullers on the one hand, and the master fullers on the other. The apprentices held that, as they laid out in a letter, no one could have work done in his house without taking apprentices, . . . For they complained of fulling masters who had their children work in their houses, without standing [for jobs] in the public square like the other apprentices, and they begged——[1] that their letter be answered. The fulling masters stated certain arguments to the contrary. The aldermen sent for both parties and for the Twenty also and asked the masters if indeed they kept their children as apprentices; each master said he did. It was declared by the aldermen that every apprentice must remain in the public square, as reason demanded.

[1] The text is corrupt here.

SOURCE Translated from *Recueil de documents relatifs à l'histoire de l'industrie drapière en Flandre*, I, 204.

Done in the year of grace 1344 [1345], in the month of February, and through a full sitting of the aldermen.

56

NAVIGATION RIGHTS OF THE COMMUNE OF ROUEN

1274

The network of tolls, fines and other payments hindering free passage of goods in the kingdom of France is evident in this document. Even a duke has to defer to the privileges of the Commune of Rouen. While these tariffs were profitable to local lords or regional officials, they had the effect of dampening commercial exchange from one region to another. Severe in the medieval period, the effects of this economic malaise were not fully felt until the seventeenth century.

John, Duke of Brittany, to his beloved men, the mayoralty and commune of Rouen, greeting and affection. Whereas we intend to send wine to Paris to our estate by Robin of Dorsoult our servant, for our own use and to share with our friends, we entreat your judgment in which we fully confide, concerning this wine which Robin brings—forty barrels of it—that you shall graciously permit it to be transported under Rouen bridge and to pass on toward Paris. And, out of due politeness, we do not wish nor intend that your authority or the liberty of your city

SOURCE Translated from *Documents relatifs à l'histoire de l'industrie et du commerce en France*, ed. Gustave Fagniez, *Collection de textes pour servir à l'étude et à l'enseignement de l'histoire*, Vol. I (Paris: Alphonse Picard et Fils, 1898), 276–77.

be in any way diminished; moreover, because you have accommodated us before in similar cases, we give you many thanks for your past and present help. Given in the month of June in the year of the Lord 1274, witnessed by our seal.

57

THE SLAVE TRADE

· 1248

The trade in slaves was both common and profitable in the early Middle Ages, although by the thirteenth century a slave was an expensive luxury in the West. The following agreement involves a slave girl, perhaps of Moslem parentage, from the Christian island of Malta; the agreement is somewhat unusual in that the girl gives her own consent to the sale.

Genoa, May 1, 1248

I, Giunta, son of the late Bonaccorso of Florence, sell, give and deliver to you, Raimondo Barbiere, a certain white slave of mine, called Maimona, formerly from Malta, for the price of £5 s.10 Genoese, which I acknowledge that I have received for her from you. . . . And I call myself fully paid and quit from you, waiving the exception that the money has not been counted and received. I acknowledge that I have given you power and

SOURCE From Robert S. Lopez and Irving W. Raymond, *Medieval Trade in the Mediterranean World,* Columbia University Records of Civilization (New York: W. W. Norton & Co.), 116.

physical dominion [over the slave], promising you that I shall
not interfere nor take away the aforesaid slave in any way, but
rather I shall protect [her] for you and keep her out [of the
power] of any person [under penalty] of £20 Genoese which
I promise you. . . . And I, said Maimona, acknowledge that
I am a slave, and I wish to be delivered and sold to you, Raimondo. And I acknowledge that I am more than ten [years
old]. Witnesses called: Oberto de Cerredo, notary, and Antonio
of Piacenza, notary. Done in Genoa behind the Church of Saint
Laurent, 1248, fifth indiction, on May 11, before terce.

58

A MEDIEVAL UNIVERSITY ON STRIKE:
PARIS IN THE THIRTEENTH CENTURY
HENRY III INVITES
THE SCHOLARS OF PARIS TO ENGLAND

*Just as the university was a medieval invention, so too was the
concept of the student strike, used effectively against the gover-
nors of the University of Paris in 1229. Strikes frequently led
to the founding of new universities; however, an invitation to
the students and masters of Paris issued by the outstanding patron of learning, Henry III, did not result in the establishment
of a new university.*

SOURCE   Translated from *Chartularium Universitatis Parisiensis*,
ed. Henri Denifle and E. Chatelain, Vol. I (Paris, 1889), 118, 119.

PARIS IN THE THIRTEENTH CENTURY

1229

In the name of the Father and Son and Holy Spirit. We the appointed trustees, following the common agreement and will of the university, order and, in ordering, declare that unless, in our judgment, sufficient satisfaction has been made to the masters and students of the university for the most horrible injuries inflicted on them by the mayor of Paris and his accomplices and certain others who were also in on the deed within a month after Easter Day [April 15], it will no longer be permitted for anyone to remain in the city or diocese of Paris by reason of his studies, either to be instructed or to teach, for the next six years, beginning with the end of the month mentioned above. And while awaiting the emendation of these conditions, no one is to lecture publicly or in private. Nor shall anyone be allowed to return after six years, unless sufficient satisfaction has been made concerning the injuries mentioned above. So that this remains a firm condition, we have made this charter a joint statement by affixing our seals to it. Done in the year of the Lord 1228, in the month of March, the Tuesday after the Lord's Annunciation.[1]

HENRY III INVITES THE SCHOLARS OF PARIS TO ENGLAND

July 16, 1229

The king [Henry III of England] to the masters and students of the University of Paris, greeting. Because of the many tribu-

[1] It is in this case 1229 by our calendar since the medievals frequently changed the year at Easter. (Ed.'s note.)

lations and difficulties you have undergone under the evil law of Paris, we, humbly suffering with you, desire, out of reverence for God and the holy church, piously to aid you in restoring your condition to its due liberty. Therefore we announce to your community that, if it pleases you to come to our kingdom of England and make this the permanent center of your studies. Whatever cities, boroughs or towns you choose to elect we shall assign to you, to be set aside for that purpose, and we shall in every way give you cause to rejoice, as is fitting, in the liberty and tranquillity which is pleasing to God and which ought to be fully sufficient for you. In whose, etc. By the king's witness at Reading, the sixteenth day of July.

59

A THIRTEENTH-CENTURY RITUAL OF KNIGHTHOOD

As the military functions of knighthood became less and less important in the High Middle Ages, the knightly class grew more and more anxious to preserve and enhance its self-consciousness as a group. The knightly aristocracy attempted to make itself ever more exclusive, and to glorify entry into its ranks by elaborate ceremonies. The following liturgy of knighthood is an example not only of the increasingly elaborate ceremonial, but also of the growing emphasis on the knights' non-military functions—their spiritual and chivalric responsibilities to society.

SOURCE Translated from Michel Andrieu, *Le Pontifical Romain au Moyen-Âge*, Vol. II, *Le Pontifical de la Curie Romaine au XIIIe siècle* (Città del Vaticano, 1940), 579–81.

Ritual to be followed when anyone is knighted in the basilica of the most blessed Peter, prince of the Apostles, in Rome

First he who is to be knighted ought to keep a vigil through the night in the basilica itself, and to spend his time in prayer in the chapel he has chosen. In the morning, after he has heard mass, the archpresbyter, if he is present, or the prior of the canons of that basilica, dressed in the cape and accompanied by his fellow-canons and the other clerics of the church, should speak thus:

Verse: Our help is in the name of the Lord. Response: Who made heaven and earth.

Verse: Blessed be the name of the Lord. Response: From this time forth and for evermore.

Verse: Be thou to us, O Lord, a tower of strength. Response: In the presence of our enemies.

Verse: O Lord, save thy servant. Response: My God, in thee have I trusted.

Verse: The enemy shall avail nothing against him. Response: And the son of evil shall not rise up to harm him.

Verse: O Lord, hear my prayer. Response: And let my cry come unto thee.

Verse: The Lord be with thee. Response: And with thy spirit. Prayer. We ask thee, O Lord, by thy assistance to initiate and by thy aid to sustain our actions, so that all our prayer and procedure may ever begin with thee and what was begun with thy aid may be finished. Through our Lord Jesus Christ. . . . Another prayer. Stretch out thy right hand of heavenly aid to thy servant N., that he may search for thee with all his heart and that he may be worthy to follow that which he worthily requests. Through Jesus Christ thy son our Lord, who lives and rules with thee for all ages. . . .

Then the lord archpresbyter or prior of the canons gives the candidate for knighthood the blow. Having done this, he says a prayer over him.

God, who from heaven has ever gained the victory for thy faithful men, grant, we ask, to this man N., thy servant and to all who go into battle, through thy power to overcome the evil of the invisible enemy, and to trample the wantonness of the visible attackers under foot, so that, with both prideful enemies put to flight, thy church may enjoy unity and rejoice in peace. Through Jesus Christ, etc.

Then the candidate should respond by swearing his oath, [with his hands between those] of the lord archpresbyter or the prior of the basilica, to defend all other churches, widows, children, and orphans in their every need, and to fight for and aid them with all his strength.

This accomplished, they should proceed to the high altar or, if he prefers out of devotion, to the altar of confession of the blessed apostle Peter, where they should find a drawn sword, which the lord archpresbyter, or, if he should wish it, the prior, should give to the new knight, saying:

Accept, from our unworthy though consecrated hands, the sword from above, taken from the body of blessed Peter, by the very authority of the apostles, granted to thee in a soldierly manner and divinely ordained to thy use, through the office of our blessing, in defense of this universal church, in punishing evildoers, in praise of good. And be mindful of that which the psalmist prophesied, saying: "Gird on thy sword about thy thigh with power," so that the same force you exert as a knight [riding into battle], you use powerfully to destroy the mass of iniquity, to defend and protect the holy church of God and his faithful, to execrate and scatter those enemies who falsely bear the name of Christians, to help and defend widows, children and orphans, as you have promised, and to restore what has been desolated, preserve what has been restored, and avenge what has been wrongly judged, confirm what has been rightly disposed; and in so doing, as a glorious attainer of virtue, an outstanding upholder of justice, you may deserve to reign without end with the savior of the world, whose image you bear in your name. Who with God the Father etc.

And he girds on the sword, saying:

Gird on thy sword on thy thigh with power, and pay heed,

for the saints conquered kingdoms not through the sword but through faith.

Then the lord archpresbyter or the canons' prior of the basilica gives him the kiss of peace, and says: Go and do ye as a good knight of Christ and blessed Peter, the key-bearer of the heavenly kingdom. Response: Amen.

Having made his reverence to the altar, accompanied by the lord archpresbyter, prior and the honorable band of his canons, his oblation made, he should return to his own people; first, however, he should receive his gilded spurs from the hand of an older knight at his side, on the steps of the basilica of St. Peter.

If, indeed, it had been a Roman who was to be knighted, he ought first to have been washed, naked, with rosewater and to have slept, naked, on a bed prepared for the occasion, according to the customs of his country, and then dressed in gilded vestments lined with fur; after that he ought to have kept his vigil, praying, in the church, and, the following morning, to have been knighted according to the ritual described above.

60

A MARRIAGE CASE

1293

The following record, taken from a 1293 case heard before the commissary court of the diocese of Canterbury, England, deals with an attempt to secure an annulment on grounds of

SOURCE   I am grateful to the Dean and Chapter, Canterbury Cathedral, and to Richard Helmholz for permission to quote this passage from his transcription and translation of this canon law case from the Dean and Chapter Archives, Canterbury, *Sede Vacante* Scrapbook III, no. 37.

consanguinity. It illustrates, first, the difficulties associated with identifying kinship in a society without written records of births and marriages; secondly, it suggests one reason why the wide-sweeping rules of the canon law against incest and marriage between relations caused less difficulty in medieval practice than has long been assumed, since people were often very uncertain of who was related to whom, and they were not always well-informed about the degrees of consanguinity (determined by counting back along each side of the family to the common ancestor).

In this case, the second witness, Galfred, gives a genealogy which indicates that John and Alice are related in the third and fourth degrees. Yet the common belief was that they were related in the fourth and fifth degrees. And some did not believe that they were related at all. To compound the uncertainty, the church courts required concrete proof of consanguinity before a marriage would be dissolved—it was not enough merely to allege rumors of kinship. In the case, no such proof from first-hand witnesses was forthcoming, nor was there any pre-existing public gossip that the marriage was within the prohibited degrees. As a result, John and Alice were declared to be lawfully, and indissolubly, married.

Osbert Crotehele, sworn and diligently examined on the consanguinity which is said to exist between John son of Simon Twyford and Alice widow of William Tannator, says that he does not know how to determine grades of consanguinity. He has heard it said, however, by old and trustworthy men that the said John and Alice are related in the fourth and fifth degree of consanguinity. This he heard after the start of the law suit. There is public voice and fame of it in the neighborhood of Bennington, and he firmly believes that it is true. He deposes neither corrupted nor instructed,[1] and he is not related by consanguinity to either John or Alice.

[1] I.e., he gives his deposition as a witness honestly.

Galfred Lillysdenne, sworn and questioned on the said consanguinity, says that there was a certain Richard Henxdenne, the ancestor, from whom was born Matilda, from whom Cecilia, from whom Alice, from whom John about whom the suit deals. Also from the ancestor was born Emma, from whom Muriel, from whom Alice about whom the suit deals. Asked if he has seen all those he names, the witness says no, except Alice and John on one side, and on the other Emma and Muriel and Alice. Asked if they conducted themselves as relations, he says that he does not know. Asked from whom he learned to determine grades of consanguinity, he says from several old and trustworthy men, and this after the start of the suit. Asked what the fame of the country is on the said consanguinity, he says that some say they are related by consanguinity, some say they are not. There was no fame on the consanguinity between them until after the publication of the banns. And he believes that they are related as he deposed above. And he is related by consanguinity to the woman about whom the suit deals.

John Ydenne, sworn and questioned on the said consanguinity, says that he does not himself know of any consanguinity between the aforesaid parties. He says, however, that some say they are related in the fourth and fifth degree, and some the third and fourth degree. And in what degree they are related, he does not know. Asked as to his belief, he replies that he does not know; but he says that the elders of the whole country say that they are related in the fourth and fifth degree of consanguinity. He is not related.

In the name of God, Amen. Having heard and fully understood the merits of the cause of marriage and divorce before us, brother R. de Clyve commissary general of Canterbury *sede vacante*, . . . having invoked the grace of the Holy Spirit and by the counsel of experts in the law assisting us, having pondered those things which are to be pondered, because we find that the said impediment of consanguinity is in no way proved, and the marriage between John and Alice was legitimately contracted, we pronounce that John and Alice may be coupled in marriage, and adjudge John to Alice as her man and husband and Alice to the said John as his legitimate wife by the same sentence.

61

GIOVANNI VILLANI, CHRONICLE OF FLORENCE
c. 1308 – 48

The banker Giovanni Villani (c. 1275–1348), prominent in the commercial and political life of fourteenth-century Italy, began his chronicle in about 1308. It was intended to survey world history from a Florentine perspective, and provides a vivid description of the city's political factions, as well as of the infamous French attack on Pope Boniface VIII in 1303.

How the city of Florence was first built

After the city of Fiesole was destroyed, Cæsar with his armies descended to the plain on the banks of the river Arno, where Fiorinus and his followers had been slain by the Fiesolans, and in this place began to build a city, in order that Fiesole should never be rebuilt; and he dismissed the Latin horsemen whom he had with him, enriched with the spoils of Fiesole; and these Latins were called Tudertines. Cæsar, then, having fixed the

SOURCE From Giovanni Villani, *Villani's Chronicle: being selections from the first 9 books of the Chronicle Fiorentine of Giovanni Villani*, ed. Philip Wicksteed, trans. by Rose E. Selfe (London: Archibald Constable & Co. Ltd., 1906), 27, 29, 141, 142, 346–51. Copyright © by Constable & Company Limited 1970.

boundaries of the city, and included two places called Camarti and Villa Arnina [of the Arno], purposed to call it Cæsaræa from his own name. But when the Roman senate heard this, they would not suffer Cæsar to call it after his name, but they made a decree and order that the other chief noble Romans who had taken part in the siege of Fiesole should go and build the new city together with Cæsar, and afterwards populate it; and that whichever of the builders had first completed his share of the work should call it after his own name, or howso else it pleased him. . . . And the said lords each strove to be in advance of the work of the others. And at one same time the whole was completed, so that to none of them was the favour granted of naming the city according to his desire, but by many it was at first called "Little Rome." Others called it Floria, because Fiorinus, who was the first builder in that spot, had there died, he being the *fiore* [flower] of warlike deeds and of chivalry, and because in the country and fields around where the city was built there always grew flowers and lilies. Afterwards the greater part of the inhabitants consented to call it Floria, as being built among flowers, that is, amongst many delights. And of a surety it was, inasmuch as it was peopled by the best of Rome, and the most capable, sent by the senate in due proportion from each division of Rome, chosen by lot from the inhabitants; and they admitted among their number those Fiesolans which desired there to dwell and abide. But afterwards it was, through long use of the vulgar tongue, called Fiorenza, that is "flowery sword." . . .

In the said times when Frederick was in Lombardy, having been deposed from the title of Emperor by Pope Innocent, as we have said, in so far as he could he sought to destroy in Tuscany and in Lombardy the faithful followers of Holy Church, in all the cities where he had power. And first he began to demand hostages from all the cities of Tuscany, and took them from both Ghibellines and Guelfs, and sent them to Samminiato del Tedesco; but when this was done, he released the Ghibellines and retained the Guelfs, which were afterwards abandoned as poor prisoners, and abode long time in Samminiato as beggars. And forasmuch as our city of Florence in those times was not among the least notable and powerful of Italy, he desired especially to vent his spleen against it, and to increase the accursed parties of the Guelfs and Ghibellines, which had begun long time before through the death of M. Bondelmonte, and before, as we have already shown. But albeit ever since this the said parties had continued among the nobles of Florence (who were also ever and again at war among themselves by reason of their private enmities), and albeit they were divided into the said parties, each holding with his own, they which were called the Guelfs loving the side of the Pope and of Holy Church, and they which were called the Ghibellines loving and favouring the Emperor and his allies, nevertheless, the people and commonwealth had been maintained in unity to the well-being and honour, and good estate of the republic. But now the said Emperor sent ambassadors and letters to the family of the Uberti, which were heads of his party, and their allies which were called Ghibellines, inviting them to drive their enemies, which were called Guelfs, from the city, and offering them aid of his horsemen; and this caused the Uberti to begin dissension and civil strife in Florence, whence the city began to be disordered, and the nobles and all the people to be divided, some holding to one party, and some to the other; and in divers parts of the city there was fighting long time. . . .

How the king of France caused Pope Boniface to be
seized in Anagna by Sciarra della Colonna,
whence the said Pope died a few days afterwards.

After the said strife had arisen between Pope Boniface and King Philip of France, each one sought to abase the other by every method and guise that was possible: the Pope sought to oppress the king of France with excommunications and by other means to deprive him of the kingdom; and with this he favoured the Flemings, his rebellious subjects, and entered into negotiations with King Albert of Germany, encouraging him to come to Rome for the Imperial benediction, and to cause the Kingdom to be taken from King Charles, his kinsman, and to stir up war against the king of France on the borders of his realm on the side of Germany. The king of France, on the other hand, was not asleep, but with great caution, and by the counsel of Stefano della Colonna and of other sage Italians, and men of his own realm, sent one M. William of Nogaret of Provence, a wise and crafty cleric, with M. Musciatto Franzesi, into Tuscany, furnished with much ready money, and with drafts on the company of the Peruzzi (which were then his merchants) for as much money as might be needed; the Peruzzi not knowing wherefore. And when they were come to the fortress of Staggia, which pertained to the said M. Musciatto, they abode there long time, sending ambassadors and messages and letters; and they caused people to come to them in secret, giving out openly that they were there to treat concerning peace between the Pope and the king of France, and that for this cause they had brought the said money; and under this colour they conducted secret negotiations to take Pope Boniface prisoner in Anagna, spending thereupon much money, corrupting the barons of the country and the citizens of Anagna; and as it had been purposed, so it came to pass; for Pope Boniface being with his cardinals, and with all the court, in the city of Anagna, in Campagna, where he had been born, and was at home; not thinking or knowing of this plot, nor being on his guard, or if he heard anything of it, through his great courage not heeding it, or perhaps, as it pleased God, by reason of his great sins,—in the month of September, 1303, Sciarra della Colonna, with his mounted followers, to the number of 300, and many of his friends on foot, paid by money of the French king, with troops of the lords of Ceccano and of Supino, and of other barons of the Campagna, and of the sons of M. Maffio d'Anagna, and, it is said, with the consent of some of the cardinals which were in the plot, one morning early entered into Anagna, with the ensigns and standards of the king of France, crying: "Death to

Pope Boniface! Long life to the king of France!" And they rode through the city without any hindrance, or rather, well-nigh all the ungrateful people of Anagna followed the standards and the rebellion; and when they came to the Papal Palace, they entered without opposition and took the palace, forasmuch as the present assault was not expected by the Pope and his retainers, and they were not upon their guard. Pope Boniface—hearing the uproar, and seeing himself forsaken by all his cardinals, which were fled and in hiding (whether through fear or through set malice), and by the most part of his servants, and seeing that his enemies had taken the city and the palace where he was—gave himself up for lost, but like the high-spirited and valorous man he was, he said: "Since, like Jesus Christ, I am willing to be taken and needs must die by treachery, at the least I desire to die as Pope"; and straightway he caused himself to be robed in the mantle of St. Peter, and with the crown of Constantine on his head, and with the keys and the cross in his hand, he seated himself upon the papal chair. And when Sciarra and the others, his enemies, came to him, they mocked at him with vile words, and arrested him and his household which had remained with him; among the others, M. William of Nogaret scorned him, which had conducted the negotiations for the king of France, whereby he had been taken, and threatened him, saying that he would take him bound to Lyons on the Rhone, and there in a general council would cause him to be deposed and condemned. The high-spirited Pope answered him, that he was well pleased to be condemned and deposed by Paterines such as he, whose father and mother had burnt as Paterines; whereat M. William was confounded and put to shame. But afterwards, as it pleased God, to preserve the holy dignity of the Popes, no man dared to touch him, nor were they pleased to lay hands on him, but they left him robed under gentle ward, and were minded to rob the treasure of the Pope and of the Church. In this pain, shame and torment the great Pope Boniface abode prisoner among his enemies for three days; but, like as Christ rose on the third day, so it pleased Him that Pope Boniface should be set free; for without entreaty or other effort, save the Divine aid, the people of Anagna beholding their error, and issuing from their blind ingratitude, suddenly rose in arms, crying: "Long live the Pope and his household, and death to the traitors"; and running through the city they drove out Sciarra della Colonna and his followers, with loss to them of prisoners and slain, and freed the Pope and his household. Pope Boniface, seeing himself free, and his enemies driven away, did not therefore rejoice in any wise forasmuch as the pain of his adversity had so entered into his heart and clotted there, wherefore he departed straightway from Anagna with all his court, and came to Rome to St. Peter's to hold a council, purposing to take the heaviest vengeance for his injury and that of Holy Church against the king of France, and whosoever had offended him; but, as it pleased God, the grief which had hardened in the heart of Pope Boniface, by reason of the injury which he had received, produced in him, after he was come to Rome, a strange malady so that he gnawed at himself as if he were mad, and in this state he passed from this life on the 12th day of October in the year of Christ 1303, and in the church of St. Peter, near the entrance of the doors, in a rich chapel which was built in his lifetime, he was honourably buried.

We will further tell of the ways of Pope Boniface.

This Pope Boniface was very wise both in learning and in natural wit, and a man very cautious and experienced, and of great knowledge and memory; very haughty he was, and proud, and cruel towards his enemies and adversaries, and was of a great heart, and much feared by all people; and he exalted and increased greatly the estate and the rights of Holy Church, and he commissioned M. Guglielmo da Bergamo and M. Ricciardi of Siena, who were cardinals, and M. Dino Rosoni of Mugello, all of them supreme masters in laws and in decretals, together with himself, for he too was a great master in divinity and in decretals, to draw up the Sixth Book of the Decretals, which is as it were the light of all the laws and the decretals. A man of large schemes was he, and liberal to folk which pleased him, and which were worthy, very desirous of worldly pomp according to his estate, and very desirous of wealth, not scrupulous, nor having very great or strict conscience about every gain, to enrich the Church and his nephews. He made many of his friends and confidants cardinals in his time, among others two very young nephews, and his uncle, his mother's brother; and twenty of his relations and friends of the little city of Anagna, bishops and archbishops of rich benefices; and to another of his nephews and his sons, which were counts, as we afore made mention, to them he left almost unbounded riches; and after the death of Pope Boniface, their uncle, they were bold and valiant in war, doing vengeance upon all their neighbours and enemies, which had betrayed and injured Pope Boniface, spending largely, and keeping at their own cost 300 good Catalan horsemen, by force of which they subdued almost all the Campagna and the district of Rome. And if Pope Boniface, while he was alive, had believed that they could be thus bold in arms and valorous in war, certainly he would have made them kings or great lords.

62

CHANGE IN THE FEUDAL ORDER:

A FIEF-RENTE CHARTER

A THIRTEENTH-CENTURY MONEY FIEF

In feudal Europe a fief usually consisted of a piece of land and its appurtenances. In the later Middle Ages, however, the fief-rente appeared, which provided for annual installments of money paid by the lord to the vassal in exchange for his traditional military and political services. The fief-rente is one indication of a reviving money economy which was gradually to undermine the feudal system. That the money fief could be granted to ordinary workers is evident from the description of the fief of the carpenter Leobinus.

A FIEF-RENTE CHARTER

August 23, 1289

I, Raoul of Clermont, constable of France and lord of Nesle, make known to all who shall see and hear these present letters that I have received from that high and noble man, my dear lord Guy, count of Flanders and marquis of Namur, in good coins, well counted and numbered, 221 pounds in the money of Tours for the term of the Feast of St. John the Beheaded next

SOURCE Translated from Bryce D. Lyon, *From Fief to Indenture* (Cambridge: Harvard University Press, 1957), 283.

approaching; which money my said lord the count owes me as my fief, and which I received from him for the aforementioned term at the fair of Lille. . . . In witness of which I had ordered these present letters to be drawn up, sealed with my own seal. Written in the year of grace 1289, on the eve of St. Bertremil the apostle.

A THIRTEENTH-CENTURY MONEY FIEF

THIS IS THE FIEF OF LEOBINUS THE CARPENTER

He has a payment of fifty *solidi* . . . [in return] for which he is required to do carpentry, in his own person, according to the amount of work there may be to do, in the bishop's palace, or in the place where his wine is pressed. And on the days in which he works, he ought to have sufficient grain and a midday meal and wine at noon, and in the evening, at his home, he ought to be given two white loaves and half a pint of wine, and he ought to be given the same provisions on Sundays and feast days, except for the grain and wine at noon.

While he is working he ought to have all his *scopellos*, which could not be used in his work, and he ought also to have a room of his own in which to keep his tools or *scopellos*. And at the grape harvest he ought to have a small measure of grape clusters and a pint of new wine. Those of his tools which are broken or damaged while he is working for the bishop are to be repaired at the bishop's expense. And each day that the Bishop of Chartres is at Chartres, he shall dine at the bishop's court, if he likes, at his companions' table. At harvest time he ought to serve in the wine cellar day and night, and for this he ought to receive adequate pay—two pennies per night *por haste*—and for

SOURCE Translated from *Documents relatifs à l'histoire de l'industrie et du commerce en France*, ed. Gustave Fagniez, *Collection de textes pour servir à l'étude et à l'enseignement de l'histoire*, Vol. I (Paris: Alphonse Picard et Fils, 1898), 334-35.

each day he remains in the cellar, he ought to receive, to be sent to his home, two white loaves and a half a pint of wine. At the feast of blessed Mary, at Christmas, at Easter, on Rogation Thursday, at Pentecost and at the feast of All Saints he ought to receive four white loaves and one pint of wine, to be sent to his home; on Tuesday in Lent, four white loaves and one pint of wine and a cock and a portion of salted meat.

63

PEASANT REVOLTS: FROISSART, *CHRONICLES*

late fourteenth century

A member of a French merchant family, Jean Froissart (1337–1410) spent his life traveling and recording his observations with the intention of writing a chronicle of the great events of his century. In his Chronicles, *which span the history of Western Europe from 1325 to 1400, Froissart devoted much space to describing the feudal nobility, whose courtly and refined manners he instinctively admired. But his Chronicle gives evidence of the decline of the feudal system in the fourteenth century, and to the desperate peasant rebellions that made its decline even more apparent. The Jacquerie and English Peasant Revolt were the products of a period of severe economic distress, made more acute by the tax burdens of the Hundred Years' War.*

source From *Chronicles of England, France, Spain and the adjoining countries from the latter part of the reign of Edward II to the coronation of Henry IV*, by Sir John Froissart. Trans. from the French editions by Thomas Johnes, Esq. Vol. I (London: Wm. Smith, 1844), 240–41, 652–54.

THE COMMENCEMENT OF THE INFAMOUS
JACQUERIE OF BEAUVOISIS

Soon after the deliverance of the king of Navarre out of prison, a marvellous and great tribulation befel the kingdom of France, in Beauvoisis, Brie, upon the river Marne, in the Laonnois, and in the neighbourhood of Soissons. Some of the inhabitants of the country towns assembled together in Beauvoisis, without any leader: they were not at first more than one hundred men. They said, that the nobles of the kingdom of France, knights, and squires, were a disgrace to it, and that it would be a very meritorious act to destroy them all: to which proposition every one assented, as a truth, and added, shame befal him that should be the means of preventing the gentlemen from being wholly destroyed. They then, without further council, collected themselves in a body, and with no other arms than the staves shod with iron, which some had, and others with knives, marched to the house of a knight who lived near, and breaking it open, murdered the knight, his lady, and all the children, both great and small; they then burnt the house. . . . They had chosen a king among them, who came from Clermont in Beauvoisis: he was elected as the worst of the bad, and they denominated him James Goodman.[1]

They did the like to many castles and handsome houses; and their numbers increased so much, that they were in a short time upwards of six thousand: wherever they went, they received additions, for all of their rank in life followed them, whilst every one else fled, carrying off with them their ladies, damsels, and children, ten or twenty leagues distant, where they thought they could place them in security, leaving their houses, with all their riches in them.

These wicked people, without leader and without arms,

[1] Jacques Bon Homme.

plundered and burnt all the houses they came to, murdered every gentleman, and violated every lady and damsel they could find. He who committed the most atrocious actions, and such as no human creature would have imagined, was the most applauded, and considered as the greatest man among them. I dare not write the horrible and inconceivable atrocities they committed on the persons of the ladies. . . .

When the gentlemen of Beauvoisis, Corbie, Vermandois, and of the lands where these wretches were associated, saw to what lengths their madness had extended, they sent for succour to their friends in Flanders, Hainault, and Bohemia: from which places numbers soon came, and united themselves with the gentlemen of the country. They began therefore to kill and destroy these wretches wherever they met them, and hung them up by troops on the nearest trees. The king of Navarre even destroyed in one day, near Clermont in Beauvoisis, upwards of three thousand: but they were by this time so much increased in number, that had they been altogether, they would have amounted to more than one hundred thousand. When they were asked for what reason they acted so wickedly; they replied, they knew not, but they did so because they saw others do it; and they thought that by this means they should destroy all the nobles and gentlemen in the world. . . .

While these conferences were going forward, there happened in England great commotions among the lower ranks of the people, by which England was near ruined without resource. Never was a country in such jeopardy as this was at that period, and all through the too great comfort of the commonalty. Rebellion was stirred up, as it was formerly done in France by the Jacques Bons-hommes, who did much evil, and sore troubled the kingdom of France. It is marvellous from what a trifle this pestilence raged in England. In order that it may serve as an example to mankind, I will speak of all that was done, from the information I had at the time on the subject.

It is customary in England, as well as in several other countries, for the nobility to have great privileges over the commonalty, whom they keep in bondage; that is to say, they are bound by law and custom to plough the lands of gentlemen, to harvest the grain, to carry it home to the barn, to thrash and winnow it: they are also bound to harvest the hay and carry it home. All these services they are obliged to perform for their lords, and many more in England than in other countries. The prelates and gentlemen are thus served. In the counties of Kent, Essex, Sussex and Bedford, these services are more oppressive than in all the rest of the kingdom.

The evil-disposed in these districts began to rise, saying, they were too severely oppressed; that at the beginning of the world there were no slaves, and that no one ought to be treated as such, unless he had committed treason against his lord, as Lucifer had done against God: but they had done no such thing, for they were neither angels nor spirits, but men formed after the same likeness with their lords, who treated them as beasts. This they would not longer bear, but had determined to be free, and if they laboured or did any other works for their lords, they would be paid for it.

A crazy priest in the county of Kent, called John Ball, who, for his absurd preaching, had been thrice confined in the prison of the archbishop of Canterbury, was greatly instrumental in inflaming them with those ideas. He was accustomed, every Sunday after mass, as the people were coming out of the church, to preach to them in the market place and assemble a crowd around him; to whom he would say,—"My good friends, things cannot go on well in England, nor ever will until every thing shall be in common; when there shall neither be vassal nor lord, and all distinctions levelled; when the lords shall be no more masters than ourselves. How ill have they used us! and for what reason do they thus hold us in bondage? Are we not all descended from the same parents, Adam and Eve? and what can they show, or what reasons give, why they should be more the masters than ourselves? except, perhaps, in making us labour and work, for them to spend. They are clothed in velvets and rich stuffs, ornamented with ermine and other furs, while we are forced to wear poor cloth. They have wines, spices, and fine bread, when we have only rye and the refuse of the straw; and, if we drink, it must be water. They have handsome seats and manors, when we must brave the wind and rain in our labours in the field; but it is from our labour they have wherewith to support their pomp. We are called slaves; and, if we do not perform our services, we are beaten, and we have not any sovereign to whom we can complain, or who wishes to hear us and do us justice. Let us go to the king, who is young, and remonstrate with him on our servitude, telling him we must have it otherwise, or that we shall find a remedy for it ourselves. If we wait on him in a body, all those who come under the appellation of slaves, or are held in bondage, will follow us, in the hopes of being free. When the king shall see us, we shall obtain a favourable answer, or we must then seek ourselves to amend our condition." . . . Numbers in the city of London having heard of his preaching, being envious of the rich men and nobility, began to say among themselves, that the kingdom was too badly governed, and the nobility had seized on all the gold and silver coin. These wicked Londoners, therefore, began to assemble and to rebel: they sent to tell those in the adjoining counties, they might come boldly to London, and bring their companions with them, for they would find the town open to them, and the commonalty in the same way of thinking; that they would press the king so much, there should no longer be a slave in England.

These promises stirred up those in the counties of Kent, Essex, Sussex and Bedford, and the adjoining country, so that they marched towards London; and, when they arrived near, they were upwards of sixty thousand. They had a leader called Wat Tyler, and with him were Jack Straw and John Ball: these three were their commanders, but the principal was Wat Tyler. This Wat had been a tiler of houses, a bad man, and a great enemy to the nobility. When these wicked people first began to rise, all London, except their friends, were very much frightened. The mayor and rich citizens assembled in council, on hearing they were coming to London, and debated whether they should shut the gates and refuse to admit them; but, having well considered, they determined not to do so, as they should run a risk of having the suburbs burnt.

The gates were therefore thrown open, when they entered in troops of one or two hundred, by twenties or thirties, according to the populousness of the towns they came from; and as they came into London they lodged themselves. But it is a truth, that full two-thirds of these people knew not what they wanted, nor what they sought for: they followed one another like sheep, or like to the shepherds of old, who said they were going to conquer the Holy Land, and afterwards accomplished nothing.

64

THE FRANCISCAN VISION: UBERTINO DA CASALE, *THE TREE OF LIFE OF CHRIST CRUCIFIED*

1305

Ubertino da Casale, after 1298 leader of the radical "Spiritual" Franciscans, wrote The Tree of Life *on Mount Alverna during a period of enforced withdrawal from the world in 1305. He poured into his enigmatic treatise many of the strongest beliefs of the Spiritual faction—that Francis had been sent as another Jesus to save the world from corruption, that his true followers had to stand outside the institutionalized church, in opposition to it, and that Europe in the fourteenth century was on the threshold of a new and less materialistic era, foreshadowed by the gentle herald Francis.*

The pilgrim church was abounding, at the end of the fifth age of the world, in the asses of wantonness, the reptiles of avarice, and the vulgar beasts of pride, with her modest behavior totally befouled by all this, and also corroded by a hypocritical mass of heretical impiety. Then the jealous lovers of Jesus became angered at His vice-ridden spouse, inclining, as many of

SOURCE Translated from Ubertino da Casale, *Arbor Vite Crucifixe Iesu* (Venice: 1485; reprinted, Turin: Bottega d'Erasmo, 1961), 421–22, 424.

her numbers were, toward adulterers. Yet He did not restrain His mercy by His wrath, but sent down a final summons to the church of the fifth age, raising up in her midst men of the highest truth, annihilators of greed, exterminators of lust, refusers of honors, haters of duplicity, defenders of truth, aflame with love, restorers of honesty, and uniquely, beyond all others, imitators of Christ Jesus. . . . Among these, like another Elias and Enoch, Francis and Dominic shone with singular brightness—the former, cleansed with a seraphic coal, inflamed with heavenly ardor, seemed to set the whole world on fire; the latter, looming up like a cherub and protecting by the light of his wisdom and by the word of preaching, shone out the more clearly over the shadows of the world.

Wherefore now we undertake to treat of him whose stature is being especially assailed, who now and from the beginning showed forth the evangelical life more strongly amid the corruptors, and who, despite the attacks of sly masters, stood as an examplar of the highest poverty. For that reason we turn our attention to him, of whom alone it can be said that he was the sign of similitude to the life of Christ, in his searching after His behavior, his height of contemplation of Him, his lavishness of admiration for Him, and above all his privilege of being sealed with the wounds of His most sacred passion. For if we speak of his demeanor, who is able to tell with what emulation he sought to imitate the life of Christ, a life capable of suffering? For all his energy, both public and private, was bent toward this: that he should renew the desired and forgotten path of Christ in himself and others. And this was the singular privilege of that blessed Francis, that he was the first man worthy to give to the holy church the life of Jesus, carefully set out, and for all, in the form of a common and lasting order. . . .

And I heard from a solemn doctor of this order that brother Bonaventure, at that time General Minister, . . . in the presence of the aforementioned doctor, solemnly preached in the Chapter of Paris that he was certain and had been assured that blessed Francis was the angel of the sixth seal, and that the evangelist John referred literally to him and to his position and order. . . .

And to those brothers who persecuted him, [Francis] answered with a great wail, wondering why they were unwilling to undergo all things with deep humility—"O my brothers, O my brothers, you would steal from me victory over this world! For Christ sent me to conquer the world in profound subjection to all men, so that I might draw souls to Him by love, through the example of humility." And he added, "O my brothers, because you shall humble all men, you shall convert them, and those who impiously persecute you shall by your proven patience be converted to Christ, and they shall be satisfied who merely kiss the prints of your feet. . . ." Similarly he spoke to the brothers, desiring them to avoid all churchly ostentation, and to serve in humility. Because of this he called them minorites, that they might not presume to become men of major importance; and he did not want them to seek the status of prelates by any means.

65

WILLIAM OF OCKHAM, *WHETHER PRINCES MAY TAX THE GOODS OF THE CHURCH*

1338 – 39

The Franciscan William of Ockham (c. 1280–1349), began his career as a lecturer at Oxford from 1320 to 1324. He was then summoned to Avignon to answer charges of heresy. He was able, however, to escape and join forces with the Holy Roman Emperor, Louis of Bavaria, in the emperor's struggle against the papacy. William of Ockham wrote widely against papal power. Along with other Franciscan critics, he insisted that the church as a whole must embrace the Franciscan ideal of poverty. Such a disentanglement from worldly affairs, he felt, would lead to perfection in the spiritual life of churchmen. In this passage William argues that the church in any state should be subject to taxation by the king, particularly when the state is in danger; papal authority, he asserts, does not extend to temporal goods.

Whether a Prince, in Time of Need, that is, in Time of War,
can Take Back the Goods of the Church,
even against the Pope's Will

Having now shown that the pope does not have such plenitude of power as many attribute to him, it remains to be shown

SOURCE   Translated from *An Princeps Pro Suo Succursu, Scilicet Guerrae, Possit Recepere Bona Ecclesiarum, Etiam Invito Papae,* in *Guillelmi de Ockham Opera Politica,* ed. J. G. Sikes *et alii* (Manchester: Manchester University Press, 1940), Vol. I, 242, 255–57, 261.

that, despite any papal statute, prohibition or precept, sentence or order, those prelates and clerks subject to the English king are bound to aid him, even where the goods of the church are concerned, in his just war; secondly, that the pope cannot prohibit them from doing this by any statute, prohibition, precept, sentence or order. Above all, however, certain important points must be established. The first is that the prelates and clerics subject to the English king possess no temporal goods, particularly superfluous goods, by divine law, but by human law proceeding from the same king himself, which Augustine states explicitly in the first part, near the end of the sixth sermon, of his treatise on John, and as the decrees say. . . .

Therefore, all possessions, above all superfluous ones, which they have, have been donated to them by the king and by his subjects, so that they possess what they have by royal law. . . .

We have shown that clerics are bound to give the king a financial aid in his just war, even from their ecclesiastical goods. Now we must show that they are obliged to do this despite any papal statute, prohibition or precept, sentence or order, even if it comes from the supreme pontiff himself. To prove this it should be noted that the pope has no legal power over temporal goods, particularly not over superfluous goods, which have been donated by kings and other faithful members of the church by divine law, but solely by human law, if the givers should concede any power over them to him; for this reason whatever power the kings of England or those superior to them (or their single superior) gave to the pope concerning ecclesiastical property donated by them to the churches, the pope has this much power and no more. . . .

Not only does the judgment of the pope in the aforementioned case in no way bind the English clergy but, if a judgment were to be issued against the king himself, resulting from that which his law requires, even if it were to come from the highest pontiff, it would be wholly devoid of effect, nor would the king or any of his adherents be bound by it, unless perhaps they were burdened with a guilty conscience.

66

THE CONTROVERSY BETWEEN
THE PHILOSOPHERS AND THEOLOGIANS:
JOHN DUNS SCOTUS,
PROLOGUE TO THE *ORDINATIO*

c. 1304–1308

Duns Scotus (c. 1270–1308) studied and taught chiefly at Oxford until 1302, when he went to Paris and then to Cologne. It was while he was at Paris that the scholastic Ordinatio was written. In it, he denies the fundamental premise elaborated for over a century and a half by earlier scholastics: that theology and philosophy arrive at the same conclusions by different methods. By admitting that their viewpoints were irreconcilably different, Scotus destroyed the delicate balance between reason and faith that thinkers such as Thomas Aquinas had so painstakingly constructed, and expounded a radically different theology which was skeptical of intellectual knowledge and helped to encourage a return to irrational faith.

PART I. *The Necessity of Revealed Knowledge*
Does man in his present state need to be supernaturally inspired with some knowledge?

The question is raised whether man in his present state needs to be supernaturally inspired with some special knowledge he could not attain by the natural light of the intellect.

SOURCE From Allan Wolter, O.F.M., "Duns Scotus and the Necessity of Revealed Knowledge. Prologue to the *Ordinatio* of John Duns Scotus," *Franciscan Studies*, XI, Nos. 3–4 (Sept.–Dec. 1951), 241–45, 256–58.

That he needs none, I argue as follows: . . .

Furthermore, the sense needs no supernatural knowledge in its present state; therefore, neither does the intellect. The antecedent is evident. Proof of the consequence: "Nature leaves out nothing necessary" (*On the Soul*, III).[1] Now, if this is true of things that are imperfect, all the more does it hold for things that are perfect. Consequently, if the inferior faculties lack nothing necessary for their function and the attainment of their end, all the more is this true of the higher faculty. Therefore, etc. . . .

To the Contrary:

"All doctrine divinely inspired is useful for arguing. . . . etc." (Tim. 3).[2]

Furthermore, it is said of wisdom: "No one can know its way, but He who knows all things knows it." (Bar. 3).[3] Therefore, no other can have wisdom save from Him who knows all things. So much for the necessity of revelation. As to the fact thereof, he adds: "He [God] gave it to Jacob, His child, and to Israel, His beloved," referring to the Old Testament and the following: "After these things, He was seen on earth and talked with men," referring to the New Testament.

I. Controversy between the Philosophers and Theologians

In this question we are faced with the controversy between the philosophers and theologians. The philosophers insist on the perfection of nature and deny supernatural perfection. The theologians, on the other hand, recognize the deficiency of nature and the need of grace and supernatural perfection.

A. Opinion of the Philosophers

The philosophers, then, would say that no supernatural knowledge is necessary for man in his present state, but that all the knowledge he needs could be acquired by the action of

[1] Aristotle, *On the Soul*, III, ch. 9.
[2] II Timothy 3, 16.   [3] Baruch 3, 31.

natural causes. In support of this, they cite from various places both the authority and the reasoning of the Philosopher[4]. . . .

Furthermore, speculative science is divided into mathematics, physics and metaphysics according to the *Metaphysics*, VI.[5] And from the proof for this, which is given there, no other speculative science seems possible, since in these sciences the whole of being is considered, both in itself and in all its divisions. Now just as a speculative science other than these three would not be possible, neither is any practical science possible other than those acquired sciences that have to do with functional and productive activity. Consequently, practical acquired sciences suffice to perfect the practical intellect and speculative acquired sciences, the speculative intellect. . . .

Refutation of the Opinion of the Philosophers

Three arguments can be raised against this opinion. (Note:[6] By natural reason nothing supernatural can be shown to exist in the wayfarer, nor can it be proved that anything supernatural is necessarily required for his perfection. Neither can one who has something supernatural know it is in him. Here then it is impossible to use natural reason against Aristotle. If one argues from beliefs, it is no argument against a philosopher since the latter does not concede a premise taken on faith. Hence, these reasons which are here urged against him have as one premise something believed or proved from something believed. Therefore, they are nothing more than theological persuasions from beliefs to a belief.)

[First principal argument] The first way is this. Every agent who acts knowingly needs a distinct knowledge of his destiny or end. I prove this, because every agent acting for the sake of an end, acts from a desire of the end. Now everything that is an agent in virtue of itself acts for the sake of an end. Therefore, every such agent seeks its end in a way proper to itself. Just as an agent that acts by its nature must desire the end for

4 Aristotle. 5 *Meta.*, VI, ch. 1.
6 Marginal note added by Scotus.

which it must act, so also the agent that acts knowingly. For the latter is also an agent in virtue of itself, according to the second book of the *Physics*.[7] The major then is clear.

But man can have no definite knowledge of his end from what is natural; therefore, he needs some supernatural knowledge thereof. . . .

[Fourth principal reason] A fourth argument is this. Whatever is ordered to some end towards which it is not disposed, must be gradually disposed for this end. Man is ordered to a supernatural end towards which he is of himself indisposed. Therefore he needs to be gradually disposed to possess this end. This takes place by reason of some imperfect supernatural knowledge, which is maintained to be necessary. Therefore, etc. . . .

Objection to the opinion of the Theologians

That no such knowledge, however, is necessary for salvation, I prove: Let us assume that someone is not baptized. When he grows up, he has no one to teach him. The affections [of his will] such as he is capable of, are good and in accord with what his natural reason tells him is right. What reason reveals to him as evil, he avoids.

Although God could visit such a one, teaching him the common law by man or angel even as He visited Cornelius, still let us assume that such an individual is taught by no one. Nevertheless he will be saved. . . .

[Reply] It could be said that such an individual, by willing what is good in general, merits *de congruo*[8] to be justified from original sin, and God does not deprive such a one of this gift of His liberality. Hence, He gives him the first grace without using the sacrament, because God is not constrained to make use of the sacraments. But grace is not [ordinarily] given with-

[7] *Physics*, II, ch. 5.

[8] Theologians distinguish between that which merits a reward *de condigo* viz. in strict justice, and that which merits it *de congruo*, strict obligation in justice.

out the habit of faith. Hence, such an individual actually possesses the habit of theology, even though this habit could not
be reduced to act. . . .

67

BERNARD GUI, *THE INQUISITOR'S HANDBOOK*

c. 1321

*The expansion of heretical sects such as the Waldensians, Hu-
miliati and Cathars during the twelfth century provoked the
church to reorganize the means of suppressing heresy. In 1233
Pope Gregory IX founded the papal Inquisition. The Order of
Preachers, or Dominicans, which had been founded with the
goal in mind of winning back the heretics through persuasive
argument, continued this task as leaders of the Inquisition. One
of their number, Bernard Gui (c. 1261–1331), became an inquisitor in 1307; his manual provides excellent information on
the inquisitorial process, as well as on the beliefs of heretical
groups, most of whose own writings were destroyed. Much of
the manual consists of a series of formulas for documents, with
the names left blank to be filled in at need.*

SOURCE Translated from Bernardus Guidenis, *Practica Inquisi-
tionis Heretice Pravitatis,* ed. C. Douais (Paris: A. Picard, 1886),
1, 5, 150, 209, 235–37, 240.

The first part of the treatise follows in which the various forms of letters of summons or of seizure of persons guilty or suspected of the crime of heresy are collected, according to the variety, diversity or quality of the guilt and of the faults. . . .

1. *General form of summons*

Brother Bernard Gui, of the order of Preachers, inquisitor into heretical perversity in the kingdom of France, deputy of the apostolic see, to the chaplain of such and such a church or to him who holds his place, greeting in the name of the author of faith, Lord Jesus Christ. By the aforesaid apostolic authority in the name of which we act, we order you to summon on our behalf your parishioner _____ to appear on such a day in person before us in the house of inquisition near the town of Narbonne, at Toulouse, to answer the full truth concerning those things which pertain to faith and to the office of the inquisition entrusted to us, in the matter and cause of faith, and to do whatever else shall seem needful. Return this letter by the bearer with your seal added to it (or thus: and, as a sign of your reception and fulfillment of our command with your seal appended to it). Given at Toulouse, under our seal, on the Kalends of April, in the year of the Lord 1315. . . .

Form of a letter for arresting anyone defamed as a heretic, or suspected.

Brother Bernard Gui of the order of Preachers, to the bailiff of _____ or to him who holds his place, and to all others holding rights of jurisdiction, power, or office of rule on behalf of our lord the king of France, or of any other lords whatever, who were sufficient (or thus: to whom this letter shall come) greeting, in the name of the author of faith Lord Jesus Christ. By the apostolic authority in the name of which we act, and on behalf of our lord the king of France, we require and order you (and your underlings, whosoever they be) on our behalf to seize _____ of _____, and bear him as a captive to _____ messenger of our (or, to _____ notary of ours, or, to _____ castle sentry of the inquisitor of Toulouse), the bearer of these presents, whom we sent especially for this purpose, [and we order you] through him to bring [the accused] to us under the guard of loyal and faithful men, to answer us truthfully concerning [his] faith and concerning those things which pertain to faith and to the office of inquisition entrusted to us, in the matter and cause of faith. . . . (And so on for all similar circumstances and cases. . . .)

Form of a sentence of degradation and imprisonment against any mischievous religious or presbyter, fortuneteller or idolator, who sacrificed to demons, and who ought to have been degraded and imprisoned for that, since the aforesaid charges, together with the greatest profanation or sacrifice made to demons, involve error and are, because of their nature and the manner of doing them, manifestly heretical.

In the name of the Lord, Amen. We, _____, by God's grace bishop of _____, when recently we heard that brother _____ of _____ order or _____ presbyter of _____, in _____ perpetrated certain mischievous deeds, both fortunetelling, necromancy, devil worship and several other detestable acts, which seemed to constitute error and heresy against the doctrine of the faith, and which were said to spot the purity of the faith in that district or vicinity. A diligent inquisition having been made against the same brother _____ (or presbyter)—and the oaths of witnesses having been received in a trial in our presence—we had the same brother (or presbyter) seized and brought into our presence, in order to question him and find out the truth more certainly concerning the things mentioned above, and related matters. And in that tribunal held in our presence, having received there from the accused an oath to tell the full and simple truth in all the matters of inquisition in the cause of the faith and for the sake of its purity; when many questions had been asked of him, at last through the investigation we made, and also by the confession of the same brother (or presbyter) made in the court, we judged and are legitimately resolved that the same brother _____ (or presbyter) did, etc. (in this place the sins, extracted from his confession, are described and summarized again one by one).

Moreover, the said brother _____ (or presbyter), detected in the act of performing those crimes, was unwilling from the beginning to confess to them of his own accord, and, when he was called before the tribunal, he denied the truth many times against his own oath: for example, he deceitfully changed the account of his crime many times in the confessions made before the tribunal in our presence. . . .

It follows from the first two subjects—namely, the commission of the office of the inquisition and its power—that we must now treat thirdly of its execution. Here two matters arise: the first is the freedom to carry out his office unimpeded, by which freedom every obstacle is removed; the second is the due form of proceeding toward the act and exercise by which he arrives at his intended end.

As to the first, it ought to be recognized that the carrying out of the office of the inquisition is free and unimpeded in five ways particularly: first, because inquisitors have no impediment from superiors who supervise them, as they are prelates; second, they have none from inferiors against whom they take action; third, they have none from officials or ministers by virtue of whose authority they act; fourth, they have none from the witnesses they call; fifth, they have none from any other contingencies which might arise or occur. . . .

The fifth and last part of the treatise follows, which deals with the method, technique and skill of questioning and examining heretics, believers and their associates, so that the deceptions, tricks and wiles which some of them hide behind can more subtly be detected in one's own questioning of single suspects (Manicheans, Waldensians, Poor Men of Lyons, or those of the sect of False-Apostles who exploit the name of apostles of Christ though they are rather apostles of Antichrist, and those others of the pestiferous sect which has appeared recently who simulate perfect evangelical poverty—though they have not assimilated it —and call themselves the paupers of Christ, claiming to be of the Third Order or the Third Rule of St. Francis, which Third Order is commonly called Beguines in the vernacular) and [this section shows how to deal] no less with those who, having converted from the perfidy of the Jews to the faith of Christ, afterward returned to the vomit of Judaism. Finally it touches on the plague or pestiferous error of fortunetelling, divination and the invocation of demons and other matters, and also the various and proper methods of abjuring heresy in the tribunal are described.

GENERAL PROCEDURE

When anyone is being given a hearing, or is under examination, whether he came of his own volition, or was summoned, whether he was called into question as a suspect, or denoted, or defamed, or even accused of the crime of heresy, or of abetting heresy, or of receiving heretics, or of committing other acts which are under the jurisdiction of the office of inquisition into heretical perversity or contingent to it in any way, he shall be examined and heard out: the inquisitor (or his substitute) first of all having questioned and warned him gently and modestly, he swears on the bible to tell the full and simple truth, acting as a witness, and about the instance of heresy and anything to do with it, and about anything pertaining to the office of inquisition in any way, either concerning himself, as prime instigator, or concerning other persons living or dead. When he has sworn, he is urged and exhorted to volunteer the truth of whatever he knows or knew or heard about the instance of heresy. If, moreover, he should request time to deliberate so that he could give a more considered answer, it may be granted him, if it seems expedient to the inquisitor, especially if he seems to ask it honestly, not out of trickery; otherwise, he is asked to reply immediately about his own acts. Afterward the date of his appearance is to be registered by a public notary, this way: the year, the Kalends, _____, or _____ town or village, _____ diocese, coming willingly, or having been summoned, or called into question as a suspect; appearing before a tribunal constituted in the presence of that man of religion N., inquisitor into heretical perversity in the kingdom of France, commissioned by the apostolic see, swore on the bible to tell the full and simple truth, as a witness, about the instance or the crime of heresy and all things relating to it, either concerning himself, as prime instigator, or concerning other persons living or dead; he testified and was confessed, etc.

It must be noted, though, that if anyone disputes openly and manifestly against the faith, bringing in reasons and authorities on which heretics are accustomed to rely, such a one would easily be proven heretical by the learned men of the church, since he already perceives himself to be heretical in that he relies on error to defend himself. But since modern heretics seek and strive to palliate their errors in secret, rather than to confess them openly, the learned men cannot prove them wrong through their knowledge of the scriptures, because they slip out by means of verbal trickeries and astute logical contrivances; and because of this, the learned men are more often bested by them, and the heretics, glorying in this, are strengthened all the more, seeing that they can mock the learned men thus, and then cleverly hide from them by their sly tricks, stratagems and tortuous circumlocutions. For nothing is worse than to capture heretics who will not openly confess their error but disguise it, or who cannot be convicted by certain and sufficient testimony, in which case the questioner is attacked by difficulties on all sides: his conscience tortures him, on the one hand, if he punishes a man who has neither confessed nor been convicted; on the other hand, his mind tortures him even more, instructed as it is, through frequent experience, in the falsity, subtlety and malice of such men, if they, because of their foxy cleverness turn out to be an injury to the faith, because from this they are strengthened and multiplied and made even more clever. What is more, lay Christians take from this sort of incident matter for scandal, if once an inquisitorial process has been begun against someone, it is broken off amid some embarrassment: and they are in a sense weakened in their faith when they observe learned men being made the sport of rustics and villagers. For the laity believe us to have at hand lucid and obvious explanations of dogma, so that no one could argue against us without our knowing at once how to convince him, in such a way that even the laymen themselves could clearly understand the explanations; and for that reason it is better in those cases not to dispute with such astute heretics concerning the faith in the presence of laymen. . . .

OF THE ERRORS OF THE MODERN MANICHEANS

The sect and heresy of the Manicheans, and its erroneous followers, assert and admit that there are two Gods or two Lords, that is, Gods of good and evil, maintaining that all visible and corporeal things were not made by God the heavenly father, whom they call the God of good, but by the devil and Satan, a maleficent God, since they call him the God of evil and the God of this temporal sphere and prince of this world; and in this way they assert two creators, God and the devil, and two creations, one of invisible and incorporeal things, the other of visible and corporeal things. . . .

Also, they never eat or even touch meat, nor do they eat cheese or eggs, nor anything which is born of the flesh by way of generation or conception. Also, they do not kill any animal or bird, since they maintain and believe that the spirits of those who have died, and have not been received into their sect and order by the laying on of hands according to their ritual, are present in brute animals and even in birds, and [they believe] that those spirits pass from one body into another. Also, they do not touch women. Also, at the beginning of a meal, whether they are among Believers or among others of their own kind, they bless a loaf or a portion of a loaf, holding the loaf in their hands with a towel or some other white cloth hanging from their neck, saying the paternoster and breaking the loaf into little pieces; and this bread they call the bread of holy prayer and the broken bread; and the True Believers call it blessed bread or marked bread, and they eat of it as a communion at the beginning of the meal and distribute it also to the Believers. . . . They preach that to die an evil death is to die in the faith of the Roman Church; a good death, "in the hands of the faithful of Christ," they say is to be received, on one's deathbed, into their sect and order, following their ritual; and this they say is a good end. The reverence mentioned above [genuflection to the *perfecti*] they say is made not to them but to the Holy Spirit, whom they maintain is within them, and by whom they are received into their sect and order.

68

_____

MARSILIUS OF PADUA, *THE DEFENDER OF PEACE*

1324

The extravagant claims to power in worldly affairs made by Boniface VIII and John XXII were anachronistic in the early fourteenth century, when both governments and their citizens

SOURCE From Marsilius of Padua, *The Defender of Peace*, Vol. II, trans. by Alan Gewirth, Columbia University Records of Civilization, XLVI (New York: Columbia University Press, 1956), 426–29.

were developing a growing consciousness of their own inde-
pendence. By far the most extreme opponent of papal power
was Marsilius of Padua (c. 1275–1342), whose thoughts on
government and political theory have a strikingly modern tone.
He was rector of the University of Paris, where The Defender
of Peace was written in 1324. Following the discovery of his
writings in 1326 he was forced to flee to Germany, where, like
Ockham, he joined the court of Louis of Bavaria, and quickly
became the most forceful imperial propagandist in Louis' employ.

*In which are Explicitly Inferred Certain Conclusions
which Follow Necessarily from the Results Set Forth
in the First Two Discourses. By Heeding These Conclusions,
Rulers and Subjects Can More Easily
Attain the End aimed at by this Book*

Of the conclusions to be inferred, we shall place this one first:

1. For the attainment of eternal beatitude it is necessary to
believe in the truth of only the divine or canonic Scripture, together with its necessary consequences and the interpretations
of it made by the common council of the believers. . . .

2. Doubtful sentences of divine law, especially on those matters which are called articles of the Christian faith . . . must be
defined only by the general council of the believers, or by the
weightier multitude or part thereof; no partial group or individual person . . . has the authority to make such defini-
tions. . . .

6. Only the whole body of citizens, or the weightier part
thereof, is the human legislator. . . .

7. The decretals or decrees of the Roman or any other pontiffs, collectively or distributively, made without the grant of the
human legislator, bind no one to temporal pain or punishment. . . .

10. The election of any elective ruler or other official, especially if such office carries coercive force, depends upon the
expressed will of the legislator alone. . . .

14. A bishop or priest, as such, has no rulership or coercive jurisdiction over any clergyman or layman, even if the latter be a heretic. . . .

17. All bishops are of equal authority immediately through Christ, nor can it be proved by divine law that there is any superiority or subjection among them in spiritual or in temporal affairs. . . .

32. Only the general council of all the faithful has the authority to designate a bishop or any metropolitan church highest of all. . . .

69

MYSTICAL RELIGION:
JOHN TAULER

SERMON FOR THE SECOND SUNDAY
AFTER THE EPIPHANY

THE BOOK OF THE POOR IN SPIRIT
BY A FRIEND OF GOD

The Dominican John Tauler (c. 1300–1361) is among the most important of the Rhineland mystics of the fourteenth century. His writings were in many ways a direct response to the laity's need for a deeper spirituality; much of his time was spent as preacher and chaplain to nuns in Strasbourg. He wrote in German and much of his work is as concerned with practical ad-

SOURCE From John Tauler, *Sermon for the Second Sunday After the Epiphany, The Sermons and Conferences of John Tauler,* trans. by Walter Elliott (Apostolic Mission House, Brookland Station, Washington, D.C., n.d.), 124, 126–27.

282

vice on leading a Christian life in the world as it is with his own mystical speculation. When reading Tauler it should be remembered that mystical language is often allegorical; Tauler uses the most concrete terms to describe the most intangible of experiences.

SERMON FOR THE SECOND SUNDAY
AFTER THE EPIPHANY

c. 1350

"And on the last and great day of the festivity, Jesus stood and cried: If any man thirst, let him come to Me and drink." John vii, 37.

What is the thirst of which our Lord Jesus Christ here speaks? Nothing else but this: When the Holy Ghost enters a soul, that soul feels a fire of love; indeed, a very conflagration of love burns in that soul, causing a fiery thirst after God; that is to say, an interior longing to possess Him. And it often happens that such a soul is mystified and cannot account for its condition, knowing only that it suffers interior emptiness and anguish, and that it loathes all created things.

Three kinds of men experience this thirst, and each kind differently, one kind being beginners, the second those who are making some progress, and the third are perfect, as far as may be in this life. King David says: "As the hart panteth after the fountains of water, so my soul panteth after Thee, O God!" (Ps. xli, 1). When the hart is driven by the hounds through forests and over mountains, he is burnt with a consuming thirst and longs for water more than any other kind of animal. Now, beginners in the spiritual life, much more than any other class, are pursued by heavy trials and temptations, and they are like the hart hunted by hounds. . . .

And now that the hart has shaken off and distanced all the hounds, he comes to a clear stream of water; he joyfully plunges down into it and drinks all he wants and is fully refreshed. So it is with the soul at the waters of Divine consolation. When, without Lord's help, he has driven off his temptations and at last comes to God with all confidence, what shall he do but drink deep of God's love and joy? And then he is so filled with God, that in his happiness and peace he forgets himself and thinks that he can work great miracles; he is ready joyously to go through fire and water for God, and to face a thousand drawn swords; he fears neither life nor death, neither pleasure nor pain. And so it would seem that he is intoxicated with God's love.

This is the joy of jubilee. Sometimes such a one weeps for joy; sometimes he laughs, and again he sings. Men about him, whose only guide is natural reason, cannot understand all this, knowing nothing of the wonderful ways of the Holy Spirit with elect souls. Look at this strange conduct, they exclaim; and they at once sit in judgment upon these chosen spirits and harshly condemn them. But meantime these enjoy unspeakable happiness; happiness comes to them from everything that occurs. Do what you please to them, visit them with good or evil, it is all one. They rest wholly unconcerned, free and contented. Whatever happens without, the joy of God glows bright within them, a delicious thirst for God rules their souls without intermission, and is as constantly gratified. Some of them die of jubilation, their hearts quite overcome with love for our Lord. For, dear children, it is a mark of God's greatest work in their souls, that they can no longer endure its bliss and live in the body. Many a one of these favored men has yielded up with such entire abandonment to this wonderful visitation of God, that poor, weak human nature has given way and death has followed.

Dear children, when our Lord sees men thus intoxicated with His spiritual gifts, He acts like a prudent father of a family, whose children, taking advantage of their father's being in bed asleep, go down into his cellar and drink to excess the good wine he has stored there. When the father wakes up and sees what has happened, he goes out and cuts a good, strong switch, and he comes and gives his children a severe whipping, and afterwards he gives them nothing but water to drink till they are perfectly sobered again. So does God deal with His chosen ones. While they drink to excess the delights of His love, He is, as it were, asleep. But presently he punishes them by withdrawing the strong, sweet wine of His joy, for their want of moderation has hindered its benefiting them. . . .

THE BOOK OF THE POOR IN SPIRIT
BY A FRIEND OF GOD

1350

The author of this work was, like Tauler, a member of the Rhineland school of mystics. Written around 1350, it ranks among the best works of this school and contains its essential thoughts. The author was a Dominican, but beyond this fact it is difficult to say anything definite about him. The expression "Friend of God" was often used to denote one who practiced a spiritual rather than formalistic religion. It could also indicate, however, that the author belonged to an actual group called by that name, set apart from all others by their unique relationship with God. The author of The Book of the Poor in Spirit *advocates what was a common program for mystics in the fourteenth century; abandonment of material things and of reason, withdrawal into the self, and then a "violent" search for union with God.*

CHAPTER I: *True Spiritual Poverty is Detachment*

Spiritual poverty is a God-likeness. What is God? God is a being detached from all creatures. He is a free power, a pure act. In the same way spiritual poverty is a state of being detached

SOURCE From *The Book of the Poor in Spirit by a Friend of God*, C. F. Kelly (London and New York: Longmans, Green & Co., 1954), 53, 54, 59.

from all creatures. And what is detachment? That which clings to nothing. Spiritual poverty clings to nothing and nothing to it. . . .

Detachment from all that is Creaturely

What use, then, is it for one to have in himself a reasonable discernment in images and forms, if it will not bless him? Further, if he must become wanting in the power to reason, shall he then become poor? I answer that reason is useful as long as man has not yet attained true spiritual poverty; as long as he is weighed down with multiplicity, so must he make use of this power of discernment. Thus is it useful and must not be discarded. But when a man comes to the point where he is made simple and stripped of multiplicity, and hence attains genuine poverty, he then must forsake all discernment through images and transfer himself with One into One, without any unlikeness.

If a man remained on the level of discernment, he would make many mistakes and would not be really poor. Also this power of reason is useful since in this way only can man be taught. Thirdly, since man is in time, he must be active in time in accordance with the outer man. Hence, in order that man may not altogether remain in time and that the outer man may be properly subordinated to the inner, a reasonable discernment is needed. . . .

CHAPTER II: *True Spiritual Poverty is Freedom*

Freedom is a perfect purity and detachment which seeks the Eternal. Freedom is a withdrawn and separated being, similar to God or wholly attached to God. Now spiritual poverty is also an isolated condition, apart from creatures, and in this sense it is free. A free soul sets aside all feeble and created things and penetrates into the uncreated good—God. And this she attains by violence, as Christ says: "The kingdom of heaven suffereth violence, and the violent bear it away." To the soul, God is the kingdom of heaven; hence, when she withdraws from all things and adheres only to God, she attains God by violence. . . .

70

MINNESINGER POETRY:
THE SONGS OF PRINCE WIZLAW OF RÜGEN

c. 1285–1325

Wizlaw (ca. 1265) was prince of the Baltic island kingdom of Rügen. The Minnesänger were wandering minstrels who sang of the courtly ideals of passion, sacrifice and devotion to the Virgin or some unattainable lady. Although Wizlaw's poetry was written late in the Minnesinger tradition, it still contains an excellent expression of the ideals of Germanic chivalry.

> Mary, thy humility
> brought a great reward to thee
> when the angel Gabriel
>   cried, 'Ave, blessed Mary!'
> And thy virtue was so great
> that thou didst not hesitate,
> but replied, 'God's will be done.'

SOURCE From *The Songs of the Minnesinger Prince Wizlaw of Rügen*, trans. by Wesley Thomas and Barbara Garvey Seagrave. University of North Carolina Studies in the Germanic Languages and Literatures, No. 59 (Chapel Hill: University of North Carolina Press, 1967), 101–2, 109–10.

The angel did not tarry.
Thou, undefiled,
didst bear a child.
God's son, divine and stainless,
appeared on earth;
his human birth
was laborless and painless.
Thus, Virgin, was thy infant born,
whom we did crucify with scorn,
who suffered for our sins and died
    to give us sanctuary. . . .

'Whate'er befalls me, small or great,
was meant to be and is my fate.'
This saying causes many men
    to reach a false conclusion.
'Twas meant to be' and 'Fate' are fools
and those who hear them are their tools,
but, though they spread throughout the world
    much sorrow and confusion,
they can't be harmed,
their lives are charmed,
for all they take the credit.
This should not be,
give ear to me;
no one has ever read it
in any book, of this I'm sure.
How can these fools be so secure
when they deceive the people thus
    with lies and self-delusion?

71

_____

LITURGICAL DRAMA: *THE THREE MARYS*
fourteenth century

The Three Marys, *taken from a fourteenth-century manuscript
in the French monastery of D'Origny Sainte-Benoîte, was a
popular play celebrating the resurrection of Jesus. Its origin was
a tenth-century addition to the Easter Mass in which the angel
guarding the sepulcher announced to the three Marys that Jesus
was no longer there; by the fourteenth century this simple addition to the mass had been lifted out of the service to become the
core of a lengthy drama with spoken dialogue, interspersed with
secular songs and characters such as the unguent seller. The
mixture of sacred and secular elements in the liturgical drama
is typical of much of late medieval popular culture.*

Mary Magdalene and the other Mary, at the break of day,
bore spices to the tomb, seeking their Lord where He lay. . . .

The Three Marys:
    Let us go out, then, and buy
    Oils to anoint the lovely body.
    In him was true health and true love.
       Alas! we'll see him no more!

SOURCE Translated from E. de Coussemaker, *Drames Liturgiques
du Moyen Âge* (Paris: Librairie Archéologique de Victor Didron,
1861), 271–73, 275, 277–79.

Here Mary Magdalene remains behind, and the other two Marys approach the merchant. The merchant says:

Come nearer, you who love so well.
There is unguent here, if you wish to buy it.
With it you can anoint our Lord,
His holy body which you sacredly attend.

In the same place the Two Marys say:

Tell us, good, true and loyal merchant,
The unguent you wish to sell us—
What price have you in mind?
    Alas! we'll never see him again!

The Merchant says:

This ointment moves you to greedy desire
You'll give me five besants of gold for this
Or I didn't bring it.

The Two Marys:

Alas! we'll never see him again!

The Merchant says:

I have another very fine ointment,
It's yours for just a talent;
Much more dear than the others.

The Two Marys:

Gentle Merchant, we want your best,
The more you charge, the more we want it.
To anoint our great Lord from heaven we want it.

The Merchant says:

You have spoken well, valiant ladies,
I'll give it to you for two good besants
For the Lord you adore so.

The Two Marys:

Wise Merchant, we ask you for God's sake
That you sell us enough of the very finest
That he who is all Good may bear a good odor.
    Alas!

The Merchant says:

Take this, the age knows none better:

You can anoint your very great Lord.
Ask his mercy, good women, for me. . . .
Here the angels should arrange themselves around the sepulcher,
some at the head, the others at the foot, dressed in white vestments; and they should chant together:

O thou Christians, whom do you seek, sorrowing thus?
And whom do you desire to anoint with holy oils? . . .
These words our Lord sings to Mary Magdalene but Mary
doesn't see him at all:

Woman, why weep ye? Whom seek ye?
Mary Magdalene bows down and says:

O Sir, if you have taken him away, tell me where you
    have lain him:
Alleluia! And I will take him again. Alleluia!
Our Lord says: Mary!
Mary Magdalene says, at the feet of our Lord:
    Rabboni! . . .
The Three Marys say:
    To his tomb we came, weeping,
    We saw an angel of God sitting there,
    And saying that Jesus was risen. . . .
    We know Christ is indeed risen from the dead,
    Have mercy on us, conqueror King!

72

THE ROMANCE OF THE ROSE

1230 – c. 1300

The Romance of the Rose spans the thirteenth century both chronologically and culturally. Begun in 1230 by Guillaume de Lorris and completed late in the century by Jean de Meun (d. 1305), it was, among other things, a romance, an allegory of the psychology of courtly love, and a compendium of learned treatises on various subjects; as such it was intended to be read and enjoyed on many levels.

When I the age of twenty had attained—
The age when Love controls a young man's heart—
As I was wont, one night I went to bed
And soundly slept. But then there came a dream
Which much delighted me, it was so sweet.
No single thing which in that dream appeared
Has failed to find fulfillment in my life,
With which the vision well may be compared.
Now I'll recount this dream in verse, to make
Your hearts more gay, as Love commands and wills;

SOURCE From *The Romance of the Rose* by Guillaume de Lorris and Jean de Meun. Trans. by Harry W. Robbins, ed. Charles W. Dunn, 3–5, 35, 40, 64, 67, 169–71, 210, 334, 337, 440–41, 462, 464. Eng. trans. copyright © 1962, by Florence L. Robbins. Copyright © 1962, by E. P. Dutton & Co., Inc. Reprinted with permission of the publishers.

And if a man or maid shall ever ask
By what name I would christen the romance
Which now I start, I will this answer make:
"*The Romance of the Rose* it is, and it enfolds
Within its compass all the Art of Love.". . .
    Five years or more have passed by now, I think,
Since in that month of May I dreamed this dream—
In that month amorous, that time of joy,
When all things living seem to take delight,
When one sees leafless neither bush nor hedge,
But each new raiment dons, when forest trees
Achieve fresh verdure, though they dry have been
While winter yet endured, when prideful Earth,
Forgetting all her winter poverty
Now that again she bathes herself in dew,
Exults to have a new-spun, gorgeous dress;
A hundred well-matched hues its fabric shows
In new-green grass, and flowers blue and white
And many divers colors justly prized.
The birds, long silent while the cold remained—
While changeful weather brought on winter storms—
Are glad in May because of skies serene,
And they perforce express their joyful hearts
By utterance of fitting minstrelsy. . . .
When I'd advanced a space along the bank,
I saw a garden, large and fair, enclosed
With battlemented wall, sculptured without
With many a figure and inscription neat. . . .
The God of love, who, ever with bent bow
Had taken care to watch and follow me,
Beneath a fig tree lastly took his stand;
And when he saw that I had fixed my choice
Upon the bud that pleased me most of all
He quickly chose an arrow; notching it,
He pulled the cord back to his ear. The bow
Was marvelously strong, and good his aim,

And when he shot at me the arrow pierced
My very heart, though entering by my eye.
Then such a chill seized me that since that day
I oft, remembering it, have quaked again
Beneath a doublet warm. Down to the ground
I fell supine; thus struck, my heart stopped dead;
It failed me, and I fainted quite away.
Long time I lay recovering from my swoon,
And when I gained my senses and my wits
I still was feeble, and supposed I'd lost
Great store of blood, but was surprised to find
The dart that pierced me drew no drop of gore;
The wound was dry. With both my hands I tried
To draw the arrow, though it made me groan,
And finally the feathered shaft came out.
But still the golden barb named Beauty stayed
Fixed in my heart, never to be removed.
I feel it yet, although I do not bleed. . . .
    At that, with clasped hands I became his man.
Most proud was I when his lips touched my mouth;
That was the act which gave me greatest joy. . . .
Long time I lingered near the place, distraught,
Till Reason from her observation tower,
On which she scans the country all about,
Came forth, approaching nigh to where I stood.
She's not too young or old, too tall or short,
Too fat or lean. Her eyes like two stars shone.
She wore a noble crown upon her head.
A queen she might have been, but more did seem,
To judge by her appearance and her face,
An angel come, perhaps, from Paradise.
Nature could hardly frame a work so fair.
'Twas God himself, unless the Scriptures lie,
Who in his image and his likeness formed
This godlike one, and her with power endowed
To rescue men from rash and foolish acts.

Provided that her counsel they'll believe.
Reason addressed me as I madly wept:
"Fair friend, your youth and folly brought this pain
And this dismay, when on an ill-omened day
You yielded to the springtime's pleasant spell
Which so bewitched your heart. 'Twas evil hour
At which you came into that shady park
Of which the key is kept by Idleness.
Who ope'd the gate for you. One is a fool
Who makes acquaintance with that tempting maid.
Whose sweet companionship is perilous.
You've been deceived and brought to grief by her;
For had not Idleness conducted you
Into the garden that is named Delight
The God of Love had never seen you there.
Recover from your foolishness at once—
For foolishly you've acted—be on guard
That never more such counsel you accept,
By which you have been made to act the sot.
Unwise is he who would chastise himself!
But 'tis no wonder; men are fools in youth.
Now I should like to give you this advice:
Into oblivion consign that god
Who has so weakened, tortured, conquered you.
I see no other way to healthful cure;
For felon Danger lies in wait for you,
And you should wish to test his might no more.
Yet Danger's not to be compared with Shame,
My daughter, who the blooms defends and guards,
Aided by Fear, who surely is no fool,
But one whom all most surely should beware.
With these is Evil Tongue, who none permits
To touch the roses. . . .
Writings that emphasize degeneracy
Prove that in our first parents' early days
Loyal and true was love—not mercenary.

Most precious was that glorious Golden Age!
Men were not greedy for fine clothes or food.
They gathered acorns in the woods for bread;
In place of fish and flesh, they searched the glades,
Thickets, hills, and plains for fruits and nuts:
Apples and pears, chestnuts and mulberries,
Sloes and the seed pods of the eglantine,
Red strawberries, and blackberries and haws.
As vegetables, peas and beans and herbs
And roots they had. They gathered heads of grain.
The grapes that grew upon the fields they picked,
Nor put them in the wine press or the vat.
Abundantly on honey they could feast;
It fairly dripped from stores within the oaks.
No claret or spiced honey wine they drank
Nor any mixture—only water pure.

    "No plowing was then needed by the soil,
But by God's care it foisoned by itself,
Providing all the comforts that men wished.
They ate no pike or salmon; and they wore
But shaggy skins, or made their clothes of wool
Just as it came from off the backs of sheep.
Nor did they dye it scarlet, green or blue.
The cottages grouped in their villages
Were roofed with broom or branches, or with leaves;
Or else they made their homes in earthly caves.
Sometimes they refuge took among the rocks
Or in the hollow trunks of mighty trees,
When tempests made them fear the stormy blasts
And warned them that for safety they must flee.
At evening when they wished to go to sleep
In place of beds they brought into their homes
Great heaps of moss or leaves, or sheaves of grass.

    "Whene'er as if 'twere everlasting spring
The wind had been appeased, and soft and sweet
The weather had become, with pleasant breeze,

So that each morning every bird essayed
In his own language to salute the dawn,
All this inspired their hearts with joyous love. . . .
Nor yet had king or prince brought despotism
To pinch and rob the folk. All equals were.
Not yet for private property they strove.
Well did they know this saying is no lie
Or foolishness: 'There's no companionship
'Twixt Love and Seignory.' Whom Love unites
Either's supremacy will quickly separate." . . .
The God of Love, awaiting neither time
Nor fitting place, summoned his baronage
By letters begging or commanding them
To meet in parliament. They all appeared
Without excuse, ready to do his will
As each was able. I will name them all
Disorderly, as best befits my verse.
    Dame Idleness, the garden keeper came
Beneath the biggest banner; Noble Heart
Came next with Wealth and Franchise and Largesse,
Hardihood, Pity, Honor, Courtesy,
Gladness, Simplicity, Companionship,
Youth, Mirth, Security, and Fond Delight,
Humility and Patience, Jollity,
Hidewell and Beauty and Forced Abstinence,
Who led False Seeming, who'd not come alone.
These were the chieftains who their forces led
With willing hearts. . . .
Venus her meinie summoned, then gave word
Her chariot to prepare, for in the mud
She would not go afoot. Her car was bright,
Rolling on four gold wheels begemmed with pearls.
In place of collared horses, six fair doves
She chose from out her dovecots for the shafts.
    All things are ready, so she mounts her car
And starts to wage her war with Chastity. . . .

Then did Dame Venus tuck her skirts up high
And like an angry woman seize her bow
And cock the shaft, well fitted at the notch,
Drawing the bowstring backward to her ear
(The arrow was not more than fathom long!)
And like a skillful archeress take aim,
Pointing it at a loophole in the tower
That Nature had with cunning workmanship
Seated between two columns, visible
In front, indeed, but not on either side. . . .
Tormented by my labors, I approached
So near the rose tree that I could at will
Lay hands upon her limbs to pluck the bud.
Fair Welcome begged me, for the love of God,
That no outrageous act I should perform,
And to his frequent prayers I gave assent
And made a covenant with him that I
Would nothing do beyond what he might wish.
   I seized the rose tree by her tender limbs
That are more lithe than any willow bough,
And pulled her close to me with my two hands,
Most gently, that I might avoid the thorns,
I set myself to loosen that sweet bud
That scarcely without shaking could be plucked.
I did this all by sheer necessity.
Trembling and soft vibration shook her limbs;
But they were quite uninjured, for I strove
To make no wound, though I could not avoid
Breaking a trifling fissure in the skin,
Since otherwise I could have found no other way
To gain the favor I so much desired. . . .
   This, then, is how I won my vermeil Rose.
Then morning came, and from my dream at last I woke.

73

THE DANCE OF DEATH

early fifteenth century

This fifteenth-century English poem expresses the macabre fatalism many men felt in the wake of the repeated waves of plague which swept all of Europe beginning in the midfourteenth century and continuing throughout most of the fifteenth. The poet stresses the inevitability of death, its utter disregard for distinctions of wealth and rank, and its ever present warning that youth, beauty and all human triumphs pass quickly.

I

O yee folkes / harde herted as a stone
Which to the world / haue al your / advertence[1]
Like as hit sholde / laste euere in oone
Where ys youre witte / where ys youre providence
To see a-forne the sodeyne / vyolence
Of cruel dethe / that ben so wyse and sage
Whiche sleeth allas / by stroke of pestilence
Bothe yonge and olde / of low and hie parage.[2]

SOURCE From *The Dance of Death,* edited by Florence Warren, and published by the Oxford University Press for the Early English Text Society (Oxford, 1931), 2, 8, 14, 20, 22, 50, 68, 70.
[1] give all your attention   [2] lineage

II

Dethe spareth not / lwo ne hye degre
Popes kynges / ne worthi Emperowrs
When thei schyne / moste in felicite
He can abate / the fresshnes of her flowres
Ther bryt sune clipsen[3] / with hys showres
Make hem plownge / from theire sees lowe
Maugre[4] the myght / of al these conquerowres
Fortune hath hem / from her whele [y] throwe. . . .

IX

First me be-houeth / this daunce for to lede
Whiche sate yn erthe / hyest yn my see
The state ful parilous / who so taketh hede
To occupie / Petirs dignitie
But for al that / deth I mai not flee
On his daunce / with other for to trace
For whiche al honoure / who prudently can see
Is litel worthe / that doth soo sone pace.[5]

X

Sir Emperowre / lorde of al the grounde
Soueren Prince / ande hyest of noblesse
Ye most forsake / of golde yowre appil rounde
Sceptre and swerde / and al yowre hie prouesse
Be-hinde leue / yowre tresowre & richesse
And with other / to my daunce obeie
Ayens[6] my myght / is worth noon hardynesse
Adames children / alle thei mosten deie. . . .

XIV

O noble Kynge / moste worthi of renown
Come forth a-noon / for al yowre worthinesse
That somme-tyme had / a-bowte yow envroun[7]

[3] eclipse   [4] in spite of
[5] pass   [6] against   [7] in your surroundings

Grete (r)ialte / and passynge hye nobless
But right a-noon / al yowre grete hyenesse
Sool fro yowre men / yn haste ye schul hit lete[8]
Who most haboundeth / here yn grete richesse
Shal bere with him / but a single shete.[9] . . .

XXII

Ye that amonge / lordes and barouns
Hau had so longe / worship & renoun
Forgete yowre trumpettes / & yowre clariowns
This is no dreme / ne symulacioun[10]
Somme-tyme yowre custome / & entencioun
Was with ladies / to daunce yn the shade
But ofte hit happeth / In conclusioun
That oo[11] man breketh / that another made. . . . .

XXIV

Come forth a-noon / my lady & Princesse
Ye most al-so / go vp-on this daunce
Nowt mai a vaile / yowre grete straungenesse[12]
Nowther yowre beaute / ne yowre grete plesaunce
Yowre riche a-rai[13] / ne yowre daliaunce
That somme-tyme cowde / so many holde on honde
In loue / for al yowre dowble variaunce
Ye mote as now / this foting understonde. . . .

XLVIII

Sire monke also / with yowre blake abite[14]
Ye mai no lenger / holde here soioure[15]
Ther is no thinge / that mai yow here respite[16]
Ayeyn my myght / yow for to do socoure

---

[8] leave   [9] i.e., a winding sheet
[10] simulation   [11] one   [12] aloofness, haughtiness   [13] array
[14] habit—i.e., monk's robe   [15] sojourn   [16] nothing can keep
you here

Ye mote accounte / towchyng yowre laboure
To erthe and asshes / turneth eueri floure
The life of man / is but a thynge of nowght. . . .

LXXI

Sire Cordelere[17] / to yow my hande is rawght[18]
To this daunce / yow to conueie[19] ande lede
Whiche yn yowre prechynge / hau ful ofte tawght
How [that] I am / moste gastful[20] for to drede
Al-be that folke / take ther of none hede[21]
Yitte[22] is ther noon / so stronge ne so hardi
But dethe dar reste / and lette for no mede
For dethe eche owre / is present & redy.

LXXIII

Litel Enfaunt / that were but late borne
Schape yn this worlde / to haue no plesaunce
Thow moste with other / that gon here to forme
Be lad yn haste / be fatal ordynaunce. . . .
Lerne of newe / to go on my daunce
Ther mai non age / a-scape yn sothe ther fro[23]
Late eueri wight / haue this yn remembraunce
Who lengest leueth / moste shal suffre wo.

17 cord-wearer—i.e., Franciscan friar
18 reached
19 convey
20 frightful
21 although no one pays any attention
22 yet
23 in truth, no age can escape from it

74

THE LAW SCHOOL OF BOLOGNA: FREDERICK BARBAROSSA'S AUTHENTIC "HABITA"

1158

This document allows the law students of Bologna to claim the privilege of imperial protection on their way to and from the city of their studies. The emperor in this way reciprocated the legal help he received from Bolognese lawyers. The document incorporates for the first time the concept of the "studium generale" (a technical phrase used later to designate a university) to refer to an aggregate of schools.

Emperor Frederick.

Having ordered a diligent examination to be made into this matter by our bishops, abbots, dukes and all the judges and nobles of our sacred palace, we grant this privilege to all itinerant scholars who travel by reason of their studies, and especially, because of our piety, to those who teach the canon or holy law, so that both they and their underlings may travel

SOURCE   Translated from *Authentica Habita,* quoted in H. Koeppler, "Frederick Barbarossa and the Schools of Bologna," *English Historical Review,* LIV (1939), 607.

safely to the places where they carry on the study of letters, and dwell in them securely. For, we consider [it worthwhile] that, because those who do good deserve our praise and protection, with special affection we defend from all injury those by whose knowledge the world is illumined, and by whose lives students are molded in obedience to God and to us, His minister. Who among them is not pitied, exiled for his love of learning? Once wealthy, they now waste themselves away to paupers, exposing their very lives to all manner of dangers, and often—which is difficult to bear—they suffer senseless physical attacks at the hands of the lowest sort of men.

Therefore we decree by an eternal and inviolable general law, that no one be found hereafter daring enough to presume to injure scholars in any way, nor to make them any charge on account of a debt owed by someone else from their province, which we have heard is done from time to time, following a perverse custom.

Be it known to all those who violate this holy law, and throughout their lands, that if they neglect to promulgate this to the officials of those places, restitution of the confiscated property will be required of them four times over, and, when the infamy inflicted by this law is known, they shall forever lose their offices. . . .

We therefore order this law to be inserted among the imperial constitutions, under the rubric "lest the son on behalf of the father, etc."

75

ACADEMIC HERESY: GILES OF ROME,
ON *THE ERRORS OF THE PHILOSOPHERS*

c. 1270

Giles of Rome (1247–1316), a student of Thomas Aquinas at Paris from 1269 to 1272 and a member of the Order of the Hermits of St. Augustine, here gives a critical analysis of the works of Greek and Moslem philosophers whose conclusions were injurious to Christian belief. Giles' work represents one of the earliest reactions against the writings of the non-Christian philosophers, which had been embraced with such eagerness by twelfth- and earlier thirteenth-century scholars at Paris and elsewhere.

Here Begin the Errors of the Philosophers Aristotle,
Averroës, Avicenna, Algazel, Alkindi and Rabbi Moses
(Maimonides), Compiled by Brother Giles of the Order
of St. Augustine

As it is the case that many wrong conclusions follow from one faulty statement, so the Philosopher has drawn many errors from one faulty principle.

For he believed nothing to be disposed in some condition

SOURCE   From Giles of Rome, "On the Errors of the Philosophers," in *Medieval Philosophy*, trans. by Herman Shapiro, 386–87, 392–93. Copyright © 1964 by Random House, Inc. Reprinted by permission of the publisher.

in which it previously was not, except it came to be that way through a preceding motion. He held, moreover, that there is no novelty except where there is change, taken properly. Because, therefore, every change taken properly is a terminus of motion, there can be no novelty without a preceding motion. Now from this principle he concluded that motion never began to be; since if motion began, the motion was new. But nothing is new except through some preceding motion. Therefore there was motion before the first motion, which is a contradiction.

Further: he erred because he posited time never to have begun. Now time always follows on motion. If, therefore, motion never began, neither did time. Moreover, it seemed to him that the principle of time involved a special difficulty. For since an instant is always the end of the past and the beginning of the future, a first instant cannot be given, because there was a time before every instant, and before any assigned time there was an instant. Time, therefore, did not begin, but is eternal.

Further: because of what has already been stated, he was forced to posit a mobile to be eternal and the world to be eternal. For as one cannot give a time without motion, and motion without a mobile, if time and motion are eternal, the mobile will be eternal, and so the world would never begin. All of this is clear from Book VIII of the *Physics*.

Further: he was forced to posit the heavens to be ungenerated and incorruptible, and never to have been made but always to have been. For since among the varieties of motion only the circular is continuous—as is clear from Book VIII of the *Physics* —if any motion is eternal, the circular will be eternal. And since circular motion is proper to the heavens—as is shown in Book I *On the Heavens and the Earth*—it then follows that the heavens are uncreated and that they were never made. . . .

A Compilation of the Errors of Averroës

Now the Commentator[1] agrees in all the errors of the Philosopher. Indeed, he spoke even more ironically and with greater pertinacity than the Philosopher against those who posited the world to have begun. He is to be argued against incomparably more than against the Philosopher, because he more directly impugns our faith, holding to be false that which could not contain falsity as it is based upon the First Truth.

He went beyond the Philosopher's errors because he scorned all law, as is clear from Book II and XI of the *Metaphysics,* where he mocks the law of the Christians, or our Catholic law, and even the Saracen law, because they too posit the creation of things and that something can be created from nothing. . . .

Further: he erred saying in Book XII that God is neither solicitous, nor does He have care, nor does He provide for individuals existing in the sublunary world. For, as he says, "this is neither permissible to, nor consonant with, Divine Goodness."

He erred further, denying a Trinity to be in God, saying in Book XII that some men "held a Trinity to be in God, but they sought by this device to be evasive and to really say that there are three Gods and one God; still, they don't even know how to be evasive properly, because when substance is numbered, the aggregate will still be one through the one added intention."

Because of this, according to him, if God were three and one, it would follow that He would be a composite, which is contradictory.

[1] Averroës.

76

THE RECEPTION OF ARISTOTLE: ROGER BACON, *COMPENDIUM OF THE STUDY OF THEOLOGY*

1292

Roger Bacon (c. 1214–1294) was among the English scholastics of the thirteenth century whose center was at Oxford. It was here that he studied under Robert Grosseteste at the Franciscan house. He then studied and lectured on Aristotle in Paris, and on his return to England, joined the Franciscan Order and continued teaching at Oxford. In this passage Bacon describes in his characteristically critical style his own view of the reception of Aristotle's works at Oxford and Paris. His remarks imply that, although the initial effect of the rediscovery of Aristotle's works may have come in the twelfth century, nothing like total absorption and understanding of them existed before the late thirteenth.

The knowledge of Aristotle's philosophy has come slowly into use among the Latins, since his works on natural philosophy and metaphysics, and the commentaries of Averroës and others have been translated only in our own times, and [only recently] the Parisian[1] was excommunicated before the year of the Lord 1237 for [his doctrines on] the eternity of the world and of

SOURCE Translated from Roger Bacon, *Compendium studii Theologiae*, quoted in Hastings Rashdall, *The Universities of Europe in the Middle Ages*, Vol. II, Part II (Oxford: The University Press, 1895), 754.

[1] Siger of Brabant.

time, for his book on the divination of dreams, which is the third book [of Aristotle's] *On Sleep and Wakefulness,* and because of many errors of translation. Also, the *Logic* was slow to be received and read,[2] for blessed Edmund, Archbishop of Canterbury, was the first to read the *Book of Refutations* at Oxford within my lifetime, and I saw Master Hugh, who was the first to read the *Posterior Logic,* in person, and I attended his lectures.

Therefore there were few out of the multitude of Latins who were well versed in the aforesaid philosophy of the aforesaid Aristotle, in fact very few—and almost none until this year of our Lord 1292—for whom it was fully and clearly understandable in its progressions.

And the *Ethics* of Aristotle has only recently been known and read by the masters, and then but rarely: moreover, the rest of his philosophy, a thousand volumes in length, in which he treated all the sciences, has not yet been translated or made known to the Latin world.

[2] placed in the curriculum.

77

ROGER BACON, *OPUS MAIUS*

c. 1260 – 77

After denouncing the tyrannies of authority, custom, public opinion and hypocrisy over men's minds, Roger Bacon, in a passage strikingly similar to the thought of his seventeenth-century compatriot Francis Bacon, in this passage seeks to solve the problem

SOURCE Reprinted with the permission of Charles Scribner's Sons from *Selections from Medieval Philosophers,* 8–9, 14–19, ed. and trans. by Richard McKeon. Copyright 1929 Charles Scribner's Sons; renewal copyright © 1957.

of reconciling the "new knowledge" of Aristotle and other pagan and Jewish writers with Christian orthodoxy. Despite ecclesiastical prohibitions, the "dangerous" works of non-Christian philosophers continued to be read by medieval students and scholars alike; it was often members of the mendicant orders, like Bacon, who attempted to place the new learning in proper perspective to the old.

There are, indeed, four chief hindrances to the understanding of truth, which stand in the way of every man, however wise, and permit hardly any to arrive at the true title of wisdom; to wit, (1) the example of frail and unsuited authority, (2) the long duration of custom, (3) the opinion of the unlearned crowd, and (4) the concealment of one's own ignorance in the display of apparent wisdom. Every man is involved in these difficulties, every condition of man is held by them. For every one in all the acts of life and study and every occupation uses three of the worst arguments to the same conclusion; namely, (1) this has been exemplified by our ancestors, (2) this is the custom, (3) this is the common belief: therefore, it must be held. But the opposite to the conclusion follows far better from the premises, as I shall prove in many instances by authority and experience and reason. . . . Moreover, all the evils of the human race come from these deadly plagues; for the most useful and the greatest and most beautiful instances of wisdom and the secrets of all the sciences and arts are ignored; but what is even worse, men blinded by the mist of these four arguments do not perceive their own ignorance, but cover and conceal it with all caution so that they find no remedy for it; and finally, what is worst of all, they think they are in the full light of truth when they are in the densest shadows of error; because of this they hold the most true to be in the bounds of falsity, the best to be of no value, the greatest to possess neither weight nor worth; and on the contrary they honor the most false, praise the worst, extol the most vile, blind to the truth that all the brightness of wisdom is other than these, disdainful of what they can attain with great ease. . . .

Whatever has been proved by authorities is determined even more certainly from the experience of any man. . . . The world indeed is full of examples of this sort, and one example of true perfection easily finds ten thousand imperfect. Nature, in fact, has formed for us in numbers the fitting illustration of perfection and imperfection. For a number is said to be perfect the sum of whose divisors, added, equal the number itself, and there is only one such number beneath ten, namely six, and one between 10 and 100, namely 28, and one between 100 and 1,000, namely 496, and one between 1,000 and 10,000, namely 8,128, and so on; and would that it were thus with man and that this was accorded to the human race! But this never was the case, neither in life nor in knowledge, nor will it ever be, even to the final destruction of sin, since not only is there the scarcity of those who are perfect in all virtue and knowledge, but of those who have arrived at the perfection of one virtue or knowledge. The first are and will be and have always been very rare. For they are the truly perfect, but of 10,000 men not one is found so perfect in either condition of life or profession of wisdom. . . . Of the crowd moreover the judgement is the same. For the multitude of the human race has always erred in the truth of God, and only the small group of christians has received it; and we know that the great mass of christians is imperfect, for the paucity of the saints shows that. Similarly in the case of philosophical doctrine, for the crowd has always lacked the wisdom of philosophy. The slight number of philosophers, in fact, declares that. And the ordinary run of those who philosophize has always remained imperfect. For of famous philosophers only Aristotle, together with his followers, has been called philosopher in the judgement of all wise men, since he ordered all the parts of philosophy so far as it was possible in his times, but still he did not come to the limit of wisdom, as will be made sufficiently manifest below. . . .

The Affinity Of Philosophy With Theology

Chapter I

Having banished to infernal regions, then, the four general causes of all human ignorance and having removed them completely from this demonstration, I want in this second distinction to show that one wisdom is perfect and that it is contained in sacred letters; all truth has grown from the roots of this wisdom. I say, then, that either there is one science the mistress of the others, namely theology (to which the rest are entirely necessary; and without the others it can not attain to its effect; their excellence it claims as its right; the rest of the sciences obey its nod and authority), or better, there is only one perfect wisdom which is contained wholly in the sacred Scriptures, to be explained by canon law and philosophy. . . . For, although it is spread out by sciences as if in the palm of the hand, yet of itself it brings all wisdom together in the grasp of the fist, for all wisdom was given by one God and to one world and for one end. . . . The way of salvation is one, although there may be many steps; but wisdom is the way to salvation. . . . Since, therefore, the sacred Scriptures give us this wisdom, which is of Christ, it is manifest that all truth is included here. But if wisdom is so called elsewhere and if it is contrary to this, it will be erroneous, nor will it have anything save the name of wisdom; or if it is not said to be contrary, it is nevertheless diverse. But diversity, although it does not induce contrariety elsewhere, does here, as is evident from evangelical authority, "He who is not with me, is against me." So it is true of this wisdom that what is not bound to it, is proved to be against it, and therefore to be avoided by the christian.

78

THOMAS BRADWARDINE,
TREATISE ON PROPORTIONS

c. 1320 – 44

Thomas Bradwardine (c. 1290–1349) taught at Oxford from 1325 to 1335, and was famed for his learning in mathematics, astronomy, moral philosophy and theology. Although in the last year of his life he was appointed Archbishop of Canterbury, it was for his intellectual achievements that he was most esteemed. The Treatise on Proportions, *a key work in the history of science, was widely read in England and on the Continent during the fourteenth century. Bradwardine's willingness to throw over Aristotle's theory of motion in favor of empirical judgment widened a chink in the Philosopher's armor.*

INTRODUCTION

Since each successive motion is proportionable to another with respect to speed, natural philosophy, which studies motion, ought not to ignore the proportion of motions and their speeds, and, because an understanding of this is both necessary and extremely difficult, nor has as yet been treated fully in any branch of philosophy, we have accordingly composed the following work

SOURCE From *Thomas of Bradwardine His Tractatus de Proportionibus*, ed. and trans. by H. Lamar Crosby, Jr. (Madison: The University of Wisconsin Press; © 1967 by the Regents of the University of Wisconsin), 65, 87, 89.

on the subject. Since, moreover (as Boethius points out in Book I of his Arithmetic), it is agreed that whoever omits mathematical studies has destroyed the whole of philosophic knowledge, we have commenced by setting forth the mathematics needed for the task in hand, in order to make the subject easier and more accessible to the student. . . .

CHAPTER TWO

Having looked into these introductory matters, let us now proceed with the undertaking which was proposed at the outset. And first, after the manner of Aristotle, let us criticize erroneous theories, so that the truth may be the more apparent.

There are four false theories to be proposed as relevant to our investigation, the first of which holds that: *the proportion between the speeds with which motions take place varies as the difference whereby the power of the mover exceeds the resistance offered by the thing moved.*

This theory claims in its favor that passage from Book I of the *De Caelo et Mundo* (in the chapter on the "infinite") in the text which reads: "It is necessary that proportionally as the mover is in excess, etc." . . .

The present theory may, however, be torn down in several ways:

First, according to this theory, it would follow that, if a given mover moved a given *mobile* through a given distance in a given time, half of that mover would not move half of the *mobile* through the same distance in an equal time, but only through half the distance. The consequence is clear, because, if the whole mover exceeds the whole *mobile* by the whole excess, then half the mover exceeds half the *mobile* by only half the former amount; for, just as 4 exceeds 2 by 2, half of 4 (namely, 2) exceeds half of itself (that is, 1) by 1, which is only half of the former excess.

That such a consequence is false is apparent from the fact that Aristotle proves, at the close of Book VII of the *Physics,* that: "If a given power moves a given *mobile* through a given distance in a given time, half that power will move half the *mobile* through an equal distance in an equal time." Aristotle's reasoning is quite sound, for, since the half is related to the half by the same proportion as the whole is to the whole, the two motions will, therefore, be of equal speed. . . .

In the third place, it would follow that a geometric proportion (that is, a similarity of proportions) of movers to their *mobilia* would not produce equal speeds, since it does not represent an equality of excesses; for, although the proportions of 2 to 1 and 6 to 3 are the same, the excess of the one term over the other is 1 in the first case and 3 in the second case.

The consequence to which we are thus led is, however, false and opposed to Aristotle's opinion, as expressed at the close of Book VII of the *Physics* and in many other places, . . .

Nor can it be legitimately maintained that, in the passages cited, Aristotle and Averroës understand, by the words "proportion" and "analogy," arithmetic proportionality (that is, equality of differences), as some have claimed. Indeed, in Book VII of the *Physics* Aristotle proves this conclusion: "If a given power moves a given *mobile* through a given distance in a given time, half that power will move half the *mobile* through an equal distance in an equal time, because 'analogically,' the relation of half the mover to half the *mobile* is similar to that of the whole mover to the whole *mobile*." Such a statement, interpreted as referring to arithmetic proportionality, is discernibly false (as has already been made sufficiently clear in the first argument raised against the present theory). . . .

The above thesis of Aristotle may be demonstrated geometrically as follows: As is the whole mover to half the mover, so is the whole *mobile* to half the *mobile*. . . . And this is what was to have been proved. . . .

79

NICOLAUS OF AUTRECOURT,
FIRST LETTER TO BERNARD OF AREZZO

c. 1327–50

Nicolaus of Autrecourt (c. 1300–after 1350) studied at the University of Paris from 1320 until 1327. His writings met with strong papal disapproval, and were condemned in 1346. Nicolaus was required to burn his works and recant the condemned theses. He complied in 1347, and was dismissed from the teaching faculty of Paris. This letter is among his few surviving writings. Although his thought represents an extreme position, Nicolaus' radical skepticism shows the ultimate result of the nominalist revival.

With all the reverence which I am obligated to show to you, most amiable Father Bernard, by reason of the worthiness of the Friars, I wish in this present communication to explain some doubts—indeed, as it seems to some of us—some obvious contradictions—which appear to follow from the things you say, so that, by their resolution, the truth may be more clearly revealed to me and to others. For I read, in a certain book on which you lectured in the Franciscan school, the following propositions

SOURCE   *Nicolaus of Autrecourt's Critique of Causality and Substance,* trans. by Ernest A. Moody, Copyright © 1964 by Random House, Inc. Reprinted from *Medieval Philosophy* 510–15, ed. by Herman Shapiro and published by Random House, Inc. By permission of Ernest A. Moody.

which you conceded, to whoever wished to uphold them, as true. The first, which is set forth by you in the first book of the *Sentences*, Dist. 3, Qu. 4, is this: *"Clear intuitive cognition is that by which we judge a thing to exist, whether it exists or does not exist.* Your second proposition, which is set forth in the same place as above, is of this sort: *The inference,* 'An object does not exist, therefore it is not seen' *is not valid; nor does this hold,* 'This is seen, therefore this exists'; *indeed both are invalid, just as these inferences,* 'Caesar is thought of, therefore Caesar exists,' 'Caesar does not exist, therefore he is not thought of.' The third proposition, stated in that same place, is this: *Intuitive cognition does not necessarily require the existing thing."*

From these propositions I infer a fourth, that every awareness which we have of the existence of objects outside our minds, can be false; since, according to you it [the awareness] can exist whether or not the object exists. And I infer another fifth proposition, which is this: By natural cognitive means we cannot be certain when our awareness of the existence of external objects is true or false; because, as you say, it represents the thing as existing, whether or not it exists. And thus, since whoever admits the antecedent must concede the consequent which is inferred from that antecedent by a formal consequence, it follows that you do not have evident certitude of the existence of external objects. And likewise you must concede all the things which follow from this. But it is clear that you do not have evident certitude of the existence of objects of the senses, because no one has certitude of any consequent through an inference which manifestly involves a fallacy. But such is the case here; for according to you, this is a fallacy, "Whiteness is seen, therefore whiteness exists." . . .

Again, you say that an imperfect intuitive cognition can be had in a natural manner, or a non-existent thing. I now ask how you are certain (with the certitude defined above) when your intuitive cognition is of a sufficiently perfect degree such that it cannot naturally be of a non-existent thing. And I would gladly be instructed about this.

Thus, it is clear, it seems to me, that as a consequence of your statements you have to say that you are not certain of the existence of the objects of the five senses. But what is even harder to uphold, you must say that you are not certain of your own actions—e.g., that you are seeing, or hearing—indeed you must say that you are not sure that anything is perceived by you, or has been perceived by you. . . .

And so, bringing all these statements together, it seems that you must say that you are not certain of those things which are outside of you. And thus you do not know if you are in the heavens or on the earth, in fire or in water; and consequently you do not know whether today's sky is the same one as yesterday's, because you do not know whether the sky exists. . . . And *a fortiori* it follows from this that you are not certain of the things which occurred in the past. . . . Again, I ask how, on this view, the Apostles were certain that Christ suffered on the cross, and that He rose from the dead, and so with all the rest.

80

CAESARIUS OF HEISTERBACH,
THE DIALOGUE ON MIRACLES

c. 1200 – 40

Caesarius (1180–1240), monk and later prior of the Cistercian abbey of Heisterbach, served for a number of years as master of the abbey's novices, during which time he collected anecdotes and wrote exemplary stories for the novices' instruction and edification. The tales were so entertaining that they circulated widely outside the monastic community.

Of certain Templars who became invisible to the pagans while repeating their hours

Not long ago six knights of the Temple prostrated themselves to a certain canonical hour in the neighbourhood of the Saracens. When the pagan army came up unexpectedly, and they wished to rise up and flee, their leader signed to them to lie still. Then a wonderful thing happened. That the King of heaven might show how clear to Him were the faith of the

SOURCE From Caesarius of Heisterbach, *The Dialogue on Miracles,* trans. by H. von E. Scott and C. C. Swinton Bland (London: George Routledge & Sons Ltd., 1929), II, 46, 158–59, 304.

leader and the obedience of the disciples He sent His angels, by whom the infidel host was thrown into confusion, some being captured and more slain. And when the Templars signed to those whom the angels had bound, and they said to them: "Where is the army which we saw just now, and by which we have been captured and slain?" they replied: "When we have need they come to our aid; when we no longer need them, they return to their tents." For they understood that those whom they themselves could not see, were the holy angels, who always stand by the worshippers of God, and guard them. . . .

Not long ago a merchant of our country, crossed the sea, and saw the arm of S. John the Baptist in the hospital dedicated to his honour, and longing to gain possession of it, he discovered that the guardian of the relics was wooing a certain woman, and as he knew that there is nothing which women of that kind cannot extort from men, he sent for her and said; "If you help me to gain possession of the relics of S. John the Baptist, which are under the protection of your lover, I will give you 140 pounds of silver."

She, eager to gain the offered money, refused to give any consent to the keeper of the hospital, until she obtained the holy arm, which she immediately handed over to the merchant, and received the promised weight of silver.

Do you see how great a mockery? Just as long ago the head of S. John was given by Herod to a wanton girl as a reward for her dancing, and by her given to her adulteress mother, so even in these days, the arm of the same saint was given to a vile woman as the reward for adultery by the keeper of the hospital, just as by wicked Herod, and by her was sold to the merchant.

But he did not bury it in the earth like Herodias, but wrapped it in purple, and fleeing to almost the uttermost parts of the earth, he came to the city of Groningen, which is on the boundary of Friesland. There he built a house, and hiding the arm in one of its pillars, began to grow very rich. One day when he was sitting in his shop, a friend of his said to him: "Behold the whole city is on fire, and already the flames are approaching your house"; but he replied: "I have no fears for my house, for I have left a good guardian in it." Nevertheless he arose and went to his house, and there for some time gazed upon the pillar which was still untouched, and then returned to his shop, while all wondered what could be the cause of such confidence. When questioned about the protector of his house, when he replied ambiguously and noticed that this very fact made his fellow citizens suspicious, he became fearful that they might perhaps use force to discover the truth; wherefore he took out the arm and gave it to a certain recluse. But she, not knowing how to keep the secret, handed over her charge to another, who gave it to the citizens. And they immediately taking the relics and carrying them to the church, roughly answered the depositor when he begged with tears to have his property restored to him. When they asked him to what saint the relics belonged, he said that he did not know his name, because he was unwilling to give them up to them. Nevertheless in his grief he left the city, and falling into poverty, not long afterwards was taken with a grievous sickness. When he was afraid of death, he disclosed to his confessor the name of the saint, and how he had obtained the relics. When the citizens learnt this, they made a silver gilt receptacle in the shape of an arm, and adorned it with precious stones, and therein they placed the relics. I myself, two years ago, saw this arm and it was still clothed with flesh and skin. I saw there also a small golden cross full of relics which had been given to this man at the same time as the arm; this cross belonged to the emperor Frederick. . . .

We have in our monastery a large molar tooth with three fangs, of the same Forerunner of the Lord. . . .

Of a priest in Hadenmare who was seen to be chewing coals when he received the sacrament

In Hadenmare a town of the diocese of Treves when a certain priest, who is still alive, was saying mass, Theodoric a monk of Eberbach, saw him chewing the blackest of coals at the moment of reception. Now this Theodoric is a priest of simple nature and upright and has been vouchsafed many divine revelations. I was living last year with my abbot in the same town; for the house of Eberbach has a grange in that town, and it looks to the aforesaid priest to supply divine offices there; the master of the grange told us saying: "I am obliged to give so much money to the aforesaid priest that he may not neglect the services; for he is a man of perverse and luxurious life, and will often celebrate three masses in the day." And the abbot replied: "I would sooner give him money not to celebrate. *For whoso eateth unworthily eats and drinks to himself condemnation*" (I Cor. xi. 29).

Novice. — What is the meaning of his being seen to chew coals? Do then the wicked actually receive the Lord's body?

Monk. — Yes they receive it just as the good do, but only sacramentally. Fire makes charcoal and charcoal which is extinct is the fuel. For whoso handles and eats unworthily the body of Christ, prepares for himself everlasting flames, and unless he repents of so great a fault *shall be for burning and the fuel of eternal fire* (Isa. ix. 5).

Of a Frisian priest who trod upon the Lord's body

A certain religious prelate in the country of Friesland, told me last year a very terrible thing about a priest. For his hands were so tremulous that he could not receive the Lord's body except by means of a tube. One day the sacrament fell from his hands to the ground and fearing that he might be seen by someone who would make known his fault, fearing indeed the authorities of the church more than his own soul, he is said to have trodden it underfoot.

Novice. — That is why Augustine says upon that passage *they gave me gall to eat* (Ps. lxix. 22), of those who crucified Him, they are like these who receive and consecrate unworthily he says. For those who despised Christ when reigning in the heavens sin more grievously than those who crucified Him when He was walking upon the earth. And that He is trodden underfoot by them, he says in another place: "He treads Christ underfoot who sins deliberately, and he who receives Him unworthily." It was for excesses of this kind that during our time Frisia was most grievously stricken, as I remember I said in the third chapter of the 7th book, where I spoke of the boxer who struck the body of Christ from the hands of the priest.

Novice. — I think that if wicked priests really believed that Christ's body was present on the altar they would never dare such things. . . .

Of the tourney of those who were slain near Montenake

The night after the army of the duke of Louvain was slain by the people of Liége, a servant of the count of Lootz near Montenake, passing by the place of slaughter, early in the night saw there a very great tourney of devils. I do not suppose that there had been such exaltation of the foul spirits, if they had not taken great spoils there. But of those who fall in tourneys, there is no question that they go to hell, if they have not been helped by the benefit of contrition. . . .

81

A CRUSADER'S LETTER:
RICOLDO DE MONTE-CROCE,
LETTER TO BLESSED QUEEN MARY

c. 1280 – 1305

Despair at the evident failure of Christian military campaigns in the East led Ricoldo de Monte-Croce, a survivor of the seige of Acre in 1291, to compose six letters from the Holy Land, including one to God, another to the celestial curia and the one included here, to Mary. The letters combine touching naïveté, deep piety and a continuation of the genuine reliance on supernatural allies so common during the early crusades of the late eleventh and twelfth centuries.

Joy and gladness be to you, O most blessed Virgin Mary, mother of God, queen of heaven and the world's advocate, that joy and gladness which the afflicted soul lacks, from the friars preachers in the East. For a long time I have been sending letters to your divine wisdom about my sadness and admiration [for you] but did not receive any sort of reply to instruct or console me. And now, most blessed queen, I have troubled tearfully to declare to you the reason for that same sadness and admiration with other words and reasons in this present letter, so that your mercy will succor my misery quickly. . . .

SOURCE Translated from *Lettres de Ricoldo de Monte-Croce sur la Prise d'Acre* (1291), ed. R. Röhricht, *Archives de l'Orient latin*, II (Paris: 1884), Documents, 271–75, 294.

Behold me then alone, afflicted and abandoned in a far-off land, weak in body, dejected at heart and nearly wholly dismayed in mind. An exile, to you I cry, not only as the son of Eve, but as the son of many; alas, O miserable me, alas, that ever I came from western lands to the orient shore to preach Christ, to baptize and to gather men to those in the bosom of holy mother church, at a time when I now perceive that those who were added lose hope and are scattered. And now I see Christians being snatched from not only the bosom but the heart of holy mother church, and being transported as slaves to Baldactum and even to the most remote eastern regions because of the multitude of the captives. . . .

O Lady, it seems now that that prophecy of the greatest liar Mohammed is being fulfilled, when he said he had been sent by God in the bravery of his arms that he might beget many sons to enlarge the Saracen race. And if other women were lacking, from whom he could beget sons, did God then give him your handmaidens, chaste virgins dedicated and espoused to you from adolescence? What more? Will Christ, thy son, grant to Mohammed, if he has handed to him His own handmaidens and brides? For we do not dare to deny that all this happened by [divine] permission and grant. And would that the Saracens knew God, and were grateful to Him who has given them such a great victory! Indeed they are for all these things mistakenly grateful to Mohammed, and say that all this has been procured for them by the merit of the Koran; moreover they debase Christ, thy most holy omnipotent Son, and say "The Christians place their faith in a certain Jesus, son of Mary, believing Him to be God, and He avails [them] nothing against Mohammed." They even address and write insulting letters to our princes and kings, saying that in these days the luck of Christ fought with the luck of Mohammed, and the luck of Mohammed prevailed. . . .

The extent of the blasphemy against you and your son in the Koran, you know better than I. I would not have believed it if I had not read it as an eyewitness. In all this I am amazed at how the mother has patiently endured such blasphemies against her son for so long, and how the omnipotent son has withstood hearing them against such a blessed mother as well as the Highest Father. Is it not true that in many places in the Arabic law and similarly in the Koran, Mohammed introduces a demonstrative argument: "It is impossible for God to have a son, because He has no wife?" Thus in brief and foolish words this seductive, obscene and most carnal blasphemy tries to remove the son from His Father and the Father and Godhead from His son. About you, moreover, he said that you, pondering your son Jesus, said: "I would rather be dead than that such a son should be born of me!" You know, O Lady, that publicly they dogmatize and preach that Jesus, the son of Mary, shall return near the end of the world and shall be made a Saracen. You know, O Lady, that when I crossed near the river of paradise, the Tigris, I found between Baldactum and Nineveh a city, which was in ancient times Baldoc, where even now they await the son of Haah, with a mule saddled and prepared respectfully, although he died six hundred years ago, and every Friday they bring back the mule prepared to receive him. In that day they say that Jesus, the son of Mary, will appear and will be made a Saracen. O Lady, I shall believe what you say of your Son and not the Saracens! Up to now, I have not been able to believe that Jesus Christ, your son, would be made a Saracen. I see manifestly, however, that He himself has given and conceded many things to the Saracens; perhaps these are but preludes. Perhaps He really will become a Saracen. . . .

It happened after all this, that on the third day, when I was no less anxious and expected a reply, and wondered greatly that they had not answered me either by messenger or in writing, or in a meaningful dream that I could understand, evil seemed to close in around me and I began to wonder even more greatly. . . . I began to be insulted enough to write them [the heavenly hierarchy] again, just because I didn't know to whom else I could write, or what to write beyond what I had already said. Besides, I feared to alienate myself so far from them, because of

my impatience or for some other reason, that I wouldn't be able
to find a messenger willing to present a letter full of such impatience at the court of the Eternal King. Nonetheless I didn't
give up, and I don't believe I could have received a refusal from
that court, where so much assistance is prepared for me, and
where the Son is before the Father, the mother before the son.
Mohammed, however, against whom I asked the protection of
God and the celestial court, seems to me to be manifestly contrary to the Father, son, mother and the entire celestial court.
And therefore I am not dispirited, but firmly believe that they
will send me a practical reply, and not just a theoretical one,
because I asked for a reply in deeds, not words. . . .

82

HENRY OF LANCASTER,
THE BOOK OF HOLY MEDICINES

1354

*Henry, first Duke of Lancaster (1310–1361) was a diplomat
and military leader during the Hundred Years' War, and exerted
a strong influence on the English King Edward III. His devotional treatise, written in French sometime after mid-century, is
filled with the sensual religious imagery of his time. It reflects
a tenderness of religious feeling not usually associated with a
soldier, yet it is just this kind of unlikely combination of emotional traits that characterizes many fourteenth-century figures.*

SOURCE From *Le Livre de Seyntz Medicines*. The Unpublished
Devotional Treatise of Henry of Lancaster, ed. E. J. Arnould (Oxford: Published for Anglo-Norman Text Society, by Basil Blackwell,
1940), *Anglo-Norman Texts*, II, 7, 8, 13, 132–33.

If a man were gravely afflicted with great wounds, even unto death, he would not be at all wise if he delayed too long in searching for a medicine with which to cure his wounds. And if the man is poor, and the medicine costly, it is too unjust if the doctor be not so chivalrous that he cure the man without taking more from him than hearty thanks, provided it be done sincerely; . . .

Ah! sweetest Lord Jesus Christ, I am that man, poor and stripped of all goods—I am most gravely afflicted with seven wounds, so foul and so perilous that I can expect nothing but death, and see! it will be the evil death, if I don't soon have comfort and help from a good doctor—and that is you, good Lord God, who are medicine and salve and refuge to all who seek you sincerely. . . .

Hear, Lord, if you will; I will show you my wounds which are seven: the first is my ear, the second my eye; the third my nostrils; the fourth my mouth; the fifth my hand; the sixth my foot; the seventh my heart.

Again, to say it all together, my whole body is full of wounds, and the wounds I spoke of before are so full of all the seven deadly sins and of venial sins that I have a grave doubt [of my salvation], but that I take comfort and assurance in your great graciousness, good Master, that you, if you please, will help me to cure it all. . . .

Good, sweet Seigneur and very noble Master, I have now come, by your holy grace, to reveal the stinking wound of my nose and nostrils with which I have so often sinned. . . .

Also I have, Lord, with great delight smelled the fragrance of women, or of those possessions of theirs for whose sake I have most often fallen into sin. Alas! good Lord God, if only I could have remembered rightly how one day she will be so foully stinking that three days after her death I would not touch her for anything. . . .

And next, sweetest Lord and Physician, I would have great need of a potion to comfort me and wipe me clean inside and purge away the filth of my wounds. The potion must be delicious to drink and strong to act to do that for which it is ordered and properly taken. Where can man find this good potion?

Sweetest Lady Saint Mary, you who distill and prepare this sweet and precious potion, I beg you, my sweet Lady, that now, in my great need, I may have enough to fill it [from your] beautiful and sweet little breasts, which are full of so precious and noble a liquor, sweet virgin's milk, the like of which was never seen before nor shall be again. Well should this sweet potion be noble, precious and miraculous: noble, for that so noble a lord as sweet Jesus drank of it and took from it the substance of humanity. And man finds precious any good thing which is rare; surely by this reasoning man ought well to hold it precious, for virgin's milk is rare, nor is there any but in you, sweetest Lady. And it is miraculous—although nothing is a miracle in the eyes of God—but it is a miraculous thing for us to think of how that high and noble lord deigned to come down among us, so low, because of His great humility. . . .

SUGGESTED READING

This list of supplementary books is organized to correspond roughly to the chronological divisions in the document sections; titles useful for the entire medieval period have in most cases been included in the first section. More titles can easily be located in the bibliographies which many of these books contain. Books available in paperback editions are marked with an asterisk.

SECTION I

Alföldi, András, *The Conversion of Constantine and Pagan Rome*, Oxford, 1948.

*Bark, William C., *Origins of the Medieval World*, Stanford, 1958.

Barker, John, *Justinian and the Later Roman Empire*, Madison, 1966.

*Barraclough, Geoffrey, *Origins of Modern Germany*, 2nd ed., New York, 1966.

*Blair, Peter Hunter, *An Introduction to Anglo-Saxon England*, Cambridge, England, 1956.

*Bloch, Marc, *Feudal Society*, London, 1961.

*Bolgar, R. R. *The Classical Heritage and Its Beneficiaries*, New York, 1964.

Brooke, Christopher, *From Alfred to Henry III*, Edinburgh, 1961.

*Brown, Peter, *Augustine of Hippo*, Berkeley and Los Angeles, 1969.

Burckhardt, Jakob, *The Age of Constantine the Great*, New York, 1949.

*Cam, Helen M., *England Before Elizabeth*, New York, 1960.

Cantor, Norman F., *Medieval History. The Life and Death of a Civilization*, New York and London, 1963.

*——, *The English*, New York, 1969.

*Cochrane, C. N., *Christianity and Classical Culture*, New York, 1957.

*Cohn, Norman, *The Pursuit of the Millennium*, New York and Oxford, 1957.

*Curtius, E. R., *European Literature and the Latin Middle Ages*, New York, 1963.

*Geanokoplos, Deano J., *Byzantine East and Latin West*, New York, 1966.

Gilson, Etienne, *A History of Christian Philosophy in the Middle Ages*, New York, 1955.

*Guillaume, Alfred, *Islam*, 2nd ed., Harmondsworth, 1956.

Hanning, R., *The Vision of History in Early Britain*, New York, 1966.

Kern, Fritz, *Kingship and Law in the Middle Ages*, Oxford, 1956.

*Knowles, David, *The Evolution of Medieval Thought*, Baltimore, 1962.

*Leff, Gordon, *Medieval Thought from St. Augustine to Ockham*, Baltimore, 1958.

Lot, Ferdinand, *The End of the Ancient World and the Beginnings of the Middle Ages*, New York, 1961.

Ross, J. B. and M. M. McLaughlin, *The Portable Medieval Reader*, New York, 1949.

Southern, Richard William, *Western Views of Islam in the Middle Ages*, Cambridge, Mass., 1962.

*Wallace-Hadrill, John M., *The Barbarian West*, New York, 1962.

——, *The Long-Haired Kings and Other Studies in Frankish History*, New York, 1962.

Watt, W. Montgomery, *A History of Islamic Spain*, Edinburgh, 1965.

White, Lynn, Jr., ed., *The Transformation of the Roman World*. Berkeley and Los Angeles, 1966.

SECTION II

Cantor, Norman F., *Church, Kingship and Lay Investiture in England 1089–1135*, Princeton, 1958.

———, "The Crisis of Western Monasticism 1050–1130," *American Historical Review* LXVI (1950).

*Fawtier, Robert, *The Capetian Kings of France*, New York, 1966.

*Ganshof, Francois L., *Feudalism*, 2nd ed., New York, 1961.

Gilson, Etienne, *The Mystical Theology of Saint Bernard*, New York, 1940.

Haskins, Charles H., *The Normans in European History*, New York, 1959.

*———, *The Renaissance of the Twelfth Century*, New York, 1957.

———, *The Rise of the Universities*, Ithaca, 1957.

*Heer, Friedrich, *The Medieval World: Europe 1100–1350*, Chicago, 1962.

Hollister, Charles Warren, *Anglo-Saxon Military Institutions*, Oxford, 1962.

———, *The Military Organization of Norman England*, Oxford, 1965.

*Leclercq, Jean, *The Love of Learning and the Desire for God*, New York, 1961.

*Petit-Dutaillis, Charles, *The Feudal Monarchy in France and England*, New York, 1964.

*Poole, A. L., *From Domesday Book to Magna Carta*, Oxford, 1951.

*Runciman, S., *The Medieval Manichee*, New York, 1961.

*———, *History of the Crusades*, New York, 1964–67.

*Southern, Richard William, *The Making of the Middle Ages*, New Haven, 1962.

——, *Saint Anselm and His Biographer*, Cambridge, England, 1963.

*Strayer, Joseph R., *Feudalism*, New York, 1965.

Tellenbach, Gerd, *Church, State and Christian Society at the Time of the Investiture Contest*, Oxford, 1940.

Vinogradoff, P., *Roman Law in Medieval Europe*, New York, 1909.

*Waddell, Helen, *The Wandering Scholars*, Garden City, New York, 1955.

*White, Lynn, Jr., *Medieval Technology and Social Change*, New York, 1966.

SECTION III

Branner, Robert, *Gothic Architecture*, New York, 1961.

*Crombie, A. C., *Medieval and Early Modern Science*, 2nd ed., New York, 1959.

*Huizinga, J., *The Waning of the Middle Ages*, New York, 1954.

Kantorowicz, E. H., *Frederick II*, New York, 1967.

——, *The King's Two Bodies*, Princeton, 1957.

*Kelly, Amy, *Eleanor of Aquitaine and the Four Kings*, New York, 1957.

*Knowles, David, *The English Mystical Tradition*, New York, 1965.

——, *The Monastic Order in England*, 2nd ed., Cambridge, England, 1963.

——, *The Religious Order in England*, Cambridge, England, 1957–62.

Lambert, Malcolm D., *Franciscan Poverty*, London, 1961.

Leff, Gordon, *Paris and Oxford Universities in the Thirteenth Centuries*, New York, 1967.

*Lewis, C. S., *The Allegory of Love*, New York, 1958.

——, *The Discarded Image: An Introduction to Medieval and Renaissance Literature*, Cambridge, England, 1964.

333

*Lovejoy, Arthur O., *The Great Chain of Being*, New York, 1960.

*Mâle, E., *Religious Art in Thirteenth-Century France*, New York, 1913.

*Mundy, John H. and P. Riesenberg, *The Medieval Town*, New York, 1958.

Owst, Gerald, *Literature and Pulpit in Medieval England*, New York, 1961.

*Panofsky, Erwin, *Gothic Architecture and Scholasticism*, New York, 1957.

Powicke, F. M., *King Henry III and the Lord Edward*, Oxford, 1947.

———, *The Thirteenth Century*, Oxford, 1953.

Rashdall, Hastings, ed., *The Universities in the Middle Ages*, 2nd ed., revised by Frederick M. Powicke and A. B. Emden, Oxford, 1936.

*Robertson, D. W., *A Preface to Chaucer*, Princeton, 1962.

Sabatier, Paul, *Saint Francis of Assisi*, Paris, 1894.

INDEX

335

336

338

51 L

341

343